Twelve Essays on Winnicott

Twelve Essays on Winnicott

THEORETICAL DEVELOPMENTS AND CLINICAL INNOVATIONS

Edited by Amal Treacher Kabesh

OXFORD
UNIVERSITY PRESS

OXFORD
UNIVERSITY PRESS

Oxford University Press is a department of the University of Oxford. It furthers the University's objective of excellence in research, scholarship, and education by publishing worldwide. Oxford is a registered trade mark of Oxford University Press in the UK and certain other countries.

Published in the United States of America by Oxford University Press
198 Madison Avenue, New York, NY 10016, United States of America.

CIP data is on file at the Library of Congress
ISBN 978–0–19–094963–1

1 3 5 7 9 8 6 4 2

Printed by Sheridan Books, Inc., United States of America

{ CONTENTS }

{ PREFACE }

Amal Treacher Kabesh

The essays assembled in this book were first published as the introductions to eleven of the volumes that make up *The Collected Works of D. W. Winnicott* (published by Oxford University Press in 2016, print and online). Initially, it was Clare Winnicott's aspiration and hope that Winnicott's works (publications, audio recordings, correspondence) would be gathered together to be available in one collection. The General Editors—Lesley Caldwell and Helen Taylor Robinson—have achieved this ambition under the auspices of the Winnicott Trust.

It was then decided to group these introductory essays into one further book as they provide a textured map of Winnicott's oeuvre and elucidate both theoretical development and clinical practice. They represent a major contribution to Winnicottian scholarship; written by renowned international Winnicottian scholars, they offer in-depth framing and discussion of Winnicott's conceptualizations of human beings and of psychoanalytic practice. Each essay covers a different period of Winnicott's life; the dates are indicated at the beginning of each contribution.

The essays published in this volume are very close to the original introductions except in one respect—repetitive biographical detail has been deleted from the original scripts or shifted into the section that furnishes biographical detail in the essay by Caldwell and Taylor Robinson (Chapter 1 in this volume). Where there is a divergence in opinion, then the original biographical account is retained. The full references to the *Collected Works* are included in this edition.

The 12 volumes of the *Collected Works* comprise previously published work along with previously unpublished texts. Each volume is presented chronologically according to date of delivery, or writing, or of first publication. The various drafts of Winnicott's work are also included to illustrate the development and interplay of an idea. This inclusion of the drafts provides a fine illustration of Winnicott's willingness to develop, refine, and reflect on his ideas and clinical practice. The *Collected Works* is thus ordered chronologically; the known date of composition or first presentation takes priority over the date of first publication. Robert Adès explains the order as follows: the chronological bibliography, following American Psychological Association style, is ordered exclusively by the year of first publication. Accordingly, a work's position in the bibliography does not always correspond to the location of the item in the *Collected Works.* In cases where this differs, the date of composition—and hence the publication's location in the *Collected Works*—is given in square brackets after the title. Uncertain or estimated dates have been indicated with "c."—when some estimation is possible—and otherwise marked "not dated" [n.d.]. Any further information on the history of a work's composition and publication, along with other pertinent information, can be found in its headnote. The introduction to Volume 12 authored by Robert Adès serves to provide a map to the *Collected Works* and, therefore, has not been included in this volume. It is accessible online.

The *Collected Works* opens with a detailed introduction written by Lesley Caldwell and Helen Taylor Robinson. This rich essay appears as Chapter 1—"The Enduring Significance of Donald D. Winnicott: A General Introduction to the *Collected Works*"—in this volume of essays and provides a multifaceted exploration of Winnicott's progressive elaboration of his theoretical and clinical positions. Caldwell and Taylor Robinson present the intellectual and institutional context of Winnicott's development into a major and significant analytic figure, elucidating key concepts such as creativity, the necessity of illusion, transitional objects and transitional phenomena, fantasy, and the psyche-soma. Winnicott was centrally preoccupied with what is required to develop a healthy self that is able to engage with the world with liveliness and authenticity. This essay offers a sustained discussion of Winnicott's "clinical directions."

Ken Robinson's essay in Chapter 2, "From Pediatrics to Psychoanalysis," provides a detailed and cogent account of Winnicott's education as a medical doctor and his growing engagement with psychological matters. Robinson's detailed account of the early years of Winnicott's work (1911–1938) traces through the various influences (individuals, concepts, clinical practice) on Winnicott's education. (Robinson points out that Winnicott preferred the word "education" to "training.") Importantly, Robinson highlights Winnicott's commitment as a pediatrician *and* as a psychoanalyst.

Christopher Reeves discusses Winnicott's theoretical development during the period 1939 to 1945 in Chapter 3, entitled " 'Two makes one, then one makes two': Early Emotional Development" (this chapter is dedicated to Christopher Reeves, who sadly died before the volumes appeared in print). He reminds the reader of the context of World War II, the conflict in the British Psychoanalytical Society (commonly referred to as "the Controversial Discussions"), and Winnicott's increasing disagreements with Melanie Klein's theoretical propositions, as all influencing Winnicott's developing theoretical perspectives. Winnicott conceptualized the infant and mother as a unit that should be understood as "two makes one, then one makes two" as the mother and baby are to be regarded as a psychic unit and then become separated though still united.

During this period Winnicott pays increasing attention to "hate" as a powerful emotion that is felt and experienced by all human beings. Hate is discussed thoroughly in Chapter 4, "Towards Different Objects, Other Spaces, New Integrations," by Vincenzo Bonaminio and Paolo Fabozzi. Bonaminio and Fabozzi open their essay thus: "*Hate.* This is the first time that a *feeling* bursts into psychoanalytic discourse with such disruptive effect on the metapsychological terrain," and thereby they equally bring the force of emotion upfront as they simultaneously explore how Winnicott also disrupted psychoanalytic discourse as he argued for the persistent strength of emotions. Movement is a theme in this chapter as Bonaminio and Fabozzi trace through the various conceptual shifts (theoretical and clinical) that Winnicott undertakes during the years 1946 to 1951.

In Chapter 5, Dominique Scarfone advocates "Reading Winnicott Slowly" in order to understand fully the complexities and movements of Winnicott's thinking. Scarfone points out that for Winnicott it is important to speak the truth of one's thoughts without compromise; in upholding this ideal, Scarfone understands Winnicott as close to Freud's spirit in not being compliant or adhering to the prevalent norms within psychoanalytic groups. During this period (1952–1955), Scarfone writes, Winnicott "appears as formidably alive and in constant motion, treating patients, writing papers, discussing those of others, writing letters to medical journals and newspapers, all with a profound sense of devotion towards whatever truth can be discovered by sound psychoanalytic practice and rigorous thinking."

In Chapter 6, "Reaching His Peak," Jennifer Johns and Marcus Johns place emphasis on Winnicott's theoretical and clinical influence. They argue that Winnicott the person is the same as Winnicott the theoretician and clinician. Winnicott had found his own idiom, and this led to a growing divergence of opinion between him and Melanie Klein. While Winnicott agreed with the "ubiquity and importance of envy in the analysis of adults and children," his view was that ego-integration was in the process of development. Jennifer Johns and Marcus Johns clarify Winnicott's understanding that envy found in adults and children is a result of what has taken place during the processes of ego-integration, individuation, and maturation. The child responds with a degree of envy due to the legacy of the mother's capacities to respond, recognize, and adapt. Critically, envy in a Winnicottian frame is understood as a response to the environment and is not an innate essence. From the early 1950s onwards, Winnicott was concerned with the various ways a child discovers reality, explores the complex interrelationships between self and other (the me and not-me), and begins to uncover fantasy and reality, and the use of objects by the developing infant. In short, recognition as a capacity and as a process that is always in process becomes central to Winnicott's understanding of what it is to be human.

Angela Joyce, in Chapter 7, "Health: Dependence Towards Independence," explores Winnicott's theoretical developments during the period 1960 to 1963. She writes that Winnicott was a theoretician of health as he was concerned to elaborate the possibilities of living and being truthful. As is well known, Winnicott paid subtle attention to the difference between the real (authentic) self and the false (compliant) self. It is when there are too many impingements, too many demands to adapt to the environment, and when there are too many failures of a good-enough environment, that the infant retreats into helplessness and despair resulting in a compliant and false self. Alongside developing his ideas about the real and false self, Winnicott was developing his conceptualization of the infant's necessary moves from absolute dependency to relative dependence and then finally towards independence. Winnicott did not believe that any human being was ever fully independent—but we can reach towards independence.

Winnicott was not willing to imbibe and repeat unthinkingly the canon of received psychoanalytic theory, as is illustrated in Anna Ferruta's essay in Chapter 8, "Object Presence and Absence in Psychic Development." Ferruta expounds the development of Winnicott's thinking during 1964 to 1966, and she explores how an extraordinary range of topics and a "courageous extension" of his thinking into primitive areas of the mind characterize his work. The volume of the *Collected Works* that this piece introduces (Volume 7) includes a range of his essays that both bring together his preoccupations and deepen our understanding of aspects of being human: integration, movement across emotional states of mind, the integration of the ego, and the treatment of borderline and psychotic patients. Winnicott was convinced that integration starts at once for the infant despite dependency on primary caretakers. Failure of integration, or disintegration, were cause of profound concern for Winnicott, and he thought through the cause and effect of these states of mind with sensitivity and compassion. The matter of integration and the expression of individuality is a theme that runs throughout his work. Winnicott argued persistently that the task of the clinician is to be available to the patient. The clinician is there to meet the transference, to give voice to unexpressed feelings and fantasies—in short, to be of service to the patient. As Ferruta points out, the material contained in Volume 7 of the *Collected Works* illustrates "Winnicott's wish to maintain his independent way of thinking while trying to avoid seeming intolerant or detached."

In 1967 and 1968, Winnicott consolidated his thinking on technique, the task of the analyst, nonverbal communication and possible mutuality of experiences between mother and infant, use of gaze, and the mother's capacity to adapt to her infant's needs. For Winnicott, it is from mothers and babies that much can be learned about the needs of psychotic patients. The importance of reliability is a theme that Winnicott stresses persistently, and he emphasizes that when reliability breaks down, which it inevitably does, then *unthinkable anxiety* overwhelms the infant. He perceives annihilation as a catastrophe that occurs as a result of extreme anxiety and primary privation. The task of the analyst, Winnicott insists, is to attend to the primitive developmental needs of his patients. His thinking about the intermediate area of experience—fluidity between internal and external—leads for Winnicott to play, to creativity, to culture itself. Psychoanalysis itself is, for Winnicott, a specialized form of play. Ann Horne's lucid contribution in Chapter 9, "Communication Between Infant and Mother, Patient and Analyst: The Years of Consolidation," provides a useful synopsis of Winnicott's achievements that were consolidated and enhanced during these two years. Horne sums these up as follows: how the infant arrives at a separate sense of self and other; the perception of reality and the object as real; delinquency as hope; the reliable environment; and playing and culture.

In his essay in Chapter 10, "Being, Creativity, and Potential Space," Arne Jemstedt expounds a number of ideas that were of crucial significance to Winnicott: creativity and the creative process, being, illusion, and transitional phenomena. Jemstedt draws our attention to Winnicott's important paper "Communicating and Not Communicating Leading to a Study of Certain Opposites" (published in Volume 6:4:8). In this paper, Winnicott argues that at the core of every human being is a silent communication, a sacred area, and crucially it is an aspect of health and an important aspect of being alive. This is a Winnicottian paradox as it is from this silent core that itself cannot (indeed, should not) be communicated that communication occurs. Paradox abounds in Winnicott's understanding of human beings and human lives as we strive to communicate and simultaneously keep our core silent and hidden; the baby creates and finds the object; we live in illusion and simultaneously inhabit relatedness with other human beings. It is in intermediate areas that the infant selects and fills the transitional object, and importantly it is the use of transitional objects that marks the beginning of the capacity to symbolize. Jemstedt writes that Winnicott places illusion, the capacity to create, and the discovery of the object as surviving intact as fundamental aspects of being alive and necessary aspects of creative living.

Essays by Marco Armellini (Chapter 11) and Steven Groarke (Chapter 12) illuminate the last works produced by Winnicott before his death, *Playing and Reality, Therapeutic Consultations in Child Psychiatry*, and *The Piggle*; these were prepared by Winnicott and published after his death in 1971. Winnicott continually revised his work on "the emotional development of the individual human being," but it remained unfinished until edited by Christopher Bollas, Madeleine Davis, and Ray Shepherd and was published posthumously, in 1988, as *Human Nature*. In "Expectation and Offer: The Challenge of Communication in Winnicott's *Therapeutic Consultations*," Armellini explores the intricacies of Winnicott's thinking as exemplified in *Therapeutic Consultations* and *The Piggle* specifically. Armellini writes that these projects represent "a complex pattern of development and maturation," and importantly these works are not "guides to the application of theory to different settings or as a demonstration of the clinical validity of theoretical concepts." Winnicott was able to tolerate gaps and uncertainties in order to "preserve the full complexity of life." While wanting to maintain openness and uncertainty, Winnicott was also able to recommend that a family needed a vacation and not analytic treatment. Frequently, Winnicott perceived that the patient needed contact and communication, not interpretation nor the omniscient knowledge of the analyst. Of vital importance is Winnicott's stringent opinion that frequently symptoms are not signs of disease but rather are the communication of the patient's developmental history and of suffering. Indeed, as Armellini writes, we (that is, clinicians) "are implicitly asked not to explain"; moreover, Winnicott's case studies illustrate "how tyrannical the intellect can be and how the mind can be a persecutory object."

Steven Groarke's essay "Winnicott and the Primacy of Life" explores the vitality of living, communicating, and making meaning. Volume 11 provides an account of Winnicott's treatment of a young toddler—Gabrielle ("Piggle")—who suffered from troubling fantasies. Winnicott describes his treatment of Gabrielle and enables readers to imagine and think through the treatment for themselves (thinking for oneself is a theme that is also taken up in Scarfone's essay "Reading Winnicott Slowly"). Groarke pays close attention to Winnicott's essay *Human Nature*. It is living, as Groarke writes, that is vital for Winnicott, who was resolved that it is living that gives life meaning. Groarke sums up the questions as follows: What did it mean for Winnicott to be on good terms with life? What kind of life did he assume a healthy person is able to live? And how might we live fuller, more meaningful lives? In short, it is reaching for, striving after, meaning that is to "reach for life." This is not, though, about the avoidance of pain; indeed, for Winnicott suffering is a way of going-on-being, and the healthier the individual the greater the capacity for suffering. What we make of life is inextricably linked with what we make of the world we inhabit, and yet again Winnicott's view is that the world has to be invented and perceived before it becomes habitable and thinkable. Of vital importance is what we make out of what we have.

These twelve essays explore Winnicott's ideas, clinical innovations and intentions, his conceptualization of what it is to be human. The authors of these essays provide a rich elucidation of his capacity to communicate, to be an engaged and concerned bystander, to rethink psychoanalytic practice and theoretical dogma, and perhaps above all to be engaged in life. The last word belongs to Winnicott, who asserted that despite the pains and struggles of being a human being and the unspeakable difficulties, we are always "urged into life by living."

{ ACKNOWLEDGMENTS }

These essays were originally published as introductions to the eleven volumes of *The Collected Works of D. W. Winnicott*. Lesley Caldwell and Helen Taylor Robinson are the General Editors of the *Collected Works*, and grateful thanks are due to them for their careful editorship and sustained stewardship of the *Collected Works* over a number of years. A large number of clinicians and academics initially reviewed the introductions, and the feedback provided was invaluable. Thanks are also due to Robert Adès, Emma Letley, Sarah Nettleton, and Clay Pearn for their work on the introductions to the *Collected Works* and for providing much-needed expertise.

I am grateful to Ann Horne and Angela Joyce for their help and support while I was editing these essays. Recognition is also due to members of the Winnicott Trust (past and present) for their unstinting enthusiasm for the publication of Winnicott's work: Barbie Antonis, Lesley Caldwell, Steven Groarke, Ann Horne, Jennifer Johns, Angela Joyce, Ruth McCall, Marianne Parsons, Helen Taylor Robinson, Judith Trowell, and Elizabeth Wolf. Camilla Ferrier, Sarah Harrington, and Hayley Singer patiently answered my queries with humor and efficiency, and I owe them a debt of gratitude. Even though most of the work was undertaken during much-needed summer vacations, the contributors willingly answered any query with alacrity and good humor. Importantly, thanks are due to the authors of this collection of essays for their invaluable contributions to Winnicottian scholarship.

{ CONTRIBUTORS }

Marco Armellini

Marco Armellini has been a practicing child psychiatrist since 1985. He completed his training in Child and Adolescent Psychoanalytic Psychotherapy with Andreas Giannakoulas and Vincenzo Bonaminio in the 1990s. His clinical experience developed with the Italian public health sector, particularly in the area of infant mental health and autistic developmental disorders. He has published several contributions about the British Independent Tradition in psychoanalysis.

Vincenzo Bonaminio

Vincenzo Bonaminio, PhD, is training and supervising analyst of the Italian Psychoanalytic Society (SPI) and works in Rome in private practice with adults, adolescents, and children. He was Adjunct Professor at the Department of Child Psychiatry, La Sapienza, University of Rome, where he taught child psychotherapy, worked clinically with children, and coordinated a research group on brief psychoanalytic psychotherapy with latency children. For over 25 years he has been Director of the Istituto Winnicott, a training program for the psychoanalytic psychotherapy of children, adolescents, and parental couples, attached to the University. He is Director of the Winnicott Centre Italia in Rome. He has been Honorary Visiting Professor at University College London. He is co-editor of *Richard e Piggle*, the *Italian Journal for the Psychoanalytic Study of the Child and the Adolescent*, and co-editor of the series Psicoanalisi Contemporanea.

Lesley Caldwell

Lesley Caldwell, General Editor of the *Collected Works*, is a member of the British Psychoanalytic Association in private practice in London. She is a guest member of the British Psychoanalytical Society and a corresponding member of LAISPS—Los Angeles Institute and Society for Psychoanalytic Studies. She is an Honorary Professor in the Psychoanalysis Unit and Honorary Senior Research Associate in the Italian Department at University College London. As Chair of the Squiggle Foundation (2000–2003) and editor of the Winnicott Studies monograph series (2000–2008), she published four edited collections on D. W. Winnicott. She was an editor for the Winnicott Trust from 2002 to 2016 and the Chair of Trustees from 2008 to 2012. With Angela Joyce, she published *Reading*

Winnicott (2011). She has a continuing interest in psychoanalysis and the arts and has written on film and the city of Rome.

Paolo Fabozzi

Paolo Fabozzi, PhD, is training and supervising analyst of the Italian Psychoanalytic Society (SPI) and works in Rome in private practice with adults, adolescents, and children. He is an adjunct professor in the Department of Dynamic and Clinical Psychology, "Sapienza," University of Rome. He has published in international reviews and edited *Al di là della metapsicologia* (1996), *Il sé tra clinica e teoria* (2000), and *Forme dell'interpretare* (2003).

Anna Ferruta

Anna Ferruta is Psychologist, Full Member and Training Analyst of the Italian Psychoanalytic Society and of the International Psychoanalytical Association. She is a member of the Monitoring and Advisory Board of the *International Journal of Psychoanalysis* and past Director of Training at the Italian Psychoanalytic Society. She works as a psychoanalyst in Milan, Italy, specializing in the treatment of severe psychic pathologies and the psychodynamics of institutional working groups. She is a founding member of Mito & Realtà: Association for Therapeutic Communities. Other appointments have included Vice-Director of *Psiche*, Lecturer in Psychiatry at the University of Pavia, and consultant at the Neurological Institute C. Besta in Milan. She is the author of several Italian and international publications, including books (*Pensare per Immagini*, Borla, 2005; *Le Comunità Terapeutiche*, Cortina, 2012; *La cura psicoanalitica contemporanea. Estensioni della pratica clinica*, Fioriti, 2018), articles ("Continuity or discontinuity between healthy and pathological narcissism," *Italian Psychoanalytic Annual*, 2012; "Setting analitico e spazio per l'altro," *Rivista di Psicoanalisi*, 2013), and chapters ("Themes and developments of psychoanalytic thought in Italy," in F. Borgogno, A. Luchetti, & L. Marino Coe [Eds.], *Reading Italian psychoanalysis*. London/New York: Routledge, 2016).

Steven Groarke

Steven Groarke is Professor of Social Thought at Roehampton University, an analyst of the British Psychoanalytical Society, and a member of the International Psychoanalytical Association. He teaches at the Institute of Psychoanalysis in London and is an Honorary Senior Research Associate at University College London and a training analyst of the Association of Child Psychotherapists. He is a member of the Editorial Board and Reviewing Panel, respectively, of the *International Journal of Psychoanalysis* and the *British Journal of Psychotherapy*. He currently works as a psychoanalyst in private practice in London.

Ann Horne

Ann Horne is a Fellow of the British Psychotherapy Foundation and an Honorary Member of the Czech Society for Psychoanalytic Psychotherapy. A former Head of the Child and Adolescent Psychotherapy Training at the British Association of Psychotherapists (now IPCAPA at the BPF), she was co-editor of the *Journal of Child Psychotherapy* and *The Handbook of Child and Adolescent Psychotherapy* (1999; 2nd ed. 2009) and of four books in her Routledge series on Independent Psychoanalytic Approaches with Children and Adolescents. Her selected papers—*On Children Who Privilege the Body: Reflections of an Independent Psychotherapist*—will be published by Routledge in September 2018. Retired from clinical practice, most recently at the Portman Clinic, London, she teaches and lectures in the United Kingdom and abroad.

Arne Jemstedt

Arne Jemstedt, MD, is a psychoanalyst with a private practice in Stockholm. He is a member and training analyst of the Swedish Psychanalytical Association. He was President of the former Swedish Psychoanalytical Association from 1997 to 2003 and the first President of the new Swedish Psychoanalytical Association (formed through the fusion of the Swedish Society and the Swedish Association) from 2010 to 2012. He is the editor of Swedish translations of several of Winnicott's books and has published articles and chapters on Winnicott's work in Swedish and international psychoanalytic journals and books. He is European Co-Chair of the project IPA Encyclopaedic Dictionary.

Jennifer Johns

Jennifer Johns is a Fellow of the Institute of Psychoanalysis in London. She came to psychoanalysis from general medical practice and was supervised during her training by Donald Winnicott. She has worked in psychotherapy departments at University College Hospital in London and at the West Middlesex Hospital. She has an interest in psychosomatic disorders. An editor and member of the Winnicott Trust for many years, she chaired the Trust from 1997 to 2008 and has taught Winnicott's work widely.

Marcus Johns

Marcus Johns is a Fellow of the Institute of Psychoanalysis in London. He studied medicine at Charing Cross Hospital and psychiatry at the Maudsley Hospital. He trained in child and family psychiatry at the Tavistock Clinic and was Director of the Child Guidance Training Centre, where he was Consultant-in-Charge of the Day Unit for disturbed children. During this time, he trained as a psychoanalyst and became Acting Director of the London Clinic of Psychoanalysis. He was an editor of the *Bulletin of the British Psychoanalytical Society.* He is past Chair of the Trustees for the International Pre-Autistic Network (IPAN).

Angela Joyce

Angela Joyce is a training and supervising psychoanalyst with the British Psychoanalytical Society and a child psychoanalyst trained at the Anna Freud Centre in London, where she has been a member of the pioneering Parent Infant Project for many years; there she jointly led the resurgence of child psychotherapy. She works in private practice in London and is an Honorary

Senior Lecturer at University College London. She is a trustee of the Squiggle Foundation and Chair of the Winnicott Trust. She has written papers and contributed to books on early development and parent–infant psychotherapy. With Lesley Caldwell she edited *Reading Winnicott*, published as part of the New Library of Psychoanalysis Teaching Series in 2011, and she edited *Donald Winnicott and the History of the Present*, published by Karnac in 2017.

Amal Treacher Kabesh

Amal Treacher Kabesh was the Managing Editor of *The Collected Works of D. W. Winnicott*. She has a longstanding interest in bringing together psychoanalytic and cultural theory in order to understand identity (especially gender and ethnicity) and she has published extensively on these topics. She is an Associate Professor in the School of Sociology and Social Policy at the University of Nottingham. Her two recently published books are *Postcolonial Masculinities: Emotions, Histories, and Ethics* (Ashgate, 2013) and *Egyptian Revolutions: Conflict, Repetition and Identification* (Rowman and Littlefield, 2017).

Christopher Reeves

Christopher Reeves (1939–2012) was a child psychotherapist who trained at the Tavistock Clinic in London and had some personal experience of Winnicott, having attended seminars at his house during the last two years of Winnicott's life. His papers on the theoretical and clinical aspects of Winnicott's work have been published in the United Kingdom and America. He edited a collection of essays, *Broken Bounds: Contemporary Reflections on the Anti-Social Tendency* (2012), and was a contributing editor to Judith Issroff's *Donald Winnicott and John Bowlby: Personal and Professional Reflections*, both published by Karnac Books. He was Director of the Squiggle Foundation from 2008 to 2011.

Ken Robinson

Ken Robinson is a psychoanalyst in private practice in Newcastle upon Tyne. He is a member of the British Psychoanalytical Society and was formerly its Honorary Archivist. He is a training analyst for child and adolescent and adult psychotherapy in the North of England and Scotland and lectures, teaches, and supervises in the United Kingdom and Europe. Before training as a psychotherapist and psychoanalyst, he taught English Literature and the History of Ideas in the university and maintains an interest in the overlap between psychoanalysis and the arts and humanities. His essay "Creativity in Everyday Life (or Living in the World Creatively)" appeared recently in *Donald Winnicott and the History of the Present* edited by Angela Joyce (Karnac, 2017). He is especially interested in the nature of therapeutic action and the history of psychoanalysis and is currently completing a book on the use in the consulting room now of basic clinical concepts rooted in the theory and practice of Freud, Ferenczi, Balint, and Winnicott.

Dominique Scarfone

Dominique Scarfone, MD, was full professor and is now honorary professor at the Department of Psychology of the Université de Montréal and training-supervising analyst at the Institut psychanalytique de Montréal (French section of the Canadian Psychoanalytic Institute). A former associate editor of the *International Journal of Psychoanalysis*, he has published five books: *Jean Laplanche* (1997; translated into Hebrew, Italian, and English), *Oublier Freud? Mémoire pour la psychanalyse* (1999), *Les Pulsions* (2004; translated into Spanish and Portuguese), *Quartiers aux rues sans nom* (2012), and *The Unpast: The Actual Unconscious* (2015). He is the author of several book chapters and numerous articles published in international journals. He is invited regularly to give seminars and conferences in various countries and was author of one of two key papers discussed in the 2014 International Congress of French-Speaking Analysts in Montreal. He will be one of the keynote speakers at the 2019 Congress of the International Psychoanalytic Association in London.

Helen Taylor Robinson

Helen Taylor Robinson, General Editor of the *Collected Works*, is Fellow of the Institute of Psychoanalysis, British Psychoanalytical Society, London, and was a clinical psychoanalyst with adults and children until her retirement. She was an Editor and Trustee of the Winnicott Trust for seventeen years and co-edited *Thinking About Children* with Jennifer Johns and Ray Shepherd. Her special interest is in the relationship of psychoanalysis to the arts, literature, and cinema. She has been Honorary Senior Lecturer at the Psychoanalysis Unit of University College London. She has contributed to books and journals in the field of psychoanalysis and to the European Psychoanalysis and Film Festival.

Twelve Essays on Winnicott

{1}

The Enduring Significance of Donald W. Winnicott

GENERAL INTRODUCTION TO THE *COLLECTED WORKS*

Lesley Caldwell and Helen Taylor Robinson

Donald Woods Winnicott is a major figure in the world of psychoanalysis. His books have been translated into many languages, his are the most frequently accessed psychoanalytic writings online, and his innovative ideas have provided a continuing focus in the training of psychoanalysts and in debate at national and international congresses. Not only was Winnicott, according to André Green, the most important psychoanalytic thinker after Freud, he was committed to making a psychoanalytically informed approach available to a wider public. No psychoanalyst before or since has been so intent or so successful in bringing psychoanalysis into public institutional and cultural life. His openness and the facility for communicating that he displayed in very different contexts extended to a willingness to debate with fellow practitioners of different orientations and approaches, professionals from related fields, and a vast general audience. In his capacity to convey highly specialized thought effectively, he made use of technical language and that of paradox and metaphor. His interest in understanding the interaction between inner and outer reality within the growing individual was sustained with increasing complexity throughout his life.

After Freud, Sandor Ferenczi, and Karl Abraham, Winnicott, with Melanie Klein and Anna Freud, is a major figure of the second generation of psychoanalysts. His writing, teaching, and broadcasting helped to take psychoanalysis forward by making it a continuingly relevant and dynamic discipline. His work in pediatrics and child psychiatry, education, child health, and development remains influential, and, more recently, associated disciplines in the humanities and social sciences have begun to use his work.

Brief Biography

Winnicott (1896–1971)[1] grew up in the prosperous business class in Devon, England, where he enjoyed a cared-for, somewhat religious upbringing, with two older loved sisters and many cousins living nearby. His father was twice mayor of Plymouth and knighted for his contribution to local politics, but it appears to have been his mother, sisters, cousins, and the family servants who constituted Winnicott's main early environment. He was sent to The Leys School in Cambridge at the age of thirteen and then began to study biology at Cambridge with a view to training in medicine. In his adolescent years, he appeared to be as good at sports, singing, and playing as at academic work. He read and admired Darwin and was already manifesting a concern for the less fortunate in the local Cambridge community. He had a short period as a volunteer medical officer on board a navy destroyer during World War I, which brought him up against death and loss at an early age.

On beginning his medical training at Bart's Hospital, London, in the autumn of 1917, Winnicott, troubled by his dreams, came across Freud and felt he had discovered something significant. In 1923, he sought analysis with James Strachey for his "inhibitions" (and his short height, he joked later). After medical qualification in 1920, he worked as a House Physician in several hospitals specializing in children's medicine before being appointed, in 1923, to Queen's Hospital, Bethnal Green, and Paddington Green Children's Hospital. He had a private practice in child medicine near Harley Street, and, at the age of twenty-seven, he married Alice Taylor.

By 1934, Winnicott had qualified as an analyst. He kept medical posts in public health until his retirement in 1961, but he was particularly committed to the psychological aspects of his work, especially with mothers and children. He completed the child analytic training in 1935, and, in 1936, he began a second analysis with Joan Riviere. He offered intensive analytic work and shorter psychotherapeutic interventions to children and adults. In 1939, he began writing radio broadcasts for mothers.

While valuing much of what he had learned, Winnicott began to break with some of his psychoanalytic mentors on the basis of what he observed daily in his clinical work. He became confident that the infant's actual dependence on the maternal/familial environment made the interactions of mother and child from birth crucial for psychic development. Despite the emphasis on the internal world of fantasy, he became more and more committed to what real babies need to develop a healthy self as the basis for a creative life.

During the period of the British Society's Controversial Discussions (see later in the chapter) and a certain polarization of ideas around the developmental model

[1] For extensive bibliographies of Winnicott's life see Adam Phillips (1988), Brett Kahr (1996), Robert Rodman (2003), and Jennifer Johns (2006).

of Anna Freud and Klein's model of the internal world's unconscious fantasy structure, Winnicott was able to maintain his own often uncompromising stance.

After his father's death in 1948 (his mother had died in 1925), he divorced Alice and married Clare Britton, who became the focus of his personal world and a professional collaborator for the rest of his life. He had worked with Clare, a gifted psychiatric social worker (and subsequently a psychoanalyst), in the Oxfordshire Evacuation Scheme, which led to their contributing to the postwar government planning of children's services. In 1948, Winnicott had his first heart attack, the condition that would lead to his death in 1971.

Winnicott was Chair of the International Psychoanalytical Association's 1953 committee of investigation of Jacques Lacan, served as President of the British Psychoanalytical Society from 1956 to 1959 and again from 1965 to 1968, and managed the Child and Adolescent Department of the London Clinic of Psychoanalysis. He was also instrumental in the establishment of the Finnish Psychoanalytic Society. He was President of the Paediatric Section of the Royal Society of Medicine (1952) and of the Association for Child Psychology and Psychiatry, and Chairman of the Medical Section of the British Psychological Society (1948). He won the James Spence Gold Medal for Paediatrics in 1968.

He published his first collected papers in 1958. As an internationally known clinician, he gave well-received lectures in America in 1962 and 1963, but, on a visit to New York at the end of 1968, his ill health caught up with him. In the last two years of his life, Winnicott prepared and planned books and, when he could, took on speaking engagements. He died in January 1971.

Psychoanalytic Writing: DWW and the Tradition

While all conscious communications are inflected with unconscious meaning for psychoanalysis, psychoanalytic writing itself is subject to this dimension. Winnicott's writing style, commented on both critically and favorably by so many of his readers, makes his works distinctive. From the very early letter about psychoanalysis to his older sister Violet [CW 1:1:11] to his late piece on "The Unconscious" [CW 7:3:29], he shows great skill in conducting a conversation between aspects of familiar and less familiar ways of engaging with an idea and an emotional experience.

The American analyst Thomas Ogden (2005, p. 109) discusses psychoanalytic writing as a literary genre that attempts to replicate "something like the analytic experience" through a continuing conversation that draws on conscious and unconscious experience. Through his or her writing, the analyst is engaged in a creative act in which "the reader in the experience of reading has a sense not only of the critical elements of an analytic experience that the writer has had with the patient, but also 'the music of what happen(ed)' " (Heaney, 1979, p. 173). For him, the best psychoanalytic writing is the expression of this "conversation" between unconscious processes and the conscious, rational, perceiving processes that draw on what takes place in the analysis and its representation through metaphor, analogy, rhetoric, and a compelling use of ordinary language. Ogden (1992) regarded Winnicott as particularly skillful in conveying what was important and how and why it mattered.

In Winnicott's letter to Violet [CW 1:1:11], he shows a readiness to "jump across" or "dive into" his subject matter and to plunge into the subconscious. He avoids a consistently logical sequence of thought in favor of building up a set of apparently unconnected areas; demonstrating the central tenets of psychoanalysis by making intuitive, free associative, barely conscious leaps; and combining parts of the unknown and less-known experiences in a style that suggests Ogden's unconstrained "conversation." Regardless of form or audience, much of Winnicott's writing seems to be addressed *to* someone and to echo the analytic process in shifting away or moving towards "something" while allowing for fluidity in its meaning. In this instance, his lively style allows ellipses in consciousness a prime place that anticipates much of his later writing. About this letter, Rodman commented that Winnicott was rare in undertaking "the description of so many phenomena that were outside the realm of the written or spoken word until he came to grips with them and found the words that enlarged our consciousness" (2003, p. 44).

By 1966, when Winnicott wrote briefly about "The Unconscious" [CW 7:3:29], he was angry and disappointed:

> It would seem to me that along with the general acceptance of certain psycho-analytic tenets such as childhood sexuality and the importance of the instincts and the over-riding importance of the individual's need to discover the self and to feel real there has appeared in the last decade or two a dilution of the concept of the unconscious. It is almost as if the idea of the unconscious no longer bothers anyone because—well, we have had all that. The implication is that we are conscious of it.

Unlike his early enthusiasm, his disillusion here accompanies a realization that the place of the unconscious in alleviating suffering could so easily be extinguished by the boredom of "Freud and all that." This has him fighting for the misrepresented unconscious, where earlier he was letting it speak for itself.

Perhaps this juxtaposition of early and late texts captures an aspect of his writing that is present throughout and particularly highlighted by the chronological framework followed in the *Collected Works*. The *Works* comprise twelve volumes of previously published and new texts, a selection of letters, and an accompanying volume of end material. Each volume is presented chronologically, following either date of delivery or writing, or first publication. Successive drafts or reworkings show the development and interplay of ideas through different versions often intended for different audiences. This offers a complementary way of ordering and understanding from that of the thematically structured published texts, the majority of which remain in print. The chronological sequence may also create some surprises for the reader accustomed to the previous volumes since only five original books have been retained: three planned by Winnicott and two that were incomplete at his death and published later.

Clinical Notes on Disorders of Childhood (1931), Winnicott's first book, a kind of handbook for child physicians, appears in Volume 1 [CW 1:3:1–20]. *Holding and Interpretation: Fragment of an Analysis*, written in 1955 but published posthumously, appears in Volume 4 [CW 4:4:1]. *Therapeutic Consultations in Child Psychiatry*, a selection of cases, sessions, interviews, and consultations with children over a ten-year period, was compiled and introduced by Winnicott and published in 1971. It appears as Volume 10 [CW 10:1:1–21]. *The Piggle: An Account of the Psychoanalytic Treatment of a Little Girl* (1977 [CW 11:2]) and *Human Nature* (1988 [CW 11:1]) each contain material written over extended periods, then edited and published posthumously. The first was prepared six years after Winnicott's death, although most of the manuscript was written while the analytic work was in progress between 1964 and 1966. *Human Nature* was worked on in two different outlines over many years, the first version from 1954, the second from 1967. It was prepared for publication in 1988. Both are unfinished works, which, in making up Volume 11 of the *Collected Works*, depart from the general chronological ordering.

Examples of early, middle, and late writings enable varied perspectives on the profound personal engagement that Winnicott maintained, not only in the consulting room but through a variety of public and professional interventions attuned to the unconscious processes that psychoanalysis addresses. Differences and similarities of style and content between early and late writing can be discerned alongside what Ogden describes, in the preface to his own book, as a lifelong attempt to write and rewrite one's first texts from a continuously developing perspective. This is reminiscent of Beckett's parallel tenet in *Worstward Ho* (1983): "Ever tried. Ever failed. No matter. Try again. Fail again. Fail better," and of Ogden's own understanding of Borges's first book of poems as another attempt at the search for meaning: meaning attempted, failed at many times over, but nevertheless attempted again.

To read Winnicott's writing chronologically is to meet new or developing ideas alongside familiar themes reexamined in ways that continue to generate further thought. He offers ways of accessing what is elusive or ungraspable often embedded in the discomfort that springs from the unconscious. This complexity forms part of what he and all practitioners recognize in the psychoanalytic encounter, where comfort may also bring an unease that grounds it in reality.

Early Writings

The work gathered in Volumes 1 and 2 of the *Collected Works* reveals Winnicott as a medical clinician already committed to a uniquely personal approach, one whose acute clinical insight will be deepened by the practice of psychoanalysis and a lifetime involvement in it. In the preface to *Clinical Notes on the Disorders of Childhood* (1931 [CW 1:3:Preface]), he says, "Indirectly to Professor Sigmund Freud I am grateful for an increasing ability to enjoy investigating emotional factors," and his later interests in the environment, in the bodily bases of the psyche, in aggression and in play, may all be found there in embryo, well before the groundbreaking statements of his paper "Primitive Emotional Development" [CW 2:7:8].

Rather than a pediatric Winnicott who then becomes a psychoanalytic Winnicott, both perspectives are consistently present, underpinned clinically and theoretically by the sustained attention to psyche and soma throughout his long career. "I am a paediatrician who has swung to psychiatry and a psychiatrist who has clung to paediatrics," he asserts ("Paediatrics and Psychiatry" [CW 3:3:2]). *Clinical Notes* is particularly interesting for its discussion of emotional development ("normally difficult and commonly incomplete") and his immersion in a psychoanalytic approach in routine medical work. He refers to a "libidinally cathected skin surface as an extension of the mind in papular urticarial" ("Papular Urticaria and the Dynamics of Skin Sensation" [CW 1:4:3]); he introduces the concept of "afterwardsness" in two cases described in Chapters 12 and 13 of *Clinical Notes*; and, again in Chapter 13, he anticipates the insights of his paper "Hate in the Countertransference" [CW 3:2:1]. He suggests that the anxiety felt by children when visiting a doctor and how the child deals with it give an indication of emotional health and aid the doctor in diagnosis. He argues against the reductionist emphasis on the environment originating in the United States, and, in insisting that "the nervous child is nervous for internal reasons," he endorses a psychoanalytic approach that he himself will extend through a far more comprehensive account of the environment.

When Winnicott began to train as a psychoanalyst and in the years after qualification and his supervision by Melanie Klein (1934–40), she was a formative influence. Freud apart, his first reference to a psychoanalytic article is to her early work "The Importance of Symbol Formation in Development of Ego" (1930), and his membership paper given to the British Psychoanalytical Society in 1935 quotes her consistently (1958 [CW 1:4:6]).

A willingness to intuit and to speculate was one of his strengths, but it was accompanied by a sound knowledge of the empirical bases for social-scientific experimental work. "The Observation of Infants in a Set Situation" [CW 2:3:6] attempts a scientific study of the emotional foundations of infant mental health as it conjectures about psychic processes and hypothesizes the close links in the infant between the psyche and physiological development. It draws on accumulated data from the common consultative procedure for all mothers and babies attending his clinic at Paddington Green Children's Hospital. Freud and Ferenczi are important predecessors for his ideas, and there are parallels with Freud's observations of his grandchild (1920), although Winnicott describes a formal situation with a much younger baby. In putting a spatula on a table near the baby and observing the baby's reactions, his focus is on the normal situation and what constitute deviations from it across a deliberately loose age range (five to thirteen months).

In linking physical and emotional development, he makes a claim about the psychic processes in operation. In play, the baby shows a rudimentary awareness of the distinction between inside and outside while also seeming to be enjoying a process that involves completion (Reeves, 2006). The complex relationship between symptoms, anxiety, physiological processes, and unconscious states is used to argue for the baby's realization of the existence of a world outside itself. The mental conflicts produced by desire for the spatula and fear of retaliation for that desire—that is, fear of an anticipated external situation apparently present internally whether the actual mother is disapproving or not—can be dispelled by the experience with the actual mother. The expectation of disapproval may echo Klein's account (Likierman, 2001; Reeves, Chapter 03 this volume), but, even at this stage in the evolution of Winnicott's thinking, the early primitive superego forms the basis for a rather different emphasis in the matter of infantile fantasies. Its corollary, the infant's assumptions about the mother and her insides, may produce, if all goes well, a capacity for concern leading to a recognition of relationships between whole persons.

The Controversial Discussions

The theoretical issues that were the basis of the Controversial Discussions of the 1940s have had ongoing repercussions for the history of psychoanalysis in Britain and elsewhere, but their preceding history was also important. Klein's earlier reception in Europe and her intellectual isolation in Berlin after the death of her analyst, Abraham, led to Ernest Jones's inviting her to London, where she took up membership in the British Society in 1927 and in the Training Committee in 1929. Her reception in Great Britain and the interest taken in her ideas was a mixture of acceptance and questioning. A widening divergence between Vienna and London during the same period had involved theoretical differences about fundamentals in psychoanalysis. Jones, the President of the British Society, made the decision to get the Freuds, father and daughter, as well as other European analysts, to London, and, by so doing, he brought that history and its implications for the future of psychoanalysis and its heirs to London. Freud's legacy and the tenets of psychoanalytic theory would become the bases for the ten scientific meetings of the Controversial Discussions.

On one side, there was the personal history of the Freud family and of Anna and her father, his health, and his eventual death, all within the context of Nazism and persecution; on the other, there was Klein's difficult personal and professional relationship with her daughter, especially following the death of her son in 1934. Both presented painful family situations lived out on a public stage in a disastrous split between actual and psychoanalytic families in the British Society. Personal and theoretical claims to the ownership of the legacy of psychoanalysis were further complicated by concrete economic issues due to the war (there were fewer analytic patients to treat), and, in the face of the wish of the various parties to control the Society's administrative procedures on committees, a widely recognized need for the reorganization of procedures prevailed (King & Steiner, 1991).

The outbreak of war in 1939 loomed over these disputes, but, historically, the 1941–45 Controversial Discussions and their compromise resolution originated in earlier theoretical differences. In a letter to Kate Friedlander (January 8, 1940 [CW 2:2:1]), Winnicott argued that the concept of the inner world is not taken on by Anna Freud and her adherents: "This method of stating things involves this concept of the *inner world*, the fantasy which is *located* in the individual's unconscious fantasy, and which is related to intake, retention and excretion experiences. This in my opinion is the part of the psycho-analytic theory which I do not find represented in the Viennese Group's way of looking at things, and I believe this special bit of theory will come up again and again for discussion until we each understand exactly where the other stands."

The developmental model of Anna Freud, as against Klein's of an internal world whose unconscious "positions" and fantasy structure ascribed less importance to developmental or constitutional genetic forces, divided the British Society, creating schools of theory and practice that remain a major area of psychoanalytic debate.

Winnicott was one of the five Kleinian training analysts at this time, and his resolution to the Second Extraordinary Business Meeting on the scientific aims of psychoanalysis and his plea for not restricting the truth-value of Freud's work to nonscientific repetitions was seconded by Klein ("Resolution K: On Scientific Aims in Psychoanalysis" [CW 2:4:1]). But his rather background presence throughout (something he himself acknowledged in his presentation of his ideas, "D. W. W. on D. W. W." [CW 8:1:2]) suggests a distance from Klein that gathers strength in the following years. In the discussion that followed Klein's own contribution (March 1944), he voiced the doubts about some areas of her theory that he would go on to investigate in depth. He questioned if a baby's first cries could be called "sad" and doubted Marjorie Brierley's use of the word "depressive." He found Sylvia Payne's description of the baby as "helpless" problematic, and he endorsed the mother–baby unit as presented in Merrell Middlemore's 1941 book *The Nursing Couple* (King & Steiner, 1991, p. 820). When Paula Heimann insisted that "the infant was an individual from birth" (p. 821), he agreed that the infant was a personality from birth but emphasized its dependence (p. 821).

The Environment and Infantile Development

Winnicott's presentation of his own approach to psychoanalysis and to the constitution of human experience in "Primitive Emotional Development" [CW 2:7:8] is extraordinarily bold in its conception of the human being and of human subjectivity—the "facilitating or thwarting of the satisfactory growth of life-creating activities" (Deri, 1978, p. 48). Infantile development is here grounded in a particular understanding of the environment as constitutive of both interiority and exteriority. With far-reaching implications for psychoanalytic practice, the primacy attributed to the environment in the establishment of psychic reality extends the foundations of individuality and its psychic determinants through the relationship with others.

From its seemingly casual, almost conversational inversion of the links between child development and psychoanalysis, "Primarily interested in the child patient, and the infant, I decided that I must study psychosis in analysis" [CW 2:7:8], to his clinical observation of the psychoanalytic types who present for analysis, Winnicott presents a schema of psychoanalysis as embedded in the fantasies of the patient about the analyst, the analyst's work, and the analyst's own areas of depression. This work, which necessarily happens and can only happen within the analytic frame, proposes that the analytic couple is formed together in a way that anticipates Bléger (1967), the Barangers (2008), and Ferro's (1992) developments of the analytic field. Thomas Ogden takes this paper as his model for reading Winnicott and, significantly, psychoanalysis after Winnicott (Ogden, 2001). Bonaminio and Fabozzi (Chapter 04 this volume) describe it as "a master plan" for a new approach to psychoanalysis and to human experience.

In his model, the baby has to encounter himself or herself as a separate unit; the condition of that possibility is the facilitating function of the mother, what Bion (1962), borrowing from Marion Milner, later described as the mother's reverie. The infant, initially without an ego, depends upon the ego support provided through environmental/maternal provision for his or her emotional development. Stages in the process of differentiation of self—holding; the mother and infant living together; the mother, father, and infant living together—are linked to the different levels of dependence through which an infant can begin to "be," to exist in his or her own right. From the mother's desire and its embodiment in ordinary physical care, the infant gradually acquires the psychic resources that form the beginnings of a self, able to withstand instinctual impulses from inside and out and to engage with self and other. The growth of the psyche is located in the necessities of infant care, and ego psychology grows out of dependence and the psychic messages it conveys.

The conditions of earliest development provide the infant with an experience of "at-one-ness" with the mother, when, experientially, the infant and mother (maternal care) "cannot be disentangled," but healthy development demands precisely that they are. The gradual emergence of the human infant subject out of the infant–mother matrix is linked with the place and role of the object in the formation of the self. For the infant, the object is a "subjective" object, created out of his or her primary creativity; the mature outcome of the developmental process is the recognition of the object, objectively perceived. In both "Primitive Emotional Development" and in early papers on aggression

("Aggression" [CW 2:1:8]; "Aggression in Relation to Emotional Development" [CW 3:5:2]), Winnicott proposes that aggression is constitutive of the relationship with external reality, a theme that will be extensively returned to in his subsequent writings.

The beginnings of inner reality arrive through the processes of integration, personalization, and realization, but the primary relation to external reality and successful early emotional development depends upon the overlap of two experiences of being alive: that of the mother and that of the baby. The place where the infant's experience of its earliest relations with external reality comes together is not a place in the sense of a location, but an experience—the act of feeling something, a sense of coming together from an experience of living initially "in bits and pieces" (un-integration). It is the mother who provides the continuity of being that enables the baby to become part of an experience that is lived together and to move towards gradual integration. To experience something with another is the condition of a separate mother and baby; to be aware of reality involves the individual's relation to objects that are beyond the self-created world of fantasy, a state dependent on illusion. Only then can an ongoing exchange between fantasy and reality be fully appreciated and enjoyed.

Winnicott's statement, "when a human being feels he is a person related to people, he has already travelled a long way in primitive development" [CW 2:7:8] echoes one from the previous year, "when your infant shows that he can cry from sadness you can infer that he has travelled a long way in the development of his feelings" ("Why Do Babies Cry?" [CW 2:6:2]). In locating the baby's affect—sadness—in the recognition of others, Winnicott proposes that the attributes of personhood and their foundations in psyche and soma are dependent on a temporo-spatial element provided by actual maternal care.

Aguayo (2002), one of the very few Kleinians to engage with Winnicott and Klein, dates their theoretical divergence from 1946, and there is some justice to this if the challenge of "Primitive Emotional Development" (1945) is recognized. In chapter 04, Bonaminio and Fabozzi point to the sequence of Winnicott's papers from 1945 to 1947, although Klein's "Notes on Some Schizoid Mechanisms" (1946) must also be seen in the light of Fairbairn's important contributions (1941). Meira Likierman argues for Klein's paper as deriving much "in her use of the concept of schizoid" from both Winnicott and Fairbairn because of their medical and psychiatric background (2001, p. 146). She reads the paper as part of a "broader professional dialogue" about the links between infantile mental states and adult psychosis that acknowledges the importance of Winnicott's concept of "primary un-integration" (p. 150). Klein states, "More helpful, in my view, is Winnicott's emphasis on the un-integration of the early ego. I would also say that the early ego largely lacks cohesion, and a tendency towards integration alternates with a tendency towards disintegration, a falling into bits" (Klein, 1975, p. 8, quoted in Likierman, p. 163).

Winnicott's refusal to contemplate the paranoid-schizoid position that Klein had introduced in 1946 was founded in his own account of the baby and of aggression, derived from the un-integration of the infant at the beginning and the association of aggression with motility and aliveness. No destructive intention can be attributed to ruthless infantile love. It is only when the child develops a concern for the object that aggression can be turned into hate or anger against that object. For Winnicott, a natural bodily aggression precedes aggression "against the object" and the link between aggression and destructiveness. It is within the interplay between what is offered by the environment and the reactive responses of the individual that love and hate take shape. When he describes the baby's moves towards something beyond itself, the processes are a matter of the links between natural movement and active reaching out, of the beginnings of an awareness of the environment as separate and objective. His earliest discussion [CW 2:1:8] already sees the child's aggressive encounter with the environment as a way of establishing meaning. The self is in the process of being constituted through that very activity of reaching out to encounter and simultaneously create an already existing world, a world, lying there, ready, in the right conditions, for the baby to encounter and, in illusion, create.

The externality of the object is constituted by the object mother's survival of the baby`s attacks, a capacity that allows the infant to find her in the world after first having omnipotently created her there. In discovering the otherness of the (m) other, the child is able to find her of use and of interest in her own right. When the subject destroys the object in fantasy and the real object survives, the infant becomes aware of the world beyond himself or herself. The infant and later the adult goes on continually "destroying" the subjective object in unconscious fantasy, an unconscious conflict that, in health, can enrich the life of the individual. Ogden refers to the infant destroying "his own omnipotence as projected on to the omnipotent internal object" (1992, p. 622). The infant discovers the mother in the world and, through her non-retaliatory presence, discovers the limits of his omnipotence and the beginnings of a sense of "I." The world as other becomes a resource, a source of possibilities to be used through its continuing survival of those fantasized acts of destruction.

The issues fought over so traumatically and openly in the 1940s continued to exert an influence, and Winnicott's growing estrangement from Klein was linked to them and to their institutional repercussions. At least until her death in 1960 and beyond, Winnicott seems to have attempted a dialogue inside the British Society with Klein and with the Klein group, but he always regarded the groups as "disruptive" ("Letter to Money-Kyrle" [CW 5:1:1]), and he wrote to Klein and Anna Freud arguing for disbanding them [CW 4:3:15]. In letters to Roger Money-Kyrle [CW 4:1:13], Herbert Rosenfeld [CW 4:2:2], and Hanna Segal [CW 4:1:3] in the early 1950s, he regrets "the stifling of Klein's achievements" through the increasing rigidity of her followers. He proposed a session on adolescence to Charles Rycroft, when he was Chair of the Scientific Committee, as a way of bringing in Miss Freud [CW 5:2:13], and his letter to Barbara Lantos [CW 5:2:15] sees him responding to her dismissal of Klein by claiming, while taking note of where he differs, that his own practice confirms the presence of similar impulses to those Klein describes.

From the middle of that decade, Winnicott's letters reveal his interest in what Bion is developing, along with a wry sense of Bion's lack of acknowledgment of any debt to him (letters to Wisdom [CW 7:1:11] and Meltzer, [CW 7:3:24]): "Bion (1967) did not cite Winnicott once, certainly an odd occurrence in light of his theory of container–contained" (Aguayo, 2002, p. 1135).

Winnicott's own end point in relation to Kleinian theory seems to have come with her paper on "Envy" presented to the 1955 IPA Congress in Geneva (Grosskurth, 1986, pp. 413–414), and his notes on *Envy and Gratitude* insist that hatred cannot be a part of earliest infancy ("A Study of Envy and Gratitude" [CW 5:2:5]). But he continued to engage with her and acknowledge her contribution to him personally and to psychoanalysis. His discussion of her contributions reveals his sensitivity as a reader of her work even where their emphases are substantially different (Bonaminio and Fabozzi, Chapter 04 this volume). In the 1960s, he returned to his earlier discussion of envy to illustrate his own work with an envious patient ("The Beginnings of a Formulation of an Appreciation and Criticism of Klein's Envy Statement" [CW 6:3:7]), reading Klein somewhat differently.

Kristeva (2001) credits Klein with a similar wish to engage with Winnicott, and her account of "On the Sense of Loneliness" (Klein, 1963) as a response to "The Capacity to Be Alone" [CW 5:3:20] registers a rare dimension, that of their different personalities and their different approaches to theories of human nature in their continuing awareness of each other:

> We have here a good example of the back and forth exchange between Klein and Winnicott, an example that displays the originality of both analysts, as well as their debt to each other. While Winnicott situates the capacity to be alone in a world of ecstasy, Melanie never distanced herself from a tone of desolation that strikes at the very heart of the serenity she had gained. (Kristeva, 2001, p. 261)

The diminishing importance of Klein's and Winnicott's initial close collaboration finds its origins in theoretical differences, and the exclusion of his paper on "Transitional Objects and Transitional Phenomena" from the 1952 *International Journal of Psychoanalysis* Festschrift for Klein's seventieth birthday marked an open divergence. It also signaled something significant and contentious in the paper itself, since to introduce the relation to an actual external object and propose that this may extend an understanding of the psychoanalytic project implicitly challenges the language of internal objects. Radically, it makes central to psychoanalysis the desire for engagement with a world beyond the self.

Transitional Objects

The area encompassed by transitional objects and phenomena is the one for which Winnicott is best known; it is often claimed as his most significant contribution (James, 1962; Modell, 1985; Turner, 2002) and, according to Marion Milner, by Winnicott himself.[2] Introduced in a paper given to the British Psychoanalytical Society in May 1951[3] [CW 3:6:6], it was revised and published in the IJPA in 1953 [CW 4:2:21], reprinted with minor editorial changes in his first collection of psychoanalytic papers *From Paediatrics to Psychoanalysis* [CW 5:4:24], and republished in a revised version in 1971 as the first chapter of *Playing and Reality* [CW 9:3:5]. A proposed *Transitional Book* with a variety of contributors (see CW 12) never appeared. Winnicott claimed that *Playing and Reality* itself constituted the real development of the original paper and insisted that "cultural experience has not found its true place in the theory used by analysts in their work and their thinking" [CW 9:3:9]. In linking "cultural experience" and "analytic work and thought," he addressed the larger canvas of transitional, here called "potential," space.

While the 1951 transitional objects presentation [CW 3:6:6] is consistent with the later published versions (1953 [CW 4:2:21]; 1958 [CW 5:4:24]; 1971 [CW 9:3:5]) in overall theoretical emphasis, there is a stronger concentration on anxiety in the earlier version. In 1951, the transitional object was introduced primarily through its substitutive role for the infant, "when loneliness begins to be felt, when hunger threatens, when between waking and sleeping. There is one thing common to these three states, namely *anxiety*" [CW 3:6:6]. Even then, however, he advised caution "about drawing any automatic equivalence between object and mother."

Winnicott based a highly original advance in psychoanalysis on a theoretical assumption about the child's drive towards living, derived from observations in pediatric work and from the collaboration with Clare Britton, which had confirmed children's attachment to actual objects in separations from their family settings. He may also have had in mind Fairbairn's proposition (1941) that "both the 'primary identification' with the object which characterizes infant dependency, and the achievement of mature dependence in adulthood pass through a series of transitional stages." While Winnicott emphasizes the fluidity of the processes he is elaborating, Fairbairn's association of a transition stage with the abandonment of infantile dependence offers a different understanding of the object and less interest in the internal processes at work in the child (Fairbairn, 1941, 1952;

---

[2] M. Milner (BPAS Archive). Notes made by her on her analysis with D. W. Winnicott, dated September 17, 1959, "he said if he died tomorrow, tell the world the most important thing he's done is *Transitional Objects and Transitional Phenomena.*"

[3] Discussants included Melanie Klein, Michael Balint, William Gillespie, Roger Money-Kyrle, John Rickman, Clifford Scott, Masud Khan, Marion Milner, Margaret Little, and fellow pediatrician Peter Tizard.

republished 1990, p. 35). In a talk delivered to the 1952 Club late on in his life [CW 8:1:2], Winnicott acknowledged Fairbairn's influence:

> I now became aware that Fairbairn had made a tremendous contribution, even if we only take two things. One is object-seeking, which comes into the area of transitional phenomena and so on, and the other is this thing of feeling real instead of feeling unreal. Our patients, more and more, turn out to be needing to feel real, and if they don't, then understanding is of extremely secondary importance.

Winnicott extends classical theory's emphasis on anxiety and defenses in the infant's bodily explorations by introducing the creativity of the moves towards the handling of "truly Not-Me objects," "a tendency to weave 'other-than-me' objects into the personal pattern" (1953 [CW 4:2:21]; 1958 [CW 5:4:24]; 1971 [CW 9:3:5]). The later versions of the paper insist on the normality of the transitional object.

The Psyche Soma

For Winnicott, the mind's origins are located in the psychosomatic matrix created by the mother with her infant, where the movement from dependence to independence physically is accompanied by a psychical parallel: the infant, in attaining the ordinary milestones of human development, develops a way of understanding them and symbolizing them to himself or herself. Bodily achievements and how the baby makes sense of them form the foundations for internality, consciousness, and unconsciousness. The mind–body relation is implicated in a developmental approach that links the one-person model with a psychology of interdependence through the infant's initial experience, his or her "going on being"—for Winnicott, a fundamental for healthy living.

The origins and development of mind and thinking focus on two perspectives consistently repeated throughout his work. In the case of healthy development, Winnicott proposes we can take the mind for granted, assuming its primacy in a person's location of self in body as a facet of integration: "Given the necessary environmental conditions the mind is a specialized part of the overall organization of the infant's integration of psyche and soma." It does not exist separately, but is "the *imaginative elaboration of somatic parts, feelings, and functions*, that is, of physical aliveness. [It] is dependent on the existence and the healthy functioning of the brain, [but] is not, however, felt by the individual to be localized in the brain, or indeed to be localized anywhere" [CW 3:4:20].

For the infant who has to deal with environmental (maternal) failure beyond his or her capacities, there are several possibilities which result in distorted development: "(a) over-activity in mental functioning, where psyche–soma is in opposition to mind and 'thinking' results in a precociously self-sufficient child; (b) a 'without mind' state, where the self affects stupidity; (c) a 'without psyche' self, where the imagination is curtailed; (d) a 'false self' acting as a carapace to protect the hidden true self" [CW 6:1:22]. The processes of dissociation between psyche and soma may give rise to mind as a split-off phenomenon or to illness manifested in the body.

In two papers from the 1960s, "Thinking and Symbol Formation" [CW 8:2:48] and "New Light on Children's Thinking" [CW 7:2:1], probably part of the wide-spread interest occasioned by Bion's paper on thinking (1962), Winnicott returns to "Mind and Its Relation to the Psyche-Soma" [CW 3:4:20] as a still good enough account of the ontological origins of thinking. The early paper is grounded in the Freudian assumption of the ego as first a bodily ego and Winnicott's exploration of it through the bodily relationship of the baby with the mother as fundamental to the emergence of both psyche and mind. As Dodi Goldman puts it, 'before fantasy can become visual it took the form of being experienced in the body but not yet associated with the body (Goldman, 1993, p. 163).

Clinical Directions

"Primitive Emotional Development" (1945) begins from classical analysis's organization around the patient's relations with whole people and "the conscious and unconscious fantasies that enrich and complicate them" [CW 2:7:8]. After Klein, the increased realization of the importance of a patient's fantasies about his or her own inner world and its origins in instinctual experience requires "new understanding but not new technique." The work on early infantile development, however, leads to areas that do demand a different awareness, changes in the transference, and perhaps adjustments in technique. The analysis of ambivalence and the analysis of depression produce different realizations of what the patient requires. For patients whose problems stem from the pre-depressive stage and an unformulated relation to objects, Winnicott's theoretical and technical contributions still offer continuing insights for clinical work.

Patients with problems at this level place heavy demands on the analyst, and variations in technique relate to those sort of patients. This work developed from his interest in primitive development and his understanding of un-integration and integration and its determinants in the infant–environment setup. What Winnicott termed "regression to dependence" has similarities with Balint's notion of "the basic fault" (1968). Both analysts were working in the tradition of Sandor Ferenczi and his recognition that, for some patients, classical analysis hinders rather than assists. Winnicott was clear that "management" was to be undertaken only by the most experienced clinicians. He writes, "Similarly, it would seem to me that the more schizoid depressions call for a consideration of what Balint calls the basic fault—just like the more certain schizophrenias. At the level of the basic fault there is no third person and for me this makes sense" ("Remarks on a Discussion of Balint's Paper on Technique" [CW 5:3:8]). Margaret Little (1990) and Harry

Guntrip (1975), analysands of Winnicott and clinicians themselves, have written of their experiences with him, while the second case added to the 1971 version of *Transitional Objects and Transitional Phenomena* provides his own description of work of this kind (1971 [CW 9:3:5]).

In "Clinical Varieties of Transference" [CW 5:1:11], Winnicott links the importance of infant care and the notion of transference when an established ego cannot be assumed, when environmental adaptation has not been good enough, to a "pseudo-self which is a collection of innumerable reactions to a succession of failures of adaptation." He goes on to develop the idea of a false and true self with the former protecting the latter; the former "is not involved in the reacting, and so preserves a continuity of being. However, this hidden true self suffers an impoverishment that derives from lack of experience" [CW 5:1:11]. More extended discussion of the false self continues in his papers from the 1960s [CW 6:1:22; CW 7:1:1]. Work of this kind makes the psychoanalytic setting more important than the act of interpretation.

With a patient who is unable to engage in external reality "objectively," the task of the analyst becomes one of surviving repetition of the original failure situation in the transference: "We now find all these matters coming along for revival and correction in the transference relationship, matters which are not so much for interpretation as for experiencing" [CW 9:1:4]. Through repetition in the new situation of analysis, the patient moves from the era of "the subjective object" to placing/finding the analyst in the actual external world, and the analyst comes to be experienced as other. Winnicott's work in this area has suffered from much misinformation and misunderstanding, but it derives directly from his work with borderline and psychotic patients and his attention to early infantile development. The *Collected Works* provides rich evidence of extensive clinical work that demonstrates his skill and empathy with patients of all ages and all conditions.

The case history *Holding and Interpretation. Fragment of an Analysis*[4] [CW 4:4:1] demonstrates a Winnicott committed to interpretations and to the words his patient deploys as the medium of the analysis. The two concepts may be approached as alternatives, sequentially, or with each having a place from moment to moment in the work of any analysis. Where "holding" might apparently lead towards a priority being ascribed to the preverbal unconscious and its modalities, "interpretation" would appear to locate the treatment in a more classical framework of words. Winnicott presents them as two always-linked forms of the analytic process.

This patient, who is determined on talk that he counts on Winnicott to hear and share, was also the subject of the paper "Withdrawal and Regression" [CW 4:3:29], published in 1955, which addresses the period of analysis immediately preceding that described in *Holding and Interpretation*. Winnicott summarized, "I would say

[4] A version of this was published in 1972 with commentary by the American analyst Alfred Flarsheim (Giovacchini, 1972). A definitive version with an introduction by Masud Khan was published in 1986 (Karnac Books) [CW 4:4:1].

that *in the withdrawn state a patient is holding the self* and that if immediately the withdrawn state appears *the analyst can hold the patient*, then what would otherwise have been a withdrawal state becomes a regression" [CW 4:3:29].

This appears to be the pattern discernible in the dense material made available through Winnicott's note-taking in the treatment. His acceptance of the patient's withdrawal into sleep, together with how he addresses it, aims to use the withdrawals in the service of the analytic process. Both withdrawal and regression to dependence are different from the transient states of regression that analysts recognize in their more intact patients. In this approach, the reliability of the setting assumes greater importance than any other factor and may involve modifications of normal analytic practice. An unhurried transference underpins the work, and his explicit references to it identify early trauma and its effects.

In later years, Winnicott would express increasing reluctance to interpret, but, with this patient, it is words that provide the holding environment of the analysis. When the patient describes how he avoids feeling "stopped" at the end of the session, "losing or being thrown out," he says, "I usually keep quiet about it but I feel uncomfortable. It is very difficult to be stopped in midstream."

Winnicott links the patient's affect with an explicitly Freudian interpretation: "I know that the expression 'stopped in midstream' is a metaphor but it is the nearest you have come to the idea of castration. I would say that it was as if you were stopped passing water in the middle of doing so and it brings to mind three degrees of rivalry; one in which there is perfection and the only thing you can do is to be perfect, too. The second is that you and your rival kill each other; and the third, which has now been introduced, is that one of the two is maimed."

As if it were a debate, the patient says, "I accept the idea here of being stopped in the middle of passing water; it is also very much as if one were stopped in the middle of intercourse." Winnicott's interpretation brings the end of the session into a relation with its beginning, "We thus come around to your using the word impotence in describing your feelings after the end of yesterday's session. I would like to join up the idea of your being interrupted in intercourse with your own impulses as a child to interrupt your parents when they were together" [all quotes from CW 4:4:1].

Despite the Oedipal dimensions and his willingness to use them here, Winnicott consistently approaches the patient through the theoretical lens of early infantile development. He frequently states the patient's conviction of his unlovableness and his (Winnicott's) love for him: "Behind this is hopelessness about loving and being loved, and this applies now and here, in your relationship to me" [CW 4:4:1, p. 330]. "The barrier is between you and me, and one of the things that it avoids is the idea of my loving you" (p. 411). Or, on June 17, "The new situation comes from the idea which is the opposite of deprivation, that to some extent, here and now, I have love for you" (p. 436). Winnicott's assessment of the patient's having given up, very early, any belief in himself as lovable, provides the bases for the number of interpretive references he makes about his love for his patient and his decision to maintain this as an issue, perhaps the central issue of the transference.

Armellini's discussion of Winnicott's clinical work with children in *Therapeutic Consultations in Child Psychiatry* (Chapter 11 this volume) and Groarke's account of "The Piggle" (Chapter 12 this volume) reveal the depth of Winnicott's knowledge of Freud, his extraordinary ability to make relationships with children, his capacities as a clinician, and his thorough insertion into psychoanalysis. Winnicott the analyst always seems to have been interested in enabling the patient to arrive at a realization for himself or herself and, where possible, to approach analysis as a collaboration, ideas that have had immense consequences for psychoanalytic technique and its aims to this day. André Green argues that the importance of transitionality is not the object, but the account of a space lending itself to the creation "of" objects (in 1978, pp. 176–177): "The essential feature is no longer interpreting, but enabling the subject to live out creative experiences of a new category of objects."

Creativity

An undated piece by Winnicott, "Ideas and Definitions" [CW 9:4:1], takes up creativity through the symbolic dimension of the "transitional object" and the location of symbolic and creative functioning for the infant in this stage "between" an early proto-fantasy "self" and the proto-external reality "m/other." "The origin of transitional space . . . is par excellence the dimension of connectedness" (Deri, 1978, p. 50).

By arguing [CW 4:2:21; CW 5:3:20; CW 6:3:3] that the child's move towards a transitional object is an important developmental acquisition in its own right, "not so much the object used as the use of the object" (Introduction to *Playing and Reality* [CW 9:3:4]), Winnicott extends the psychoanalytic account of symbolization beyond a base in compensation or deprivation, an emphasis similar to Marion Milner's in her paper "The Role of Illusion in Symbol Formation" (formerly "Aspects of Symbolism in Comprehension of the Not-Self" [1952]). This paper is an account of her work with Klein's grandson, first published in the IJPA seventieth birthday Festschrift for Melanie Klein (1952) and republished in *New Directions in Psychoanalysis* (1955, 1987). In her sessions with her little patient and her observation of and participation in their play, Milner became increasingly convinced that "a sense of pattern and dramatic form in what he produced" had implications for how the boy himself was to be understood. While she acknowledged that his play may also have been reparative in quality, she was more interested in its relation to the initial establishment of object relationships (1987, p. 97). She thought that her patient's material and his involvement with her (what Winnicott would later describe as his "use" of her) required a special state of mind, which she likened to "a state where the spectator is at one with the work of art"

(1987, p. 97). She put together her analytic experience and her experience as an artist to propose a parallel between art and "states that are part of everyday experience in healthy infancy" (p. 98) and further suggested that "states of illusion, of oneness are perhaps a recurrently necessary phase in the growth of the sense of twoness" (p. 100). Milner thus shifted "the psychoanalytic interest from symbols representing the past, to the symbolisation used to establish and extend relations in the present" (Podro, 1998, p. 171).

Like Winnicott, Milner emphasized the value of the object created in itself, its externality, its material existence. In this, she diverged from Ernest Jones's classic 1916 paper "On Symbolism" and from Hanna Segal's reading in "A Psychoanalytic Approach to Aesthetics," originally published in the same volumes (1952, 1955). Milner's interest in the creative impulse at work in art is extended to her wider analytic concern with the foundations of human development and is very similar to Winnicott's, whose work invites us to build up a capacity for what may be termed a psychoanalytic imagination. Winnicott's whole account derives from the place of illusion in human development. In 1971, he refers to the "further idea" of "paradox," a word introduced in 1958 in "The Capacity to Be Alone" [CW 5:3:20], which, along with play and playing, cultural experience, and what transitional space enables, carries forward the concentration on aliveness, health, and its roots in experience.

Through a consistent attention to body and mind and their simultaneous shaping by both internal and external factors, creative human development is enabled through the relationship with the world first represented by maternal care. Through a reaching outwards driven by need/anxiety (its substitutive aspect) and by a curiosity and an interest related to aliveness, the division between self and other establishes inner life, ultimately fostering the capacity to be alone with and contented in oneself. In "The Capacity to Be Alone" [CW 5:3:20], Winnicott describes how the infant gains some appreciation of the mother's continued existence ("I do not necessarily mean an awareness with the conscious mind") that "makes it possible for the infant to be alone and to enjoy being alone, for a limited period."

This sense of location and groundedness in the infant and its contribution to the infant's sense of aliveness forms the basis of inner security and potential space. A space that exists between one thing and another—an intermediate, in-between area, designated as spatial, but also crucially dependent upon time—has to emerge to enable creative living. If Winnicott's later versions of "Transitional Objects and Transitional Phenomena" make a more complex statement about the place of desire in the infant's act of creating, then the original paper also drew attention to it (1951 [CW 3:6:6]). In having the illusion of bringing about the world, the infant equates feeling and doing, thus leading to a state of being that is guaranteed by the mother's holding. Her repeated recognition of the baby's spontaneous gesture leads to the capacity to use a transitional object. The baby "can gradually come to recognize the illusory element, the fact of playing and imagining. Here is the basis for the symbol which at first is *both* the infant's spontaneity or hallucination, *and also* the external object created and ultimately cathected" [CW 6:1:22].

In *On Not Being Able to Paint,* Milner asks (1950, pp. 154–156), "May there not be moments in which there is a plunge into no-differentiation, which results (if all goes well) in a re-emerging into a new division of the me-not-me, one in which there is more of the 'me' in the 'not-me' and more of the 'not-me' in the 'me'"? Winnicott's review of this book [CW 3:6:15] suggests that her claim that "wish-fulfilling illusion may be the essential basis for all true objectivity" is potentially shocking for psychoanalysts:

> She [Milner] wishes to say that [creativity] results from what is for her (and perhaps for everyone) the primary human predicament. This predicament arises out of the non-identity of what is conceived of and what is to be perceived. To the objective mind of another person seeing from outside, that which is outside the individual is never identical with what is inside that individual. But there can be, and must be, for health (so the writer implies), a meeting place, an overlap, a stage of illusion, intoxication, transfiguration. In the arts this meeting place is pre-eminently found through the medium, that bit of the external world, which takes the form of the inner conception. In painting, in writing, music, etc., the individual may find islands of peace and so get momentary relief from the primary predicament of healthy human beings.

Play, after his book *Playing and Reality*, a concept almost synonymous with Winnicott, occurs in the transitional space through which the child begins to relate psychologically and bodily with objects in the external world. "Play" and "playing" extend the psychoanalytic links to art and culture and even more to what happens in the consulting room—the very basis of analytic work. "Why Children Play' [CW 2:4:4] contains two statements that anticipate the work of the 1960s and the increasingly frequent references to transitional space: play as the continuous evidence of creativity, which means aliveness (quoted in Abram, 2007, p. 150), and play as linking the individual's relation to inner personal reality with his or her relation to external or shared reality (p. 151). References to play are consistently present throughout the *Collected Works*, but his major theoretical discussions were given in the 1960s. There, creativity in and of the self is extended by the significance ascribed to the infant's aggression and the destruction of the object (mother/analyst) in fantasy. Creativity develops as the self makes and remakes reality in its own way, and Winnicott proposes its importance in its everyday form and in great art. The capacity to play something good into existence, to master, shape, and construct reality, is a human potential in doing and making that is the growth of imagination from infancy.

Winnicott's colleagues in the Independent tradition have continued this work. Along with Marion Milner, Charles Rycroft (1968) challenged psychoanalysts to develop a nonpathological place for creativity, art, and religion. More recently,

Michael Parsons has asserted its place at the heart of his thinking: "This view, based on Winnicott, is of the creative process itself. It does not see that process as being secondary to anything, nor as any kind of corrective or compensatory activity, but as a central expression of what it means to be human" (2000, p. 170). In arguing the artist's creation of self and world, of inside and outside, through a capacity—which may also be a necessity—to make forms that fit experience, Ken Wright has proposed a changed emphasis towards the work of analysis (Wright, 2000). Perhaps it is Christopher Bollas's consistent attention to "the creative transformations of self achieved through the use of the object" (1995, p. 88) and his focus on the revolutionary possibilities of the dream, the work of art, and free association in transforming psychic reality into another register that most clearly brings together Winnicott's and Freud's discoveries: "If we cannot have singular objects to embrace for consolation's sake, we do have the body of separate forms, into which and through which we alter and articulate our being. This is the great promise of any art form. It is, often enough, the reality of the psychoanalytic method" (Bollas, 1999). To transform the world creatively so that it meets with our own experience rather than complying and capitulating to the world's demands could be an account of what life and work involve, psychoanalysis included.

In her introduction to Volume 7, Anna Ferruta comments on Winnicott's contribution as President of the British Psychoanalytical Society to the celebrations on October 8, 1966, marking the publication of the *Standard Edition of the Psychological Works of Sigmund Freud*: "He remarked that Freud 'gave new value to inner psychic reality, and from this came a new value for things that are actual and truly external.'" In other words, he reaffirmed the indissoluble link between the internal world, to which Freud gave the status of scientific existence, and the external world, which is made real and available only by the internal world.

Organization

The *Collected Works* comprises eleven volumes of previously published and new texts and a selection of letters, presented in chronological order following either the date of delivery, writing, or first publication, and an accompanying volume of end material. Some undatable items have been grouped together as the final part of Volume 9. For more information on the structure and organization of the *Collected Works*, see the Introduction to Volume 12.

This entire collection is also available online together with many of Winnicott's original audio recordings and an introduction to his collection of broadcasts to parents by journalist and author Anne Karpf.

In compiling these collected works, the editors made all reasonable efforts to preserve Winnicott's original writings and publications with minimal editorial intervention. For this reason, certain spellings and some points of style, such as citation format and figure numbering, vary from piece to piece. For the convenience of the reader, figure numbers have been added in instances where the original figures were unnumbered. All editorial notes are marked with lowercase roman numerals and, in the print edition, appear as footnotes. Winnicott's own notes are marked with Arabic numerals and appear as endnotes. Editorial interpolations in the original text and notes appear in square brackets. Cross-references to works appearing elsewhere in the *Collected Works* have been added to aid the reader. These references are indicated by an abbreviation that includes volume, part, and chapter numbers (e.g., "CW 2:7:8" for Volume 2, Part 7, Chapter 8). Chapter number is not given for whole books that make up an entire part—in these instances, only volume and part are given. While the *Collected Works* is as complete as possible a collection of Winnicott's work, it does not include works that remain inaccessible or that are protected by confidentiality restrictions.

References

Abram, J. (2007). *The Language of Winnicott: a dictionary of Winnicott's use of words'* (2nd Edition). London: Karnac.

Aguayo, J. (2002). Reassessing the clinical affinity between Melanie Klein and DW Winnicott (1935–51). *International Journal of Psychoanalysis, 83*, 1133–1152.

Balint, M. (1968). *The basic fault*. London: Tavistock.

Baranger, M., & Baranger, W. (2008). The analytic situation as a dynamic field. *International Journal of Psychoanalysis, 89*, 795–826.

Beckett, S. (1983). *Worstward ho*. London: John Calder.

Bezoari, M., & Ferro, A. (1992). Percorsi nel campo bipersonale dell'analisi: Dal gioco delle parti alle trasformazioni di coppia. In L. Nissim Momigliano & A. Robutti (Eds.), *L'esperienza condivisa*. Milano: Cortina, 63–82.

Bion, W. R. (1962). A theory of thinking. *International Journal of Psychoanalysis, 43*, pts 4/5, 306–310.

Bion, W. R. (1984/1987). A theory of thinking. In *Second thoughts. Selected papers on psychoanalysis*. Maresfield Library. London: Karnac, 110–119.

Bléger, J. (1967). Psychoanalysis of the psychoanalytic frame. *International Journal of Psychoanalysis, 48*, 511–519; reprinted 2012, *93*, 993–1003.

Bollas, C. (1995). *Cracking up*. London/New York: Routledge/Hill and Wang.

Bollas, C. (1999). Creativity and psychoanalysis. In *The mystery of things*. London/New York: Routledge. Reprinted in *The Christopher Bollas Reader*, 2011 (pp. 194–206).

Deri, S. (1978). Transitional phenomena: Vicissitudes of symbolization and creativity. In S. Grolnick & M. Barkin (Eds.), *Between fantasy and reality* (pp. 43–60). New York: Jason Aronson.

Fairbairn, R. (1941). A revised psychopathology of the psychoses and psychoneuroses. In *Psychoanalytic studies of the personality*. 1952 Tavistock Publications; reprinted 1992, 1994, Routledge 28–58.

Giovacchini P. (Ed.) (1972). *Tactics and techniques in psychoanalytic therapy*. London: Hogarth.

Goldman, D. (1993). In *One's bones: The clinical genius of Winnicott.* New York: Jason Aronson.

Green, A. (1978). Potential space in psychoanalysis: The object in the setting. In S. Grolnick & M. Barkin (Eds.), *Between fantasy and reality* (pp. 167–189). New York: Jason Aronson.

Grosskurth, P. (1986). *Melanie Klein. Her world and her work.* London: Hodder and Stoughton.

Guntrip, H. (1975). My experience of analysis with Winnicott and Fairbairn. *International Review of Psychoanalysis,* 2, 145–156; reprinted in *International Journal of Psychoanalysis,* 1996, 77, 739–754.

Heaney, S. (1979). *Song in Opened Ground: Selected Poems 1966–1996.* New York: Straus and Giroux.

James, M. (1962). The theory of the parent-infant relationship: Contribution to the discussion. *International Journal of Psychoanalysis,* 43, 247–248.

Johns, J. (2006). D. W. Winnicott; Life, work. Precis in R. Skelton (Ed.), *The Edinburgh international encyclopaedia of psychoanalysis* (pp. 498–491). Edinburgh: Edinburgh University Press.

Jones, E. (1916). The theory of symbolism. *British Journal of Psychology,* 9, 181–229. Reprinted in E. Jones, Ed. (1948), *Papers on psychoanalysis.* London: Bailliere, Tindall and Cox.

Kahr, B. (1996). *D. W. Winnicott, a biographical portrait.* London: Karnac.

King, P., & Steiner, R. (Eds.). (1991). *The Freud/Klein controversies.* London: Routledge.

Klein, M. (1946). Notes on some schizoid mechanisms. In *Envy and gratitude and other works. The writings of Melanie Klein,* Vol. 3, 1946–1963 (pp. 1–24). International Psychoanalytical Library Series, No. 103. London: Hogarth Press & Institute of Psychoanalysis.

Klein, M. (1963). On the sense of loneliness. In *Envy and gratitude,* Vol. 3, 1946–1963 (pp. 300–313). International Psychoanalytical Library Series, No. 103. London: Hogarth Press & Institute of Psychoanalysis.

Kristeva, J. (2001) *Melanie Klein.* New York: Columbia University Press.

Likierman, M. (2001). *Melanie Klein: Her work in context.* London: Continuum.

Little, M. (1990). *Psychotic anxieties and containment.* Northvale, NJ: Jason Aronson.

Middlemore, M. (1941). *The nursing couple.* London: Hamish Hamilton.

Milner, M. (1950). *On not being able to paint.* London: Heinemann Educational Books. Reprinted 2010, London/New York: Routledge.

Milner, M. (1952). Aspects of symbolism in comprehension of the not-self. *International Journal of Psychoanalysis,* 33, 11–195. London: Institute of Psychoanalysis. Thereafter, The role of illusion in symbol formation, in *The suppressed madness of sane men* (pp. 83–113). London: Routledge, 1987.

Modell, A. (1985). The works of Winnicott and the evolution of his thought. *Journal of the American Psychoanalytic Association,* 335, 113–137.

Ogden, T. H. (1992). The dialectically constituted/decentred subject of psychoanalysis, II: The contributions of Klein and Winnicott. *International Journal of Psychoanalysis,* 73, 613–626.

Ogden, T. H. (2001). Reading Winnicott. *Psychoanalytic Quarterly,* 70, 299–323.

Ogden, T. H. (2005). *This art of psychoanalysis. Dreaming dreams and interrupted cries.* New Library of Psychoanalysis, in association with the Institute of Psychoanalysis. London/New York: Routledge.

Parsons, M. (2000). *The dove that returns, the dove that vanishes. Paradox and creativity in psychoanalysis.* New Library of Psychoanalysis, in association with the Institute of Psychoanalysis. London/Philadelphia: Routledge.

Phillips, A. (1988). *Winnicott.* In F. Kermode (Ed.), Fontana Modern Masters Series. London: Fontana.

Podro, M. (1998). *Depiction.* New Haven, CT/London: Yale University Press.

Reeves, C. (2006). The anatomy of riddance. *Journal of Child Psychotherapy, 32*(3), 273–294.

Rodman, F. R. (2003). *Winnicott life and work.* A Merloyd-Lawrence book. New York: Perseus.

Rycroft, C. (1968). Beyond the reality principle. In *Imagination and reality; Psychoanalytical essays 1951–1961* (pp. 102–113). London: Hogarth. Reprinted by Karnac, London, 1987.

Segal, H. (1955). A psychoanalytic approach to aesthetics. In M. Klein, P. Heimann, & R. Money-Kyrle (Eds.), *New directions in psychoanalysis.* London: Tavistock. Republished by Karnac (pp. 384–405), 1985.

Turner, J. (2002). Illusion in the work of Winnicott. *International Journal of Psychoanalysis, 83*, 1051–1062.

Winnicott, D. W. (1931). *Clinical notes on disorders of childhood.* [CW 1:3:1–20]

Winnicott, D. W. (1934). Papular urticaria and the dynamics of skin sensation. [CW 1:4:3]

Winnicott, D. W. (1941). The observation of infants in a set situation. [CW 2:3:6]

Winnicott, D. W. (1942). Why children play. [CW 2:4:4]

Winnicott, D. W. (1945). Primitive emotional development. [CW 2:7:8]

Winnicott, D. W. (1945). Why do babies cry? [CW 2:6:2]

Winnicott, D. W. (1949). Hate in the countertransference. [CW 3:2:1]

Winnicott, D. W. (1951). Review: *On not being able to paint*, Marion Milner. [CW 3:6:15]

Winnicott, D. W. (1953). Transitional objects and transitional phenomena. [CW 4:2:21]

Winnicott, D. W. (1954). Mind and its relation to the psyche-soma [1949]. [CW 3:4:20]

Winnicott, D. W. (1955). Withdrawal and regression [1954]. [CW 4:3:29]

Winnicott, D. W. (1956). Clinical varieties of transference [1955]. [CW 5:1:11]

Winnicott, D. W. (1957). Aggression [ca. 1939]. [CW 2:1:8]

Winnicott, D. W. (1958). Aggression in relation to emotional development [1958]. [CW 3:5:2]

Winnicott, D. W. (1958). The capacity to be alone. [CW 5:3:20]

Winnicott, D. W. (1958). The manic defence. [1935]. [CW 1:4:6]

Winnicott, D. W. (1958). Transitional objects and transitional phenomena. [CW 5:4:24] [1971; CW 9:3:5]

Winnicott, D. W. (1964). *The child, the family, and the outside world.* [not reprinted in this form in *Collected Works*]

Winnicott, D. W. (1965). Ego distortion in terms of true and false self [1960]. [CW 6:1:22]

Winnicott, D. W. (1971). *Playing and reality.* [not reprinted in this form in *Collected Works*]

Winnicott, D. W. (1971). *Therapeutic consultations in child psychiatry.* [CW 10]

Winnicott, D. W. (1971). Transitional objects and transitional phenomena. [CW 9:3:5]

Winnicott, D. W. (1977). *The Piggle: An account of the psycho-analytic treatment of a little girl* (I. Ramzy, Ed.). [CW 11:2:1–17]

Winnicott, D. W. (1986). The concept of the false self [1964]. [CW 7:1:1]

Winnicott, D. W. (1986). *Holding and interpretation: Fragment of an analysis.* [CW 4:4:1]

Winnicott, D. W. (1988). *Human nature.* [CW 11:1]

Winnicott, D. W. (1989). "D. W. W. on D. W. W." [1967]. [CW 8:1:2]

Winnicott, D. W. (1989). Ideas and definitions [n.d.; early 1950s]. [CW 9:4:1]

Winnicott, D. W. (1989). Thinking and symbol-formation [1968]. [CW 8:2:48]
Winnicott, D. W. (1989). The use of an object in the context of *Moses and Monotheism* [1989]. [CW 9:1:4]
Winnicott, D. W. (1991). On scientific aims in psychoanalysis (Resolution K) [1942]. [CW 2:4:1]
Winnicott, D. W. (2016). Remarks on a discussion of Balint's paper on technique [1957]. [CW 5:3:8]
Winnicott, D. W. (2016). A study of envy and gratitude [1956]. [CW 5:2:5]
Winnicott, D. W. (2017). The unconscious [1966]. [CW 7:3:29]
Wright, K. (2000). To make experience sing. In L. Caldwell (Ed.), *Art, creativity, living* (pp. 75–96). Winnicott Studies Monograph Series. London/New York: Karnac.

{2}

From Pediatrics to Psychoanalysis, 1911–1938

Ken Robinson

In this early period of his work, Winnicott's originality emerges out of the facilitating environment of his education[1] and pediatric experience. Just as Winnicott himself put great store in taking a history, so, in this essay, I shall set out the context in which he began to develop his unique thinking and skills.

Medical Education: The Facilitating Environment at Barts and Beyond

When, after a disappointingly arid premedical training at Cambridge, Winnicott registered at St. Bartholomew's Hospital Medical College in November 1917, he had already enlisted (June 7) in the Royal Navy Volunteer Reserve as a temporary Surgeon Probationer and had sailed on the Torpedo Boat Destroyer *HMS Lucifer*.[2] He remained in the RNVR throughout the war, rising to the rank of Temporary Surgeon Sub-Lieutenant. While at Cambridge, Winnicott had already had some exposure to hospital life as a trainee in the temporary wartime hospitals. There, he was remembered for his capacity to entertain his patients with "a comic song on Saturday evenings in the ward" (Winnicott, C., 1978, p. 11). His time on *Lucifer*, however, thrust him into the immediate horror of war. It both confronted him with the limits of his knowledge in a stressful situation and taught him how to be with patients in his care. The unqualified Winnicott was the sole medical practitioner on board, unskilled in the everyday business of attending to the medical needs of the crew—he cheerfully admitted that he could not tell the difference between gonorrhea and syphilis (Anonymous, 1961, p. 137). It was fortunate that when *Lucifer* saw action he had an experienced medical orderly to help with casualties.

---

[1] Winnicott did not like the term "training," preferring "education." I have avoided using "training" as much as possible. (http://www.blundells.org/obclub/obclub/where_are_they_now.htm#davisja)

[2] For the biography of Winnicott, see Brett Kahr (1996) and F. Robert Rodman (2003).

It is not clear exactly when Winnicott began his studies at Barts, but he qualified as a doctor on February 2, 1920, becoming a Member of the Royal College of Surgeons and a Licentiate of the Royal College of Physicians in the same year. He trained in a climate of radical change in medical education that was enshrined in the Haldane Report (1913).[3] Two key figures in this change, Archibald Garrod and Francis Fraser, were influential in his education and early professional development. The Haldane Report had recommended that professorial units be established in the major London hospitals to provide the scientific foundation for medicine already in place in Germany and America. The war intervened, so that it was not until October 1919 that two units were established at Barts, one headed by Garrod, who had worked hard to import a "scientific spirit and atmosphere" into medicine and to root medical education in both the laboratory and the ward (Garrod, 1908, p. 21). Fraser was appointed as Garrod's Assistant Director. When within a year Garrod moved to take up the Regius Chair of Medicine at Oxford, Fraser took over as Director. Fraser, whom Winnicott acknowledged in the Preface to *Clinical Notes on Disorders of Childhood* (1931 [CW 1:3:Preface]), was his chief at the Professorial Unit from 1921 to 1922. It was to Fraser he owed his easy passage to MRCP in 1922.

Barts provided an environment for Winnicott's practice as a pediatrician to take root. There, he encountered Thomas Horder, one of the most respected doctors of his day, who influenced him profoundly. Horder combined clinical sensitivity with a tough-minded scientific attitude—indeed, his enthusiasm for science played a significant part in the changes that were afoot in medicine and medical education (Lawrence, 1999, pp. 429–431). In later life, Winnicott said that psychoanalysis was an extension of the discipline of history-taking that he had absorbed from Horder. Winnicott learned from him to listen to the patient's own story and to take a careful history (Winnicott, C., 1978, p. 12). "The doctor-patient relationship," Horder believed, "is the very soul of good doctoring" (Horder, 1966, p. 56). Winnicott's own insistence on the importance of history-taking is heard repeatedly in his papers: the first chapter of *Clinical Notes* is entitled "History-taking."

Horder was not alone at Barts in stressing that the patient was more than a bundle of symptoms. Garrod, too, emphasized the importance of the patient's individuality and history, not least in his classic 1902 paper on genetic inheritance (Garrod, 1902), and Fraser, who built on Garrod's research, held both that an accurate diagnosis must take into account the patient's social situation and that treating the patient included caring for the patient (Bearn, 2008, p. 29).

All three of these influential figures had worked with children. At Great Ormond Street Hospital, Horder had found his own way of getting onto terms with young patients. He reassured children who were afraid of throat inspection by training

[3] For a detailed account of the development of medical training at Barts at this time, see Waddington (2003), pp. 146–217.

a large black cat to sit on his consulting room desk and open its mouth so that he could depress its tongue with a teaspoon (Horder, 1966, p. 27). His strategy lacks the psychological subtlety of Winnicott's spatula game, but it does share a playful attention to the child's responses. A sentence from Garrod's introductory chapter to *Diseases of Children* (1913), which became a standard textbook, offers a fitting epigraph to his work: "No man can be a good children's doctor who does not have a real love of children" (Garrod et al., 1913, p. 1). It is echoed in Winnicott's description of work with children in *Clinical Notes* as requiring "a specialised form of friendship."

Another figure important in this brief account of the matrix of Winnicott's early development is his predecessor at Paddington Green Children's Hospital, Leonard Guthrie. In his introduction to *Clinical Notes* (1931), Winnicott notes four stages in the recent history of the development of treatment for "indefinite and chronic unwellness." Ten years earlier, there was a tendency to assign children to a diagnostic category according to their symptoms. Then came clinicians who "recognised and emphasised the nervous mechanisms behind the symptoms, but accounted for the nervousness along bio-chemical lines." They were followed by those "who recognise the purely psychological nature of the mechanisms underlying the symptoms but lay all the stress on the environmental factor." Finally came the discovery, recent in 1931, that "the nervous child is nervous for internal reasons. According to this view environment is of indirect importance, as, for instance, by increasing or decreasing an already existing sense of guilt or by modifying the manifestations of anxiety." In these terms, Guthrie was ahead of his time, for, in 1907, he was already arguing in *Functional Nervous Disorders in Childhood* that symptoms may be the expression of "a neurotic temperament" as a result of "*individual* instability in the nervous system" inherited from the parent(s) (p. 14).

Guthrie shares the humanity that suffuses the work of Horder, Garrod, and Fraser, as shown in his psychological understanding of early development in his chapter on "Functional Nervous Disorders" in *Diseases of Children* (1913). His work is a reminder that we must beware not to assume that all pediatricians before Winnicott were in the dark about psychoanalysis or prejudiced against it. Between 1907 and 1913, Guthrie engaged with Freud's theories of infantile sexuality and hysteria. In 1907, he was unaware that psychoanalysis might illuminate functional disorders, but, in 1913, he refers to Freud on thumb-sucking and masturbation, as well as on nail-biting, and he discusses Freud on hysteria at some length, offering an intelligent-enough précis of the theories of conflict and repression as well as outlining briefly the libidinal phases. Although he is skeptical whether "repressed complexes" are necessarily dynamically unconscious and whether all hysterical phenomena have a sexual etiology, he is far from dismissing Freud (Garrod et al., 1913, pp. 722–725 and 732). In a footnote to *Human Nature*, Winnicott paid tribute to him as a pioneer to whom he owed "the special climate at the Paddington Green Children's Hospital" [CW 11:1:Introduction and see Steven Groarke's contribution to this edition], which made possible his appointment there in 1923, following Guthrie's death. One of Guthrie's colleagues at Paddington Green described watching him at work with children. He might well have been writing of Winnicott: "A bond of sympathy and understanding was soon established, and under its influence the child unfolded and yielded up those secrets, which others had failed to obtain" (Sutherland, 1919, p. 29).

It was because of Winnicott's "leanings towards the psychological in paediatrics" that he was appointed at Paddington Green [CW 11:1:Introduction and see Groarke, Chapter 12 in this edition].

Early Experience as a Pediatrician

After qualification, Winnicott went immediately into working with children, first as Casualty Officer and Resident Medical Officer at Queen's Hospital for Children and then as a House Physician with Francis Fraser. In 1923, he took charge of outpatient departments at both Paddington Green and Queen's where, he told Robert Tod later in life:

> I saw a very large number of patients and was in charge of the L[ondon] C[ounty] C[ouncil] Rheumatism [Supervisory] Clinic which dealt with rheumatic fever and chorea and concomitant heart disease. . . . I also had experience in the early twenties of some other very bad epidemics, notably encephalitis lethargica. We also had to deal with very severe summer diarrhoea and various polio epidemics, and of course those were the days before antibiotics so that our wards were full of children with pus in the lungs or the bones or the meninges. (Letter to Robert Tod [CW 9:1:22])

As Winnicott pointed out to Tod:

> Penicillin put a stop to all that and transformed physical paediatrics into something which could afford to look at the disturbances that belong to the lives of children who are physically healthy. (Letter to Robert Tod [CW 9:1:22])

The majority of the cases discussed by Winnicott in his papers before *Clinical Notes on Disorders of Childhood* (1931) come from his work at Queen's, and, in most of these, he focuses on physical problems. It seems that in his early practice more psychological work was carried out at Paddington Green, although he was busy differentiating the psychological from the physical in both clinics. His early publications are the outcroppings of many hours of contact with children referred with rheumatism, chorea, encephalitis, and the sequelae of measles and polio. They show him at work within a scientific medical community, faithful to his education in the "new medicine." Records also show him active in discussion at professional meetings and in postgraduate medical education. He appears as a respected figure making a valuable contribution to organic medicine and not afraid to speak his mind. He became known as one of the principal investigators of the connection between measles and encephalitis. His early paper with Nancy Gibbs on varicella encephalitis and vaccinia encephalitis [CW 1:2:1] was frequently cited in the years immediately following its publication (e.g., Bender, 1927, p. 626; Turnbull, 1928, p. 334; Greenfield, 1929, p. 297).

Winnicott at Work: "Study the Child and Not the Disease"

When John Davis worked with Winnicott at Paddington Green, he had the opportunity to witness Winnicott's pediatric practice at close quarters:

> Instead of his patients and their parents being marshalled in the waiting area, to be let in one by one, his room was crowded with families who somehow found their way to his desk in the corner when their turn came for what looked like a very informal encounter—albeit he took a careful history, made a thorough physical examination (he enjoyed handling his patients and regarded it as therapeutic as well as diagnostic) and kept good notes.

In *Clinical Notes*, Winnicott advises that "the history of a case can seldom be taken in less than a quarter of an hour" ("History-Taking" [CW 1:3:1], p. 173), a long time in a busy clinic but a time that requires considerable skill. According to Davis:

> Winnicott's consultations were elegant in the sense that what was irrelevant to the case in hand was left out so that history, examination and records were pared down to the essentials and he was able to work through large numbers without getting worried or flustered. (Davis, 1993, p. 96)

Davis witnessed Winnicott at work some twenty years after the period covered by Volume 1, but, by 1946, he already worked with a similar disciplined informality (Goldman, p. 171) that would have been developing earlier. Although his interests became more psychological, he remained the pediatrician and continued to insist on physical examination: "The child must be seen naked," he advises in *Clinical Notes* ("Physical Examination" [CW 1:3:2], p. 190). Winnicott was dedicated to outpatient work: he turned down the opportunity to have beds at a time when beds meant "that one has arrived." He feared that if he became an inpatient doctor he would develop "the capacity not to be disturbed by the distress of the children" (Letter to Robert Tod [CW 9:1:22]). It may be that he was already visiting families in their homes near the hospital (Goldman, 1993, p. 107).

Most who have written about Winnicott's pediatric consultations have talked about the later periods of his work at Paddington Green, the spatula game and squiggles. Winnicott himself indicates that both these procedures were in the making as early as the 1920s ("Therapeutic Consultations" [CW 10], p. 4, and "Collected Papers," p. 52), even though only with hindsight did he understand, with his unique psychoanalytic developmental theory, all that he observed and recorded. His paper on "Appetite and Emotional Disorder" [CW 1:4:11], for example, shows him beginning to conceptualize what happens in the child's use of the spatula. In Winnicott's clinic, "there was always available a metal bowl full of sterilized spatulas, shiny silvered objects set at a right-angle bend" that he could record the child's use of. He had observed this for some time and, by 1936, understood that:

> what [the child] does with the spatula (or with anything else) between the taking and the dropping is a film-strip of the little bit of his inner world that is related to me and his mother at that time, and from this can be guessed a good deal about his inner world experiences at other times and in relation to other people and things.

He describes but had not yet conceptualized all the stages of the spatula game, but the thinking for his paper "The Observation of Infants in a Set Situation" (1941 [CW 2:3:6]) is in process.

Similarly, in the mid-1920s, Winnicott was already noticing moments of special significance when creative contact with the child was evident, although here, too, theoretical formulation lagged behind the spontaneous humanity of his interaction with his patients:

> I was a practicing paediatrician, seeing many patients in my hospital practice and giving the opportunity for as many of the children as possible to communicate with me and to draw pictures and to tell me their dreams. I was struck by the frequency with which *the children had dreamed of me the night before attending.* This dream of the doctor that they were going to see obviously reflected their own imaginative equipment in regard to doctors and dentists and other people who are supposed to be helpful. . . . here I was, as I discovered to my amusement, *fitting in with a preconceived notion.* [CW 10:1 Introduction, see Armellini, Chapter 11 in this edition]

Later, the language of the subjective object allowed him to grasp the significance of these "sacred" moments:

> In this role of subjective object, which rarely outlasts the first or first few interviews, the doctor has a great opportunity for being in touch with the child. . . . If . . . it is used, then the child's belief in being helped is strengthened. . . . so that . . . the interview has resulted in a loosening of the knot and a forward movement in the developmental process. ("Therapeutic Consultations in Child Psychiatry" [CW 10:1:Introduction], p. 30, see Armellini, Chapter 11 in this edition)

Winnicott was acutely aware as a pediatrician working with families that the extent to which such moments can be built on depends on the wider environment.

The Physical and the Psychical: The Baby as a Human Being

From 1929 onwards, Winnicott's contributions begin to be more psychological. His work rests increasingly on the careful distinction of the physical and the psychical (and recognition, as he would later term it, that patients are a "psyche-soma"). Fundamental to this distinction is his conviction that "there is no more sure guarantee against gross error in diagnosis than a clear conception of the onset of unwellness" ("History-Taking," *Clinical Notes* [CW 1:3:1]). It is at work, for example, in his "Diagnosis of Chorea" [CW 1:2:16], written when there was a campaign to prevent heart disease in children, which led to large numbers of children being referred as possibly choreic. He argues that although children may present with symptoms suggesting chorea—growing pains, tiredness, and anxious fidgetiness—where the child is "by nature nervous" and there is no history of the onset of chorea, "the disease is emotional in origin and . . . treatment, if required, would be by appropriate analysis of the emotional state," not prolonged rest in bed. William Gillespie, who knew Winnicott at this time, drew attention to how, in such work, he "risked his whole professional reputation in the interests of the children, for had one of them died this would doubtless have been ruined" (1971, p. 228).

Despite such courage, he was careful in his earlier, more psychologically oriented papers to understate the claim of psychoanalysis as a "radical treatment" for diseases of emotional origin, especially anxiety states. He was aware that many of his colleagues were neither willing nor able to recognize an emotional basis for disease. At meetings with colleagues, however, he was less guarded, as, for instance, in his contribution to a discussion on "The Difficult Child" at the Royal Society of Medicine (December 10, 1929 [CW 1:4:4 (footnote i)]). In the presence of the psychologically minded Bernard Hart, Emanuel Miller, Margaret Lowenfeld, J. R. Rees, and Mary Chadwick, he spoke uncompromisingly of "the fact that symptoms usually represented an attempt at spontaneous cure [a phrase he owed to one of his psychoanalytic teachers, Edward Glover] for a disease due to conflict in the unconscious."

Winnicott's concern with sifting psychical from physical symptoms as part of exploring the relationship of psyche and soma is central to his book *Clinical Notes* (1931 [CW 1:3]), aimed at the general practitioner. *Clinical Notes* is, as Winnicott says, written from the heart, forthright in its criticism of bad diagnosis and practice and rooted in careful physical examination and observation, as well as in listening to the child and mother as the best foundation for restoring the child to health. In this spirit, it offers a plethora of clinical vignettes designed to talk the practitioner through the challenges of different disorders, and, lightly but firmly, it presents psychoanalytic thinking as an important aid to understand "the majority of symptoms on account of which mothers would like to seek advice [which] are directly or indirectly the result of anxiety." As John Davis notes, Winnicott's book contains "many apt and original observations." If it is now "a curiosity," it is mainly "due to a shift in epidemiology rather than because his ideas were mistaken" (Davis, 1993, p. 95).

This movement towards the psychological in Winnicott's writing is consistent with his own account of how, in his analysis with James Strachey, "I became gradually able to see a baby as a human being. This was really the chief result of my first five years of analysis" ("D. W. W. on D. W. W." [CW 8:1:2]). He had begun analysis with Strachey in 1923, staying with him for ten years.

Education as a Psychoanalyst

Winnicott first encountered psychoanalytic thinking as a medical student as a result of anxiety that he could no longer remember his dreams. He sought help in the form of Oskar Pfister's *The Psychoanalytic Method* (1915) and in 1919 read Freud's *The Interpretation of Dreams* (1900). Both affected him so deeply that he recognized that psychoanalysis would play some sort of part in his future life (Winnicott, C., 1978, p. 13), even if it were only, as he put it in a letter to his sister Violet [CW 1:1:11], as a "hobby." In this letter, he instructs Violet in the nature of the unconscious, repression, the way that the repressed asserts itself unbeknown in conscious life, and the instincts (which he understands, probably following Pfister, as "natural directions in which the something which we call the life force must travel outwards" [cf. Pfister, 1915, p. 167]). He also explains the nature of psychoanalytic treatment and its role in helping the will to battle against the repressed once it reaches consciousness. The letter is an impressive document, written on limited acquaintance with psychoanalysis.

Whether Winnicott was aware of it or not, by 1919 the discipline of psychoanalysis was already established in Britain in, for example, the work of Bernard Hart, David Forsyth, David Eder, and Ernest Jones (whose first collection of *Papers* had appeared in 1913) and in the Medico-Psychological Clinic in Brunswick Square.[4] The London Psycho-Analytical Society, which had been formed in 1913 but fallen a victim of the war and internal schism, was replaced in February 1919 by the British Psychoanalytical Society (BPAS). Winnicott had discovered psychoanalysis at a point when it was entering a period of rapid growth. Jones founded the *International Journal of Psychoanalysis* in 1920, and, in the same year, the *British Journal of Medical Psychology* started. Jones quickly set about "Englishing" Freud, securing translation rights for all that was written on psychoanalysis in German, and, in 1924, he founded the Institute of Psycho-Analysis, establishing premises and opening a clinic in 1926. In the same year, the Society put in place a formal training, though it did not take candidates until 1927. Winnicott was one of the first

[4] For a detailed account of the history of the BPAS in this period see Robinson (2010).

students. A few years later, he would be one of the first to train as a child analyst along with Susan Isaacs—only Clifford Scott qualified before them. The extension of the training to work with children, formalized in 1930, was the outcome of what Jones described to Freud in 1927 as "a rather special interest taken in the problems of childhood in London" (Paskauskas, 1993, p. 628) that had existed for some years before Melanie Klein moved to London in 1926. David Forsyth had spoken on "The Psychology of the New Born Infant" at the first Scientific Meeting of the BPAS in 1919, and Nina Searl, Mary Chadwick, Sylvia Payne, Ella Sharpe, Joan Riviere, and Gwen Lewis were all interested in child analysis. Winnicott stepped into this world when he consulted Ernest Jones for "personal difficulties" ("Human Nature" [CW 11:1:Introduction], p. 2; Groarke, Chapter 12 in this volume) in 1923, the year that he married his first wife, Alice. Jones recommended that he enter analysis with Strachey. His work with Strachey gradually gave him a framework within which to tease out what he was picking up intuitively from children in his pediatric work.

Two years or so into his analysis, Melanie Klein visited London to give a series of lectures that would lead to her relocating in London the following year. Strachey and his wife, Alix, had been instrumental in introducing her work to the British Society, and he recommended it to Winnicott:

> It was an important moment in my life when my analyst broke into his analysis of me and told me about Melanie Klein. He had heard about my careful history-taking and about my trying to apply what I got in my own analysis to the cases of children brought to me for every kind of paediatric disorder. I especially investigated the cases of children brought for nightmares. Strachey said: "If you are applying psychoanalytic theory to children you should meet Melanie Klein. She has been enticed over to England to do the analysis of someone special to Jones; she is saying some things that may or may not be true, and you must find out for yourself for you will not get what Melanie Klein teaches in my analysis of you." ("A Personal View of the Kleinian Contribution" [CW 6:3:8])

Strachey seems to have given this advice not long after Klein settled in London in September 1926. It is not known when Winnicott met her, but her work had a profound effect on him. Winnicott was accepted for training in June 1927 but struggled in his analysis for the next few years so that it was not until March 1930 that he was allowed to attend lectures and take on his first adult training case, supervised by Ella Sharpe. His work went well enough for him to take on his second case, this time with Nina Searl, in January 1931. In Sharpe and Searl, Winnicott chose supervisors who were known for their work with children as well as adults and who were open to Klein's thinking. Klein acknowledged Searl's "collaboration . . . based on common conviction and personal friendship" and praised her as having done "lasting service towards the advancement of child analysis in England" (Klein, 1975, pp. xi–xii). When he took a child training case in 1932, he went to Searl for that, too—a delinquent boy whom he describes in "The Antisocial Tendency" [CW 5:2:8] as wreaking such havoc in the Clinic that he was ordered to terminate the treatment:

> . . . on several occasions I got badly bitten on the buttocks. The boy got out on the roof and also he spilt so much water that the basement became flooded. He broke into my locked car and drove it away in bottom gear on the self-starter.[5]

It was not until early 1934 that he eventually began supervision with Melanie Klein for his second child case, an adolescent, taking his final case to her daughter Melitta Schmideberg later the same year. He qualified for adult work in January 1934 and for child work in May 1935, remaining in supervision with Klein for the next five years and analyzing her son Erik during that time. He would have liked to undertake further analysis with Klein, but his work with Erik made that impossible. In 1936, he went to her follower Joan Riviere instead.

Winnicott's Integration of Psychoanalysis and Pediatrics

Around 1929, Winnicott began to see children privately for analysis and spoke out in psychoanalytic terms in his contributions at professional meetings. From November 1929, he started to attend the scientific meetings of the British Society on a regular basis, and, in May 1930, he spoke for the first time in discussion of a paper even though still in training. In February 1931, he joined in discussion again when Melanie Klein read "Early Anxiety Situations and Ego Development," a chapter from her forthcoming book *The Psychoanalysis of Children.* His papers increasingly show him prepared to display his psychoanalytic thinking. So, for example, in his presentation on "Pathological Sleeping" in 1930 [CW 1:2:19], he separates cases due to encephalitis lethargica and cases where "sleep may . . . be found to have become invested with intensely pleasurable feeling belonging to the phantasies that, because they are felt to be forbidden, are giving rise to the anxiety."[6] And in his two contributions on enuresis in the same year, he diagnoses neurosis. He seems to have been increasingly able to run the risk of hostile response from his colleagues. In *Clinical Notes* (1931), especially in his chapters on anxiety, he promotes psychoanalysis, referring his readers to Klein's book and to Strachey.

---

[5] For a further and similar account of one of his child cases in this period, see Grosskurth (1986), p. 233.

[6] The subject of pathological sleeping was close to home because Alice was prone to fall asleep even at the wheel of a car and may herself have been suffering from encephalitis lethargica (Rodman, 2003, pp. 57–60 and 389).

But if in his pediatric work Winnicott was in process of trying to "see the baby as a human being" and applying psychoanalytic thinking to what he saw, he ran up against a problem. He describes how:

> When I came to try to learn what there was to be learned about psychoanalysis, I found that in those days we were being taught about everything in terms of the 2-, 3-, and 4-year-old Oedipus complex and regression from it. It was very distressing to me as someone who had been looking at babies—at mothers and babies—for a long time (already ten to fifteen years) to find that this was so, because I knew that I'd watched a lot of babies start off ill and a lot of them become ill early . . . I thought to myself, I'm going to show that infants are ill very early, and if the theory doesn't fit it, it's just got to adjust itself. ("D.W.W. on D.W.W." [CW 8:1:2], p. 41)

His papers between 1930 and 1935 see him first applying Oedipal thinking and then, as he assimilated Klein's influence, his interest in the enduring impact of infantile experience. His publications and presentations from 1930 and 1931 (including *Clinical Notes*) are largely rooted in Oedipal thinking, especially in anxiety and guilt due to masturbation, despite his references to Klein; but in his contribution on enuresis [CW 1:2:18] and in "Child Psychiatry: The Body as Affected by Psychological Factors" [CW 1:2:23], he begins to take account of infantile development. In the first, he distinguishes between cases with Oedipal and pre-Oedipal difficulties, the latter involving "a revival of real or phantasied sensations of infancy." In the second, he highlights for further study "the infant in all-out-rage." Compared with his earlier papers on enuresis, Winnicott's 1936 [CW 1:4:9] paper on the same topic shows just how much his thinking had changed under Klein's influence. It echoes not only her *Psycho-Analysis of Children* but "A Contribution to the Psychogenesis of Manic-Depressive States" (1935), which had introduced the concept of a depressive position:

> The principal emotions expressed by bed-wetting are love, hate and reparation, and also the urge to be rid of what is felt to be bad. Enuresis may be related to unconscious persecutory fantasies, and may be connected with the attempt to get the bad out. It may also be connected with latent depression, and may be part of an attempt to fill a hole, the hole being the result, in unconscious fantasy, of the emptying of the loved mother, the container of goodness, this emptying being in turn the result of the conversion of love into greed by frustration.

He makes similar as well as more Oedipal observations in "Skin Changes in Relation to Emotional Disorder" [CW 1:4:18], while in his "Psychology of Juvenile Rheumatism" [CW 2:1:7] he regards symptoms that prove to be psychological as a defense against depression.

Winnicott had left Queens in 1934 (although he continued to run the rheumatism clinic) and had more time for psychoanalytic work and to work out where he stood theoretically. Two papers are especially important in charting the development of Winnicott's engagement with Klein's work in this period, "The Manic Defence" [CW 1:4:6], which he gave on December 4, 1935, for membership of the British Society, and "Appetite and Emotional Disorder" [CW 1:4:11], presented to the Medical Section, British Psychological Society in 1936. Both speak of Klein's influence, but both also show signs of Winnicott beginning to find his own way in working out the relation of environment to internal world in the first stages of what Jan Abram has termed his "environment-individual set-up" phase (1935–1944) (Abram, 2008, p. 1194). Winnicott had to find a way of bringing together his observations of mother-and-child in his pediatric practice with his discovery through Klein of a rich but disturbing infantile inner reality. In a footnote to "Appetite and Emotional Disorder" [CW 1:4:11], he was careful to clarify that his conviction that there was "a psychology of the newborn infant" grew fundamentally from his pediatric experience in the outpatient clinic: "Although I was all the time influenced by Melanie Klein, in this particular field I was simply following the lead given me by careful history-taking in innumerable cases."

The task that increasingly faced Winnicott was not simply what came first, theory or observation, but what role environmental provision played in infant mental health and the formation of the internal world. In a discussion of "Neurosis in the Child"[7] at the Institute of Psychology alongside Charlotte Buehler and Margaret Lowenfeld in July 1936, he articulated a clear Kleinian line:

> the environment provided by the adult could only indirectly affect the child by modifying its inner life. The psychological activities of the young human included a constant testing and retesting of the inner (fantasy) world and outer world. There was an urge to put right in external reality what became

---

[7] The report of Winnicott's contribution to "Neurosis in the Child" (*British Medical Journal, 1936*, 94) in full:

> "Dr D. W. Winnicott said that the normal child could not be distinguished from the neurotic child, and he preferred to use the vague term 'finding life difficult.' Adults were incapable of recapturing the intensity of infantile and child feeling; normality depended on forgetting it. Adults expected babies to be like the dolls of their own childhood, and were always surprised and humiliated at the individuality of the child and the fact that the environment provided by the adult could only indirectly affect the child by modifying its inner life. The psychological activities of the young human included a constant testing and retesting of the inner (fantasy) world and outer world. There was an urge to put right in external reality what became harmed in fantasy. Every normal baby experienced a wide range of emotions, and was very much at their mercy. Abnormality appeared when the symptoms of its emotional life produced an unfriendly environment or caused bodily harm; or if play were inhibited or the child became unable to deal with its difficulties by manifesting neurotic symptoms. He ought to be able to relieve himself by sulking, rage, restlessness, bed-wetting, digestive disturbances, or minor illnesses. Each method worked in its own way, but only in a popular sense could the term 'neurotic' be applied to it. The popular use of the word 'neurosis' expressed the fallacy that neurotic symptoms were in themselves abnormal. The term had a place to describe tendencies and symptoms that had no physical basis, but the psychologist could use it if he made it clear that normal children employed neurotic symptoms in their development."

> harmed in fantasy. (Winnicott, "Contribution to 'Neurosis in the Child,'" 1936, p. 94)

In "Appetite and Emotional Disorder" [CW 1:4:11], there are, however, cracks in the theory. As in "The Manic Defence," greed is seen as a defense against anxiety and depression and as "something so primitive that it could not appear in human behaviour except disguised and as part of a symptom complex," but, in a remarkable passage, Winnicott also writes of "normal greediness which is acceptable to the self." And when he describes the "inner world [as] normally a live world of movement and feelings," it reads like a foretaste of later Winnicott even though in context it is knitted into a more Kleinian argument.

"Appetite and Emotional Disorder" [CW 1:4:11] also shows the concept of play in formation. Looking back on his own development, Winnicott was aware of how in his pediatric practice he had always been aware of "play in the relationship of trust . . . between the baby and the mother." Already in "The Only Child" [CW 1:2:6], he had touched on the importance and nature of the child's play in its development, and here he goes so far as to describe a spectrum of play:

> at the normal end of the scale there is play, which is a simple and enjoyable dramatization of inner world life; at the abnormal end of the scale there is play which contains a denial of the inner world, the play being in that case always compulsive, excited, anxiety-driven, and more sense-exploiting than happy. (p. 426)

Winnicott's account of normal play is, apart from the word "enjoyable," identical to Klein's (Klein, 1929, p. 202). Whereas, however, she felt that "we do not know much about the mental structure of the normal individual or the difficulties that beset his unconscious, since he has been so much less the object of psycho-analytic investigation than the neurotic" (Klein, 1975, p. 153), Winnicott the pediatrician was in touch with "normal family-working" and came to psychoanalysis "from health, rather than from illness, pathology" (Goldman, 1993, p. 107). His early work often and increasingly shows him rescuing children from pathologizing diagnoses, whether physical or psychological, which led to the wrong treatment. The neurotic child is normally neurotic and like the "difficult child" simply "finding life difficult." The rheumatic child, the fidgety child, the child with skin problems may well also be finding life difficult and the various manifestations of their difficulties need to be understood as being on the "psycho-physical borderline." Sometimes what is a normal expression of inner conflict, "normal unwellness," may be prevented from becoming a symptom by managing the environmental response, as in the case of the little boy who, in what can remain "a passing phase . . . if left to take care of itself," is "nasty" to his mother out of fear that he will hurt her by loving school. Here the emphasis is less on reparation from the child and more on the effect of the environment on the child. When later Winnicott parted company with Klein and her group, this emphasis on the environment was a major factor.

It is perhaps significant that Winnicott seemed to be freer in "Appetite and Emotional Disorder" [CW 1:4:11] than he was in his membership paper. 1935 was a watershed in the British Society as Klein's "The Psychogenesis of Manic-Depressive States," delivered to a Scientific Meeting of the BPAS in January, ushered in the second phase of her theory. Klein had moved to a milieu in London sympathetic to her explorations of the pre-Oedipal period and infantile fantasy. Jones and the Society saw in her someone who could help take forward the interest in pregenital development that was beginning to distinguish British from Viennese psychoanalysis. There was broad support for her extension of knowledge about the contents of the unconscious and for her theory of internal objects, but there was less acceptance of her idea of the paranoid schizoid and depressive positions, especially the latter. After a period of enthusiastic exploration that carried the Society along, divisions were appearing both within the Society and between the Society and the Vienna Society. When émigrés began to arrive in 1933 in flight from Nazi oppression, they encountered a "different analytic language" (Lantos, 1966, pp. 513–514). In 1934–1935, Exchange Lectures between London and Vienna were arranged to discuss the divergences. Winnicott found himself in an increasingly unhappy situation within the Society. As Marjorie Brierley noted, there were already "bad conditions" within the BPAS well before the arrival of the Viennese in 1938 (King & Steiner, 1991, p. 625). These conditions might account in part for the fact that, after his membership paper, Winnicott did not give another paper to the Society until 1941.

Winnicott and Contemporary Work with Children: The Extended Environment

Although Winnicott was the first pediatrician to pursue psychoanalytic training and met with some opposition within pediatrics, he was educated and practiced in a context that was working through a changed conception of childhood and infancy, one with consequences for reforms in education, child welfare, and pediatrics and for the development of progressive education.[8] The focus on the child as a unit was shifting to the child within the family, to the baby as a human being[9] developing within the family, and to the mother and baby. This new emphasis found expression in a surge of childcare manuals, and it influenced the nursery school movement, the psychology of education, child psychology, and child guidance clinics. Winnicott related to all these groups. He delivered "The Only Child" [CW 1:2:6] as a lecture to the National Society of Day Nurseries; "The Teacher, the Parent and the Doctor" [CW 1:4:7] and "Shyness and Nervous Disorders in

[8] For discussions of this changed conception, see Hendrick (1994, 1997).

[9] It is interesting that one of the most popular guides to parenting at this time was entitled *Babies Are Human Beings* (Aldrich & Aldrich, 1938).

Children" [CW 1:4:17] were addressed to teachers. He knew and worked with Emmanuel Miller, who headed the London Child Guidance Clinic in 1927, and with Margaret Lowenfeld, who shared his interest in the relation of the physical and the psychic and pioneered her own brand of play therapy (see Urwin, 1991). In the medical sphere, he knew Hugh Crichton Miller, who had launched the Tavistock Clinic in 1920 and opened a child department in 1926. These figures were eclectic in their psychological approaches, but they were exploring the same areas. Within the BPAS, there were figures like Barbara Low, who had a special interest in education, and Estelle Cole, who dedicated her little book *Three Minutes Talks About Children* (1928) to "All Mothers, Prospective Mothers and Other Women." But most important were two women Winnicott trained with, Susan Isaacs and Merrell Middlemore. He enjoyed a close friendship and collaboration with Isaacs, who was to education what Winnicott was to pediatrics (see Graham, 2009). At her invitation, he lectured from 1936 on her course in Child Development at the Institute of Education. Like Winnicott, she was skilled in talking to mothers in ordinary language. Middlemore was a fellow pediatrician who worked for Winnicott for a while at Paddington Green and embarked in the mid-1930s on observations of breastfeeding, which she reported on in 1938 at the BPAS. Published posthumously in 1941 as *The Nursing Couple*, her observations form part of the background to Winnicott's first recorded statement that "there was only a baby-mother relationship" (King & Steiner, 1991, p. 820).

Finally, at the end of the period covered by Volume 1, Winnicott worked with John Bowlby. They both contributed to R. G. Gordon's *A Survey of Child Psychiatry* (1939), Bowlby sending a draft of his paper to Winnicott for comment. Together with another of the contributors, Emanuel Miller, they wrote a now-famous letter to the *British Medical Journal* [CW 2:1:6] in late 1939 warning that "the evacuation of small children without their mothers can lead to very serious and widespread psychological disorder." By this time, Winnicott had become Consultant Psychiatrist for the Government Evacuation Scheme in Oxfordshire, where he met Clare, who would become his second wife.

Recognition of Winnicott's Work

Although Winnicott faced some hostility to his psychoanalytic interests from medical colleagues, the reviews of *Clinical Notes* were mainly favorable, especially those by Sybil Yates (Yates, 1932) and David Forsyth (Forsyth, 1933). Forsyth hailed it as "a milestone in the history of British paediatrics . . . the first of its kind to give full recognition to psychological factors alongside bodily, in the production of illness in childhood" (p. 176). As editor of *On the Bringing Up of Children* (1936), John Rickman included *Clinical Notes* in his list of suggested reading, and in her contribution on "Weaning" to the volume, Klein acknowledged Winnicott (Rickman, 1936, p. 44). And clinically, too, Winnicott was recognized for his work, inside and outside of psychoanalysis. In pediatrics, he was recognized as an authority on the psychology of rheumatism, while in psychoanalysis colleagues (including Jones and Klein) referred their children to him. Soon to become a training analyst, he had already begun to act as supervisor for child training cases.

Having benefited from the facilitating environment provided by Barts and the BPAS, Winnicott was now in turn providing a facilitating environment for the next generation of pediatricians and psychoanalysts, whether as visitors to his consultations, as members of his team, or as supervisees. In the words of one of them, Peter Tizard:

> The way in which he influenced a generation . . . younger than himself and *their* students was not by doctrinal teaching but by revealing to us the possibilities for teaching ourselves about the personalities of others. (Goldman, 1993, p. 114)

References

Abram, J. (2008). Donald Woods Winnicott (1896–1971): A brief introduction. *International Journal of Psycho-Analysis, 89*, 1189–1217.

Aldrich, C. A., & Aldrich, M. M. (1938). *Babies are human beings*. New York: Macmillan.

Anonymous. (1961). Donald Winnicott. *St. Mary's Hospital Gazette, 67*, 137–138.

Bearn, A. G. (2008). *Sir Francis Richard Fraser, 1885–1964. A canny Scot shapes British medicine*. Brighton: The Book Guild.

Bender, W. L. (1927). Epidemic encephalitis—Present status of etiology and treatment. *California and Western Medicine, 27*, 626–629.

Cole, E. (1928). *Three minutes talks about children*. London: C.W. Daniel Company.

Davis, J. (1993). Winnicott as physician. *Winnicott Studies, 7*, 95–97.

Davis, J. (n.d.). Where are they now? (http://www.blundells.org/obclub/obclub/where_are_they_now.htm#davisja).

Forsyth, D. (1933). Review of *Clinical Notes on Disorders of Childhood. British Journal of Medical Psychology, 13*, 175–177.

Garrod, A. E. (1902). The incidence of alkaptonuria: A study in clinical individuality. *Lancet*, 2, 1616–1620.

Garrod, A. (1908). Individuality in its medical aspects. *St. Batholomew's Hospital Journal*, 1908–1909 (November 16), 18–20.

Garrod, A., Batten, F., & Thursfield, H. (Eds.). (1913). *Diseases of children*. London: Edward Arnold.

Gillespie, W. H. (1971). Donald W. Winnicott. *International Journal of Psycho-Analysis, 52*, 227–228.

Goldman, D. (1993). *In search of the real: The origins and originality of D.W. Winnicott*. Northvale, NJ: Jason Aronson.

Graham, P. (2009). *Susan Isaacs. A life freeing the minds of children*. London: Karnac.

Greenfield, J. G. (1929). The encephalomyelitis of measles. *Proceedings of the Royal Society of Medicine, 22*, 297–300.

Grosskurth, P. (1986). *Melanie Klein. Her world and her work*. London: Hodder & Stoughton.

Guthrie, L. (1907). *Functional nervous disorders in childhood*. London: Frowde.

Hendrick, H. (1994). *Child welfare: England: 1872–1989*. London: Routledge.

Hendrick, H. (1997). *Children, childhood and English society, 1880–1990*. Cambridge, UK: Cambridge University Press.

Horder, M. (1966). *The little genius: A memoir of the First Lord Horder*. London: Gerald Duckworth & Co.

Kahr, B. (1996), *D.W. Winnicott. A biographical portrait*. London: Karnac.

King, P., & Steiner, R. (Eds.). (1991). *The Freud–Klein controversies 1941–45*. London: Routledge.

Klein, M. (1929). Personification in the play of children. *International Journal of Psycho-Analysis, 10*, 193–204.

Klein, M. (1935). A contribution to the psychogenesis of manic-depressive states. *International Journal of Psycho-Analysis, 16*, 145–174.

Klein, M. (1975). *The psychoanalysis of children*. Trans. Alix Strachey, revised H. A. Thorner. International Psycho-Analytical Library No. 22. London: Hogarth Press and the Institute of Psycho-Analysis.

Lantos, B. (1966). Kate Friedlander: Prevention of juvenile delinquency. In F. Alexander, S. Eisenstein, & M. Grotjahn (Eds.), *Psychoanalytic pioneers* (pp. 508–518). New York: Basic Books.

Lawrence, C. (1999). A tale of two sciences: Bedside and bench in twentieth century Britain. *Medical History, 43*, 421–449.

Middlemore, M. P. (1941). *The nursing couple*. London: Hamish Hamilton Medical Books.

Paskauskas, R. A. (1993). *The complete correspondence of Sigmund Freud and Ernest Jones, 1908–1939*. Cambridge, MA: Harvard University Press.

Pfister, O. (1915). *The psychoanalytic method*. Trans. Charles Rockwell Payne. London: Kegan Paul, Trench, Trubner and Co.

Rickman, J. (Ed.). (1936). *On the bringing up of children*. London: Kegan Paul, Trench, Trubner and Co.

Robinson, K. (2010). A brief history of the British Psychoanalytical Society. In P. Loewenberg & N. Thompson (Eds.), *100 years of the IPA. The centenary history of the International Psychoanalytical Association 1910–2010: Evolution and change* (pp. 196–227). London: Karnac.

Rodman, F. R. (2003). *Winnicott. Life and work*. Cambridge, MA: Perseus Publishing.

Sutherland, G. A. (1919, January 4). Obituary. *British Medical Journal, 1919*, 29.

Turnbull, H. M. (1928, August 25). Encephalo-myelitis in virus diseases and exanthemata. *British Medical Journal, 1928*, 331–334.

Urwin, C. (1991). Child psychotherapy in historical context. *Free Associations, 2*, 371–394.

Waddington, K. (2003). *Medical education at St Bartholomew's Hospital 1923–1995*. Woodbridge, Suffolk: Boydell.

Winnicott, C. (1978). D. W. W.: A reflection. [CW 12:X:X]

Winnicott, D. W. (1926). Varicella encephalitis and vaccinia encephalitis (with N. Gibbs). [CW 1:2:1]

Winnicott, D. W. (1927). The only child. [CW 1:2:6]

Winnicott, D. W. (1929). The diagnosis of chorea. [CW 1:2:16]

Winnicott, D. W. (1930). Contribution to a discussion on "The difficult child." *Proceedings of the Royal Society of Medicine, 23*, 573–585. [CW 1:4:4 (footnote i)]

Winnicott, D. W. (1930). Pathological sleeping. [CW 1:2:19]
Winnicott, D. W. (1930). Short communication on enuresis. [CW 1:2:18]
Winnicott, D. W. (1931). *Clinical Notes on Disorders of Childhood.* [CW 1:3:1–20]
Winnicott, D. W. (1936). Contribution to a discussion on enuresis. [CW 1:4:9]
Winnicott, D. W. (1936). Contribution to "Neurosis in the child." *British Medical Journal, 1936*, 94. [CW 1:Introduction (footnote vii)]
Winnicott, D. W. (1938). Shyness and nervous disorders in children. [CW 1:4:17]
Winnicott, D. W. (1938). Skin changes in relation to emotional disorder. [CW 1:4:18]
Winnicott, D. W. (1939). The psychology of juvenile rheumatism. [CW 2:1:7]
Winnicott, D. W. (1941). The observation of infants in a set situation. [CW 2:3:6]
Winnicott, D. W. (1958). Appetite and emotional disorder [1936]. [CW 1:4:11]
Winnicott, D. W. (1958). The antisocial tendency [1956]. [CW 5:2:8]
Winnicott, D. W. (1958). The manic defence. [1935]. [CW 1:4:6]
Winnicott, D. W. (1965). A personal view of the Kleinian contribution [1962]. [CW 6:3:8]
Winnicott, D. W. (1971). *Therapeutic Consultations.* [CW 10]
Winnicott, D. W. (1988). *Human Nature.* [CW 11:1]
Winnicott, D. W. (1989). D.W.W. on D.W.W. [1967]. [CW 8:1:2]
Winnicott, D. W. (1996). Child psychiatry: The body as affected by psychological factors [c. 1931]. [CW 1:2:23]
Winnicott, D. W. (1996). The teacher, the parent and the doctor [1936]. [CW 1:4:10]
Yates, S. L. (1932). Clinical notes on disorders of childhood. *International Journal of Psychoanalysis, 13*, 242–243.

{3}

"Two makes one, then one makes two"

EARLY EMOTIONAL DEVELOPMENT, 1939–1945

Christopher Reeves

The second volume of Winnicott's *Collected Works* covers the years immediately before and during World War II. Two major theoretical papers emerge from this period and act as convenient benchmarks reflecting the progress in his thinking about infancy. The first, "The Observation of Infants in a Set Situation" [CW 2:3:6], was first published in 1941, although it was based on clinical material assembled in the immediate prewar years from his consultations at Paddington Green Children's Hospital, where he was the pediatrician in charge. The second, "Primitive Emotional Development" [CW 2:7:8], was read before the British Psychoanalytical Society in 1945, not long after the conclusion of hostilities. Two other papers from this period, "Child Department Consultations" (1942 [CW 2:4:2]) and "Ocular Psychoneuroses in Childhood" (1944 [CW 2:6:15]), subsequently appeared in the volume of his *Collected Papers* published in 1958. However, despite their incidental points of interest, these can be considered relatively minor works in the overall trajectory of Winnicott's theoretical development.

The other frame for this period is provided by the war in Europe and its preliminaries, social consequences, and political aftermath. No other phase of Winnicott's professional life was so affected by events taking place in the public domain, nor his areas of interest and output so determined by its consequences, as during these years of World War II. Indeed, when Winnicott delivered his paper "Primitive Emotional Development" [CW 2:7:8] in November 1945 to an audience of fellow psychoanalysts, they may have been more than a little surprised to hear him begin by declaring that his presentation would be based on experiences gathered from treating up to a dozen psychotic patients in analysis during the recent war. Because of this focus of endeavor, Winnicott observed, "I hardly noticed the blitz, being all the time engaged in analysis of psychotic patients who are notoriously and maddeningly oblivious of bombs, earthquakes, and floods."

The picture he paints of himself here is of someone withdrawn from the external fray, single-mindedly devoting his energies to the long-term treatment of a small group of seriously ill analytic patients to the virtual exclusion of all other professional concerns. He displays a similar wish to distance himself retrospectively from another ongoing conflict, albeit of a different sort, that was consuming the psychoanalytic community then. This occurs in another, less formal address given to a group of psychoanalysts twenty years later, where he said:

> I got completely lost in the long controversy that went on during the war and ruined all our scientific meetings, when people were fighting for the rights of Mrs. Klein. It had to be done, but it left me completely cold; and I didn't know anything about it and I kept out of the way entirely. [CW 8:1:2]

The papers contained in Volume 2 of the *Collected Works* cast doubt on the accuracy of both these statements. One may perhaps wonder why Winnicott seemed intent on proposing a narrative of his professional activities and experiences during World War II seemingly at variance with the evidence of his letters, diaries, records, and writings, as well as with the contemporary recollections of his colleagues. Since this is an introduction to his written output of the period and not a biographical sketch, it must suffice simply to record the apparent discrepancy and attend to the facts and documents available, noting as we do so that in all his copious writings of these years he never actually drew on a single item of illustrative case material explicitly derived from the treatment of a patient identified as being psychotic. The closest one gets are a number of miscellaneous clinical vignettes dating from just before the outbreak of war. Winnicott evidently jotted these down for the benefit of his own subsequent reflections or possibly in order to record the details described in them for supervision (he was still seeing Melanie Klein for this purpose in 1939). At the very least, they are far from providing incontrovertible evidence of his extensive involvement with the treatment of psychotic patients during this period.

In 1938, Donald Winnicott was forty-two years old, a noted consultant pediatrician and author of a respected yet controversial textbook on the psychological aspects of common childhood ailments. Meanwhile, since qualifying in 1935 as a member of the British Psychoanalytical Society, his clinical reputation was growing apace, especially among the followers of Mrs. Klein, within whose circle he was then counted. To the public at large he was unknown. Yet by the end of the world war, Winnicott had become a household name across Britain due to his popular BBC radio broadcasts. These dwelled on the personal and family tribulations arising from the nationwide evacuation program as well as on the consolations and challenges facing the evacuees and their families on their return home. Such was his public standing as an authority on the psychological aspects of childhood development, both normal and pathological, that he was invited, along with Clare Britton, his future second wife, to present evidence to the Curtis Commission [CW 2:7:9]. The purpose of this government-appointed commission was to make proposals to the postwar Labour administration about the future provision for children in care. These were eventually embodied in the 1948 Children Act, which, along with the 1944 Education Act and the 1947 National Health Service Act, were to become cornerstones of the new Welfare State. Winnicott's and Britton's input was to prove highly significant in determining the eventual shape of postwar children's services, and in particular in identifying the pivotal role of the future Children's Officer.

At the same time, Winnicott had begun to acquire a reputation among his psychoanalytic colleagues as an independent-minded theoretician, especially with regard to the contentious matter of the nature and development of the infant psyche, a topic over which the followers of Anna Freud and Melanie Klein continued to be at loggerheads. By 1945, his novel formulations seemed to some of his colleagues to point towards a possible middle way between the Anna Freud and Melanie Klein camps and the conceptual resolution of an impasse that threatened the very future of the British Psychoanalytical Society as a unitary organization. Winnicott had become an authority in his own right. Another decade was to pass, however, before his standing in Britain was reflected in a comparable acceptance abroad. The papers in Volume 2 chart the first part of this trajectory, from professional regard to national esteem.

As already indicated, the advent of war played an unforeseen yet vital part in this transformation. In June 1939, when armed conflict with Germany was imminent, Edward Glover, Scientific Secretary of the British Psychoanalytical Society, canvassed those colleagues who were eligible for war service about their intentions once war broke out. It appears that Winnicott's initial impulse was to rejoin the navy, in which he had served for nine months as surgeon probationer during World War I. But this plan never materialized. Instead, he made his services available to the Ministry of Information, a department of the national government set up on the outbreak of hostilities in September 1939 in the effort to maintain civilian morale.

It was as a result of this initiative that Winnicott was invited to make his first two radio broadcasts entitled, respectively, "Children in the War" and "The Deprived Mother." These were transmitted on the BBC Home Service in the autumn of 1939, shortly after the first mass evacuation of children that took place on the eve of the declaration of war. They had an immediate resonance with the public. The papers with the same titles published in Volume 2 [CW 2:2:4 and CW 2:1:4] are later amplifications of these broadcasts, the first in a series made by Winnicott during the war and in the years following.

In his radio broadcasts, Winnicott refrained from actively endorsing the evacuation program while being careful not to condemn it, something that would not have fitted his public service role. Nevertheless, during the same period he put his signature, along with that of the child psychiatrist Emmanuel Miller, to a letter drafted by Bowlby that was sharply critical of the way that the evacuation program was being planned and promoted by the central government and local authorities.

The trio were particularly critical of the indifference of civil service planners to the deleterious psychological consequences of removing young children from their parents in order to protect them from the threat of bombing. The letter, published in Volume 2 [CW 2:1:6], first appeared in the *British Medical Journal*. Bowlby's initial plan had been for *The Times* to carry an earlier draft of it (written in collaboration with his friend, the Labour Member of Parliament Evan Durbin), where it was likely to have had a greater impact. *The Times*, however, declined to publish the original letter, no doubt regarding its critical tenor as undermining the efforts of government propaganda to promote "Operation Pied Piper" (the somewhat equivocal code name given to the mass evacuation program by its organizers). Its influence, if any, on government thinking is unknown.

Winnicott's readiness to associate himself with the letter in spite of his new public profile may perhaps represent a gesture of rapprochement towards the younger Bowlby, whose full membership of the British Psychoanalytical Society he had unsuccessfully attempted to block just a few months earlier. At the time, the point at issue had been the content of Bowlby's qualifying paper. This concerned the relevance or otherwise of "environmental factors" in accounting for the psychogenesis of childhood disturbance and the appropriateness of highlighting them in a clinical presentation before the Society, and especially a membership paper. While Bowlby regarded these factors as fundamental, Winnicott, in common with his Kleinian colleagues, did not.[1] The latter's subsequent acquaintance with the psychological casualties of the evacuation program was soon to convince him otherwise.

In late 1939, Winnicott unexpectedly found himself with time on his hands. Paddington Green Children's Hospital, his main center of work in the sphere of public medicine, had been forced to close following the evacuation and would not reopen fully until the end of the Blitz two years later. Meanwhile, referrals to the Child Department of the Institute of Psychoanalysis had dried up. His teaching duties at the Institute of Education were likewise in abeyance, and he had also relinquished his post at the Queen's Hospital for Children some months previously. In addition, his analyst Joan Riviere remained in Sussex when war was declared and did not return to London to resume her practice until the beginning of the 1940s, whereas his case supervisor, Melanie Klein, had moved to Bishop's Stortford and then to Scotland to escape the threat of bombing. On top of this, some of Winnicott's own analytic patients had also either terminated or suspended their treatments, including Melanie Klein's son Eric and Marion Milner's husband, Dennis.

It is probable that Winnicott turned his attention to writing during this fallow period. Although it is impossible to be absolutely certain, it is plausible to assign to

---

[1] See Rodman (2003) for an explication of the differences between Winnicott and Bowlby in relation to their diverse conceptualization of the environment. Eric Rayner's *The Independent Mind in British Psychoanalysis* (1991) provides a useful overview.

this time the writing both of his "Memorandum on 'The Relation Between Clinical Paediatrics and Child Psychology'" (2016 [CW 2:5:3]), a document he submitted to the British Paediatric Association in 1943, and "Child Department Consultations" (1942 [CW 2:4:2]), the review of child cases submitted over the space of a year to the Child Department of the Institute of Psycho-Analysis, seen by him in his capacity of director. This latter essay formed the subject matter of a paper read by Winnicott at a Scientific Meeting of the British Psychoanalytical Society in June 1942. That no trace of any references to the war, bombings, or devastation can be found, either as contributory causal factors of the manifest disturbance or as practical impediments to providing full analysis, suggests that the period Winnicott selected for his survey was prior to the outbreak of war.

When this paper came to be presented to the Society, it proved (and may have been intended) to be an agreeably noncontentious topic for its members to discuss at a period when other, much more conflictual topics provoked by the Controversial Discussions were on their collective minds. The paper is nevertheless interesting on its own account as being an early indication of Winnicott's newfound flexibility in assessing and providing analytic treatment according to need and circumstance rather than deciding the matter on the basis of an overriding belief in the universal efficacy of analysis in relation to frequency of sessions. As such, the paper marks a significant shift from what, years later, Winnicott described as his earlier settled outlook that "only five-a-week sessions carried on for as long as necessary" would do, regardless of the financial and practical cost to the family (see "Residential Care as Therapy" (1984 [CW 9:2:9]).

During this professional quietus in late 1939 and early 1940, a period roughly coinciding with what became known as "the phoney war," Winnicott was approached by Dr. Marjorie Franklin, a fellow psychoanalyst with a special interest in the application of analytic principles to therapeutic education. She sought to interest Winnicott in becoming a visiting psychiatrist to a young people's hostel in Bicester, Oxfordshire. This residential facility was being administered by an organization called the Q Camps under the aegis of herself and like-minded colleagues and run by a charismatic pioneer of therapeutic communities, David Wills. This hostel had recently been established with Wills as its reluctant head after the demise of an earlier therapeutic community camp in Suffolk, which had closed due to lack of financial support. The hostel, the property of Oxfordshire County Council, was situated in the grounds of a former workhouse and accommodated both the adult denizens of the former therapeutic community and an assortment of younger "unbilletable" evacuees deposited there as a place of last resort by the local authorities responsible for the evacuation reception areas throughout Oxfordshire and the adjoining counties.

Winnicott initially declined Franklin's invitation but, in the absence of other work, eventually yielded to her persuasions. So in January 1940 began what, on his own admission, was to prove a transformative experience and led in due course to his extensive involvement with the Oxfordshire Evacuation Scheme. Records show that, contrary to later accounts (his own and others), Winnicott was not initially employed as a consultant by the county authorities (Fees, 2010). He only assumed that role after David Wills's sudden departure in the spring of that year. It came about after a fraught period for the Q Camp Committee, due in part to the insistence by the Oxfordshire authorities that they should choose Wills's replacement rather than accept the nominee proposed by Winnicott and Franklin. The latter indignantly objected to this intervention and disengaged herself from the project. Winnicott, however, opted to work with the new County Council-appointed wardens and the psychiatric social worker brought in by the authority to ensure that the venture ran on lines more in accordance with its concept of good administrative practice. Although Winnicott became somewhat estranged from Franklin as a consequence of this parting of the ways, he subsequently acknowledged his debt of gratitude to her for having introduced him to the therapeutic community project in general and to David Wills in particular, as is shown in a letter to her published for the first time in Volume 2 [CW 2:6:12]. Years later, he stated that it had been due to the example and teaching of Wills that he began for the first time to learn what real therapy with deprived, acting-out children involved.

The Bicester venture finally closed in April 1941, to be replaced by a hostel provision operated directly under Oxfordshire County Council control. Before transferring his allegiance to this new enterprise and meeting for the first time his recently appointed psychiatric social worker colleague Clare Britton, Winnicott wrote a closing report to the Trustees of the organization under whose auspices Bicester had operated. This hitherto unpublished document has been included here [CW 2:7:9] because it provides an insight into the extent to which the challenging and often chaotic therapeutic community experiment, short-lived though the one at Bicester was, served to shape Winnicott's understanding not just about aspects of delinquency and deprivation as individual and community issues, but also about their larger impact on and implications for society. This theme was to recur frequently in his subsequent writings on the subject.

Unlike this largely forgotten episode, the later history of Winnicott's involvement in the Oxfordshire Evacuation Hostels scheme is well known and documented thanks to the accounts provided at various times by Britton. As she later recalled, she had initially been appointed by Oxfordshire to help direct the ministrations of "the difficult but devoted doctor who comes down every week and doesn't like social workers and leaves things in a muddle" (Winnicott, 1982). One consequence of having her as a spirited colleague and able co-worker was Winnicott's growing appreciation of the role of the psychiatric social worker. This role he had previously disparaged, along with the whole apparatus of "child guidance," which he tended to regard as a shallow, non-analytic American import (see, in this connection, the closing comments in his 1937 review of Leo Kanner's *Child Psychiatry* [CW 1:4:14]). Britton's softening influence is evident in the more deferential tone he adopted in his hitherto unpublished address of January 1943, "A Doctor Looks at the Psychiatric Social Worker" [CW 2:5:1]. However, despite the increased recognition of her role and abilities (reflected among other things in his readiness to collaborate with her on a couple of joint papers describing their shared endeavors), Winnicott's opinion concerning the advantages of "solo" work over "the clinic team," forthrightly expressed in this address, was to remain unaltered throughout his career.

In the meantime, while hostilities on the battlefield were in progress and indirectly providing him with fresh responsibilities and horizons, other conflicts of a professional and personal sort were taking place nearer home that affected and challenged him no less. These conflicts centered on the British Psychoanalytical Society and were to last for the duration of the war. Their sources were complex, interweaving scientific and personal issues (King & Steiner, 1991). In the first place, there were protracted scientific disputes between Melanie Klein and her followers on the one hand, and, on the other, the recent psychoanalytic refugees from Vienna and Berlin, led by Anna Freud, who strongly objected to what they regarded as the London-centered doctrinal deviance of the Kleinian group. This conflict over theory was multifaceted and came to embroil virtually the whole Society. It was compounded by a simultaneous wave of discontent, widely shared but voiced in particular by the newer generation of British psychoanalysts, at the organizational conservatism of the established figures who had held power, overseen the training, and unilaterally determined policy within the British Psychoanalytical Society and its Institute from its foundation twenty years earlier. Such an outline was the background of strife that Winnicott subsequently claimed to have "left him cold."

It is true that, unlike other prominent members of the Kleinian group, Winnicott did not join battle directly with Anna Freud and her circle. Nor did he submit a position paper on theory (though urged to do so) in the course of the protracted Controversial Discussions that were intended to address and hopefully reconcile their scientific differences (King & Steiner, 1991). In that sense, he was a "noncombatant." He did, however, attend almost all the meetings in which these disputes and grievances were aired. Moreover, he drafted a paper, "On Scientific Aims in Psychoanalysis" [CW 2:4:1], in connection with a motion he proposed at the first Extraordinary Business Meeting in February 1942, which he read to the Society during the second Extraordinary Business Meeting the following month. In it, he called on members of whatever persuasion to respect the basic scientific aim of the psychoanalytic enterprise begun by Freud and to which the Society was committed by its statutes—namely, to countenance the untrammeled expression of views within the psychoanalytic domain and to allow science rather than dogma to determine its further progress and development. It seems that not much notice was paid by members of the rival groups to Winnicott's exhortations in the febrile atmosphere then prevailing. Although he was careful to exclude Melanie Klein herself from the charge of factionalism (indeed, she had agreed to second his motion), he was nevertheless beginning to experience the first intimations of professional, if not yet personal, estrangement from her. This was not a welcome realization for Winnicott. Klein had been the major influence on his psychoanalytic thinking for almost a decade, a talisman in charting the emotional complexities of early infant experience at a time when such complexities were largely ignored as much by traditional psychoanalysis as by the conventional pediatrics and child psychology of the day. Not surprisingly, therefore, the process of distancing himself from such an important mentor was gradual and fitful.

Ten years later, the first signs of what could only be described as an open rift with Klein and her followers can be gleaned only indirectly and by implication from Winnicott's writings of this period. It was not until the early 1950s that he made his theoretical differences with her explicit and public. At this earlier period, they tend to manifest themselves in the topics he chose to write about and the way he addressed them rather than in anything openly stated in contradiction to her teachings. In this connection, his 1941 paper "The Observation of Infants in a Set Situation" [CW 2:3:6] holds an especially significant position. It was originally given at a Scientific Meeting of the British Psychoanalytical Society in April of that year under the title of "Observations on Asthma in an Infant and Its Relations to Anxiety." (Asthma was a topic that preoccupied him at this period, one of his patients having been the severely asthmatic husband of his friend and future colleague Marion Milner.) Although two of the cases in the published version feature children suffering from asthma, the main thrust of the paper is observational and theoretical rather than clinical. First comes a description of the typical behavior of small children with their mothers in his consulting room when encountering a shiny spatula and bowl with the license to touch them. Three stages of playful contact are identified: initial hesitation, then appropriation, and finally riddance. The first term, hesitation, is self-explanatory, although much detailed attention is given to the determinants of this hesitancy. One particular feature typically distinguishes the second from the third stages according to Winnicott's account. If an attempt is made to remove the spatula from the child's hand in the second, there is protest and an attempt to hold on to it, whereas in the third stage, the child lets it drop spontaneously or else throws it away without seeking to retrieve it. The final part of the paper is devoted to a lengthy account of the unconscious significance of the first and third stages. Linked to this is a discussion of the purported origins and expression of infantile anxiety as shown in the child's typical treatment of the spatula (this last being taken as standing for the mother's breast). What is both significant and problematic here is that there appear to be two parallel accounts interwoven in the text, although the fact that there are two and that they diverge at certain points remains unacknowledged. In one account, the child's actual relationship to the feeding mother and hers to him is stressed, with initial greed, ambivalence, and fear of loss of the internalized mother giving way in the final riddance stage to the child's readiness to accept the intermittent absence or non-availability of the mother. This I take to be the theoretical underpinning to his description of the spatula theme. In the other account, the child's fear of the destruction of the internal mother in fantasy through envious attacks on the mother's breast and father's penis is accorded greater prominence, along with the urge to make reparation to forestall loss, whereas the interpretation of the unconscious dynamic of the final stage, in which the child parts company with the spatula, is refracted through a reading of the classic instance of Freud's grandson playing with a cotton reel in the version referred to by Melanie Klein (1932).[2] The fact that there are these divergent accounts, the first culminating in the unconcerned riddance of "the inside mother" and the second in the fretful repair of the damaged internal mother, lends the paper a somewhat equivocal conclusion.

In all probability, there was a diversity not only of origin but of input in the fashioning of this paper, and this may account for the aura of ambiguity that surrounds its closing pages. The attendance records of the British Psychoanalytical Society show that Klein was not present when the lecture was delivered. However, her contemporary correspondence with Winnicott affords ample evidence of her determination that he should closely reflect her teachings in his scientific communications. At this stage, she regarded him as virtually her spokesman in the affairs of the British Psychoanalytical Society and let him know as much. In line with this, she kept the manuscript he had sent her for three months after he had delivered his lecture, during which time she made a number of alterations and insertions in the text so as to fill out what she thought "you meant to say" (Rodman, 2003, p. 123). At the same time, in writing to Susan Isaacs, she privately lamented the fact that Winnicott had not dispatched his paper to her in advance for vetting in order to "avoid blunders." So a plausible explanation of the ambiguities in the published text is that Winnicott did not demur at her self-appointed editorial intervention but instead allowed some or all of Klein's alterations to stand. A fuller discussion of these detailed textual issues lies beyond the scope of this introductory essay, but the interested reader may consult a paper dealing with the matter of authorship, ownership, and allocation of the theoretical concepts contained in it in more detail (Reeves, 2005).

Leaving this matter aside, for all its occasional obscurities, the paper represents an important if intermediate stage towards Winnicott's eventual formulation of a distinctive position of his own concerning the interrelationship of inner and outer experience in the life of the infant and small child and the role of transitional objects in their conjunction.[3] In addition, the theme of riddance, first adumbrated in the last section but barely touched on in his succeeding scientific papers, was to act as a pervasive subterranean influence on Winnicott's thinking about the aim and outcome of therapeutic endeavors of many kinds and eventually to emerge as an explicit and defining issue during the last years of his life.

Winnicott's second major paper of this period, "Primitive Emotional Development" [CW 2:7:8], represents another important milestone on this journey

---

[2] For an elaborated account of anxiety and ego, see the essay by Melanie Klein, "The Significance of Early Anxiety-Situations in the Development of the Ego," in *The Psychoanalysis of Children* (1932).

[3] See Rodman (2003, Chapter 11) for an extended discussion of the different understandings between Winnicott and Klein.

of discovery and self-discovery. Its summary title, unusual for Winnicott, stakes an authoritative claim to a domain that Klein regarded as her virtual fiefdom. The boldness of statement is only partially offset by the modest opening disclaimer: "About primitive emotional development there is a great deal that is not known, at least by me."

His public status belied such modesty. By the time he came to deliver the paper at a meeting of the British Psychoanalytical Society in November 1945, Winnicott had recently completed a highly successful series of broadcasts addressed to parents—mothers especially—on aspects of childrearing. These were to form the core of his later book *The Child and the Family* (1957).[4] He had shown confidence and authority in speaking about family experiences that were meaningful to ordinary people in a language they could understand, and this despite having no children of his own. Moreover, he had reconnected with the writings of fellow pediatrician and psychoanalyst Merrell Middlemore. In 1942, the latter's posthumously published *The Nursing Couple* (1941) had been warmly reviewed by Winnicott, who applauded its author's stress on the value of, first, detailed observation and then careful classification of the behavior of the baby at the breast. In short, Winnicott was well equipped to embark on this subject. Perhaps he was also encouraged by Klein's stated commitment to the importance of evidence as the guide to theory in determining psychoanalytic issues (after all, it was she who had seconded his 1942 resolution to that effect [CW 2:4:1]). To judge from the purposeful tenor of this paper, it seems almost as though a change of roles was being aspired to: instead of her persuading him to give expression to her viewpoint, as had been the case in relation to his spatula paper, it was he who now aimed to convince Klein and her followers about the need to reappraise their theoretical elaborations concerning the presence of envy and anxiety in the genesis of infantile fantasy in relation to breastfeeding, in the light of the evidence and arguments he was able to adduce. The tone he adopts is authoritative yet not aggressively assertive. He wishes to persuade rather than to challenge. In another context, Winnicott once remarked: "So often one feels: if you don't know, how can I tell you?" ("The Ordinary Devoted Mother" [CW 7:3:3]). He had come to recognize from experience that he was able to communicate with ordinary mothers

[4] Eight chapters of *The Child and the Family* (1957) were broadcast in the two years leading up to the presentation of "Primitive Emotional Development" in November 1945. This included the seven broadcasts in 1943–1944 on "Getting to Know Your Baby" ("Getting to Know Your Baby" [CW 2:5:8], "Why Do Babies Cry?" [CW 2:6:2], "What About Father?" [CW 2:6:8], "Their Standards and Yours" [CW 2:6:9], "What Do We Mean by a Normal Child?" [CW 2:6:10], "Support for Normal Parents" [CW 2:6:11], and "Infant Feeding" [CW 2:6:13]), and two of his seven broadcasts in 1945 ("The Only Child" [CW 2:7:1] and "Twins" [CW 2:7:2]). Of the remaining 1945 broadcasts, those on wartime experiences for families were published in *The Child and the Outside World* (1957), whereas the two broadcasts on "The New Baby" were never published. They are reproduced for the first time in Volume 12: Original Broadcast Scripts [CW 12:3:4a & 12:3:4b]. For a full list of Winnicott's broadcasts, see [CW 12:3:2]. The history of the broadcasts is discussed at length in the introduction to Volume 12 [CW 12:Introduction] and in Anne Karpf's podcast introduction to the audio material [CW 12:3:3].

because he was telling them what, in a sense, they knew already but didn't know they knew. In this paper, likewise, he was perhaps hoping that he could communicate from a similar starting point. In the event, this did not happen. The difference was that whereas ordinary parents were prepared to give him credence for his insightfulness in being able to articulate what they had hitherto only partially understood, many of his fellow psychoanalysts were not.

The origins of this paper were twofold. One arose from a cherished desire, actively resisted by his analyst Riviere, to formulate a classification of differential environmental impacts in the determination of individual psychopathology. This desire may account for his choice of the adjective "primitive" in its title, conveying the unsophisticated ruthlessness of a baby's hunger and aggression, in preference to the alternatives "infantile" or "early" as used by Klein. It may also explain the rather disconcerting way in which Winnicott allows the argument to veer from the clinical to the observational to the theoretical and back again (although it should be said that this feature of Winnicott's exposition is not confined to the present paper). What justified these abrupt transitions was that for Winnicott psychopathology was, first and foremost, the expression of the immature infantile psyche—immature through unmet needs in infancy—revealing itself and its neediness in adult guise. From this basic premise, it followed for Winnicott that the different ways in which the workings of the patient's psyche presented themselves in treatment to the unconscious of the analyst, whether as emanating from a whole person, as disintegrated, or as unintegrated—that is, as not issuing from a truly coordinated self at all—were indicative of and attributable to the nature of that individual's earliest experience. Consequently, psychopathology and child development were to be considered two aspects of the same phenomenon.

The second likely impetus for the paper was circumstantial. In March 1944, Klein had presented her paper "Some Theoretical Conclusions Regarding the Emotional Life of the Infant" as part of the "Discussion of Scientific Differences" (the Controversial Discussions and her paper was published in 1952). Winnicott intervened in the open discussion following it to argue against the propriety of ascribing the term "depressive" to the infant's feelings associated with weaning on the grounds that the baby at that stage could not be considered a whole person to whom depressive feelings could properly be said to belong. It was on this occasion that he seems for the first time to have uttered the dictum that he was to repeat a number of times at intervals in his writings subsequently: "There's no such thing as a baby, only a mother and a baby." The minutes of this meeting indicate that this utterance was greeted with a degree of incomprehension, together with a request for a fuller explanation of what he meant (King & Steiner, 1991, p. 820). One can therefore discern a subsidiary purpose of Winnicott's paper as being this: to offer an explanation, away from the heat of factional controversy, about how the baby (in being "no such thing") was nevertheless to be regarded not just as a sentient and instinct-driven creature, but also as the locus of lively feelings of passion and anxiety, love, and hate, with all their accompaniments in memory and fantasy, while being still on the way to acquiring a self-center, only achievable through maternal adaptation. The linking conceptual thread in both instances, of the psychotic and the baby, was the need to become a unit with a center, the first through the holding function (rather than interpreting) of the analyst, the second through the containing, integrating function of the mother. In his paper, he used examples drawn from each interchangeably to illustrate aspects of the other.

"Primitive Emotional Development" is undoubtedly a groundbreaking paper, affording evidence of a new creative confidence in his insights and conceptualizations about the vicissitudes of early infancy. But it is also a problematic one. Previously, Winnicott had been trying to align his formulations with the conceptualizations of Klein, even when the fit was increasingly felt as not being a good one. Here, he was struggling to articulate a statement about the essential integrity of the infant ("The Baby as a Person" [CW 3:4:27] was broadcast at this time), where the uniqueness of its experience was privileged, while at the same time laying emphasis on personhood as a developmental achievement that required for its realization the presence of the maternal surround to be taken for granted by the baby as a virtual extension of its own self-boundary. The resultant formulations in this paper of the relationships between primary unintegration, integration, and disintegration, although comprehensible as formulae, are somewhat unclear as to their reference. Just what was becoming integrated and from what unintegrated elements? Was the process of disintegration a simple return to an unintegrated condition—the *status quo ante*—or was such regression something different? These questions are barely touched on. What also did not aid clarity is Winnicott's twin perspective, that of the situation of the infant in the presence of the mother and that of the psychotic patient in the presence of the analyst. In the first case, the description applies to an initial coming together, in the second to the reconstitution of something falling apart or to pieces. This difference gives rise to a number of questions: Is the *dis*integration of the psychotic the same as or different from the *un*integration of the newborn? In what, developmentally, does integration consist—the coming together of a feeling unit, able to have an experience, or the establishment of a self that can both feel and react to bodily sensations? And, if the latter is the case, is this the same as having, or being, a self? These questions are left largely unresolved in "Primitive Emotional Development." Some years were to pass before their various different strands could be more precisely delineated and dealt with. Likewise, the distinction between "concern" and what preceded the stage of concern needed further clarification. "Primitive ruthlessness," the term used in this paper to refer to the state prior to the advent of "concern," carries a connotation of purposefulness about the drive, direction, and determination being exhibited, which, on Winnicott's own premises, does not altogether fit the infantile situation he is also describing. As if aware of the anomaly, he would later opt for using the quaint but more precise term "pre-ruth."

Nevertheless, for all its shortcomings, "Primitive Emotional Development" represents a momentous shift for Winnicott. It marks the point at which he shed the one-body psychology identified by fellow analyst Rickman as the underlying paradigm of classical Freudian conceptualizations (Rickman, 1957). Henceforward, the baby was no longer thought of by him in terms of being a psychically semi-independent entity from the outset, as postulated for instance by Klein. Making this change, however, did not mean he was about to embrace the sort of two-body perspective that suited the two figures with whose thinking and formulations he is often associated, namely Bowlby and Balint. They viewed infantile and childhood experience and behavior as the outcome of interactivity between an autonomous inner self and an environment external, encompassing and largely determining it. Instead, Winnicott embraces a position between the two, in effect, a paradigm (although it would be anachronistic to ascribe this term to his thinking) that emphasizes the transitivity of experience between mother and baby at the earliest stages. By transitivity here I mean an indeterminacy, which diminishes over time, as to where an experience or the impetus towards an experience belongs. It can be formulated as "two makes one, then one makes two": first, the mother and baby are to be regarded as a psychic unit (though not in stasis); then, the baby and mother become separated off from each other (though still united interactionally on the basis of the earlier intermingling of experience). This patterning, or paradigm, unique to Winnicott and adumbrated here for the first time, was to be a recurrent organizing structure for his thinking about human psychology both developmentally and clinically for the rest of his life.

The paper is not only groundbreaking but generative. New ideas are thrown up, then set aside for future development. Thus, a brief significant section is given over to a discussion of the role of "illusion" both developmentally and as a creative resource in the life of the healthy individual. From this were later to develop the concepts of transitional phenomena and the subjective object. There is also a brief discussion of dissociation in both its healthy and pathological aspects, a theme that eventually led to his conceptualizations about creativity and the intermediate area of experience.

Nevertheless, one should not overstress the novelty of this paper. For all its originality, one can observe an underlying thematic continuity with his earlier 1941 paper "The Observation of Infants in a Set Situation." Winnicott's focus had been on the child's use of the spatula, his or her investment of it, and the meaning of that investment and subsequent divestment. One can regard the 1945 paper as effecting a change in focus away from the child making use of the spatula onto the spatula as the object of use, except that now the spatula has become alternately the analyst and the mother. In both instances, the condition for the attendant entity, human or nonhuman, of being, as it were, an adjunct or prop is to the fore. Hence, in Winnicott's discussion of the different ways in which the therapist experiences being used by the patient according to the different diagnostic levels of the patient's illness, one can detect a parallel with his earlier description of the spatula as being used either in accordance with its actual function, imaginatively as a plaything where its functionality is not denied but held in abeyance (illusion), or, finally, as a purely subjective object, where its instrumental purpose and even its existence other than as a felt extension of the person's arm is disregarded altogether (a state of delusion in the patient; a state of primary subjectivity in the case of the infant).

Another topic that began to surface in this wide-ranging paper was to become a perennial theme for Winnicott. This concerned the coincidence of love and hate as components contained within the aggressive impulse. Consequent on this perceived coincidence, and because Winnicott viewed aggression as tantamount to a vital impulse of the individual on the way to achieving identity and independence, his writings exhibit a degree of tolerance both for the phenomenon and the expression of hate that was not generally shared by his fellow analysts. This acceptance of the inevitability—even life-asserting aspect—of hate, set out most clearly in his 1939 talk to teachers, "Aggression" [CW 2:1:8], led Winnicott into often surprising and sometimes controversial formulations that appeared in a variety of contexts. One such is his "Discussion of War Aims" (1986 [CW 2:2:3]), written during the dark days of the bombing of London. In the circumstances of the time, it is a surprisingly nonpartisan piece. In it, Winnicott argues that those on both sides of the current conflict are "fighting to exist." He then goes on: "If we accept that basically in our natures we are like our enemies our task is immensely simplified. We can then fearlessly look at our natures, at our greed, and at our ability to deceive ourselves."

A similar even-handedness in his assessment of the unconscious motivations of the parties at war with each other is evident in the interesting, if rather quirky, piece "Meet to Be Stolen From" (2016 [CW 2:3:7]), which probably dates from the same period. In both, Winnicott confronts the deleterious consequences of denying the recognition of one's own capacity both for feeling hatred in oneself and for evoking hatred in the other, the latter sometimes prompted by one's actions or omissions, sometimes through being the sort of person one is, or even just through having the possessions, capacities, or functions one has. In these reflective exercises about the roots of aggression, his brief encounter with David Wills and the Q Camp experiment with "unbilletable" evacuees in Bicester was probably influential. In creating and maintaining a therapeutic environment capable of countenancing the expression of destructive vengefulness on the part of those who felt themselves emotional outcasts, what was required, as he maintained in his closing report on this experiment to its original board of trustees ("Report on Q Camps" (2016 [CW 2:3:1])), was a "fearless frankness" from those who ran the enterprise and those who, like Winnicott, provided it with practical support and guidance. One needed to acknowledge both the hatred directed at oneself by means of displacement on the part of those who felt wronged and the reactive hate aroused in oneself due to being its lightning conductor—hence, the emphasis in his communications to different individuals and bodies on the cathartic effect of frank expression. Certainly, this fearless frankness was a marked feature of a number of Winnicott's letters published here. One wonders, for instance, what Lord Beveridge, architect of the future Welfare State, made of Winnicott's frank declaration of hatred in his letter of

1946 [CW 3:1:4]. The reason for his outrage on that occasion was that Beveridge's proposals for the planned Health Service threatened, in Winnicott's view, to trespass on a sacrosanct private, professional area—namely, that of the doctor–patient relationship—by requiring the medical practitioner to become in effect a state-sponsored civil servant.

In Winnicott's theorizing, feelings of hate were closely related to the threat or the actuality of impingement, whether of one's professional autonomy, one's personal integrity, or one's bodily wholeness. In the professional sphere, he saw hatred either directly expressed or as manifesting itself in the guise of envy, the latter readily prompting either vindictiveness or compliance on the part of the target of such hatred. Thus, for instance, the caregiver feeling under attack was liable to behave hatefully towards those he or she was caring for. The alternative to reactive attack might be to take refuge in an empty, uncreative compliance, with the person in authority experienced as behaving hatefully. In either case, young people being cared for by such caregivers were liable to become the ultimate victims of the dissemination of unvoiced hatred.

Winnicott explored these unconscious ways of responding and reacting to hate in the various writings about the wartime hostels and how they should be run that are included in Volumes 2 and 3 of the *Collected Works*. His thinking on the subject also fed into his recommendations to the Curtis Committee about the management of similar hostels for displaced or disruptive youngsters to be set up after the war and the type of staff who should be recruited to run them. His overarching concern was that the wardens of such places should be regarded and treated as "practitioners," rather as "general practitioners" were regarded in the medical sphere. They were to be assessed for their personal suitability in the first place, then trained to a proper level of competence, and, finally, left to get on with the job to the best of their ability. The role of the local authority would be to give recognition, encouragement, and the right network of support to achieve this. So strongly did he feel the need for this sort of operational freedom from external impingement that he was prepared to countenance the use of corporal punishment by wardens on the children in their care if the circumstances warranted it. He made his views on this clear both in his memorandum on the subject for the Oxfordshire Authorities ("Memorandum on Corporal Punishment" (2016 [CW 2:7:6])) and later before the Curtis Committee [CW 2:7:9]. The point he was making about the dangers of administrative oversight operating as impingement was no doubt a valid one within the context of his wider concern to prevent a subterranean hate coming to pervade the system of hostel care, but it was nevertheless a one-sided viewpoint, even on his own terms, since it ignored the negative consequences for the object of the corporal punishment—the young person—in feeling physically encroached upon, even overwhelmed, by the actions of the adult.

Another manifestation of hate by those on the outside of the caregiving system that especially concerned him was the unconscious envious attack on the caregiving function on the part of its providers and overseers. Sometimes he saw this unconscious envy expressed in administrative obstructiveness, at other times—especially in the medical, psychological, and psychiatric professions—in the employment of invasive surgical interventions that were presented as being necessary or health-promoting yet were medically unwarranted. The widespread recourse among his fellow pediatricians to tonsillectomy and circumcision was one of Winnicott's prime targets here. Within the legal and social sphere, he criticized the adoption of sentimental attitudes on the part of magistrates under the pretext of seeking to be therapeutic. This disposition betrayed a confusion of purpose and role, which in his eyes was detrimental to the needs of those who were the object of such sentimentalism.

He could be especially virulent to his fellow psychiatrists. His outrage was directed towards those among them who, for misguided purposes of treatment, either induced electric shocks or carried out leucotomies on patients. He was at least as passionate in his expression of opposition to such procedures as he had been in his opposition to the thrust of Lord Beveridge's proposals for the future National Health Service. While not discounting the objective reasons behind his argument, it is worth recognizing a particular dimension to his feelings. This arose from close personal experience of the devastating consequences of electroconvulsive therapy. This came about when his wife Alice prevailed on him to accept an adolescent girl who had been the hapless recipient of such treatment at the local mental hospital into their house in Hampstead in 1943 for an indefinite period in order to recover from her ordeal. Susan, the young person in question, was to remain with them for almost six years. During this time, she went into analysis with Marion Milner, then a newly qualified psychoanalyst whose insight and clinical skills Winnicott greatly respected. Susan's treatment was paid for by the Winnicotts themselves. Milner's very full account of its evolution and outcome would eventually appear with a Foreword by Winnicott [CW 8:1:12] in her book *The Hands of the Living God* (1969), published a quarter of a century later.

Winnicott did not exclude himself from the ordinance of hate. Intellectually, he could recognize its existence in himself, yet emotionally he experienced great difficulty in acknowledging at a personal level that he could be, and be felt as being, a hating person, at least in regard to those whom he loved and was concerned for: his wife, his family in Plymouth, and latterly his colleague, and increasingly his soulmate, Clare Britton. The conflict he experienced between intellectual recognition and emotional disavowal sharpened his sensitivity to the vagaries and compromises of sentimentality, which he abhorred. This repudiation is evident in his 1943 correspondence with Lord North on the subject of the responsibilities of the magistrate and in particular of the need for the judiciary to countenance and take account of revenge feelings on the part of the public in response to criminal acts [CW 2:6:1]. The masks of sentimentality made him alive to the importance of the psychoanalyst acknowledging his or her own hate in the countertransference. This, indeed, was to be the topic for his next major psychoanalytic paper, which was completed not long after the war's end and which appears in Volume 3 [CW 3:2:1].

Before the war, Winnicott had led a professionally cloistered life. During its six-year course, he was thrust into the fray practically, intellectually, and psychologically. The country of his birth was threatened with imminent invasion, and he, like other Londoners, had witnessed the destructive impact of enemy bombing and experienced the vengeful feelings such events provoked. Like Freud before him, and like a number of his fellow psychoanalysts in Britain, notably Bowlby and Flügel, these circumstances caused him to reappraise the sources of human conflict and the causes of its eruption both in and between peoples. This raised in acute form the topic that was to become for him a lifelong subject of inquiry, the ontogenesis of the aggressive instinct. Yet while a state of war undoubtedly provided the backdrop for this inquiry, the principal affective focus for it during these years remains undoubtedly the private struggle taking place within. This was the arena where the quest for personal integrity, experienced in the professional sphere as the need to articulate an autonomous viewpoint on matters of early human development that were uppermost in his thinking, was felt as gradually putting a strain on his loyalty to Klein. At the same time, in his personal life, the complementary drive towards creativity of thought and expression, so dearly prized by him as a condition of being truly alive, found itself increasingly at odds with the obligations of love and the common expectations of marital fidelity that he regarded as equally integral to the sort of person he aspired to be. Conceptually, to acknowledge aggression as intrinsic to being human was one thing. Actually to experience oneself as "being horrid" and as felt so by someone to whom one was deeply devoted was quite another. Not surprisingly, the vicissitudes of love and hate were to be among his principal topics of reflection and writing in the years that followed.

References

Fees, C. (2010). *A fearless frankness*. (Childrenwebmag.com).

King, P., & Steiner, J. (1991). *The Freud–Klein controversies 1941–45*. New York: Routledge.

Klein, M. (1932). The significance of early anxiety-situations in the development of the ego. In *The psychoanalysis of children*. London: Hogarth.

Klein, M. (1952). Some theoretical conclusions regarding the emotional life of the infant. In P. Heimann, S. Isaacs, M. Klein, & J. Riviere (Eds.), *Developments in Psychoanalysis*. London: Hogarth.

Middlemore, M. (1941). *The nursing couple*. London: Hamish Hamilton Medical Books.

Milner, M. (1969). *The hands of the living god*. London: Hogarth.

Rayner, E. (1991). *The independent mind in British psychoanalysis*. London: Free Association Books.

Reeves, C. (2005). Singing the same tune? Bowlby and Winnicott on deprivation and delinquency. In J. Issroff (Ed.), with B. Hauptmann & C. Reeves, *Donald Winnicott and John Bowlby: Personal and professional perspectives*. London/New York: Karnac Books.

Rickman, J. (1957). *Selected contributions to psycho-analysis.* London: Karnac.
Rodman, R. (2003). *Winnicott: Life and work.* Cambridge, MA: Perseus.
Winnicott, C. (1982). D. W. Winnicott: His life and work. In J. Kanter (Ed.), *Face to face with children: The life and work of Clare Winnicott.* London: Karnac.
Winnicott, D. W. (1938). Notes on a little boy. [CW 1:4:16]
Winnicott, D. W. (1938). Shyness and nervous disorders in children. [CW 1:4:17]
Winnicott, D. W. (1940). Children in the war. [CW 2:2:4]
Winnicott, D. W. (1940). The deprived mother [1940]. [CW 2:1:4]Winnicott, D. W. (1941). The observation of infants in a set situation. [CW 2:3:6]
Winnicott, D. W. (1942). Child department consultations. [CW 2:4:2]
Winnicott, D. W. (1944). Ocular psychoneuroses of childhood. [CW 2:6:15]
Winnicott, D. W. (1945). Primitive emotional development. [CW 2:7:8]
Winnicott, D. W. (1957). Aggression [c. 1936]. [CW 2:1:8]
Winnicott, D. W. (1969). Foreword. In Marion Milner, *The hands of the living god.* [CW 8:1:12]
Winnicott, D. W. (1984). Residential care as therapy [1970]. [CW 9:2:9]
Winnicott, D. W. (1986). Discussion of war aims [1940]. [CW 2:2:3]
Winnicott, D. W. (1987). Letter to Lord Beveridge, October 15, 1946. [CW 3:1:4]
Winnicott, D. W. (1987). The ordinary devoted mother [1966]. [CW 7:3:3]
Winnicott, D. W. (1989). D. W. W. on D. W. W [1967]. [CW 8:1:2]
Winnicott, D. W. (1991). Resolution K: On scientific aims in psychoanalysis [1942]. [CW 2:4:1]
Winnicott, D. W. (1996). Mental hygiene of the pre-school child [1936]. [CW 1:4:10]
Winnicott, D. W. (2017). Delinquency: Continued [c. 1930s]. [CW 2:1:9]
Winnicott, D. W. (2017). A doctor looks at the psychiatric social worker [1943]. [CW 2:5:1]
Winnicott, D. W. (2017). Evidence given to the Home Office Committee on Children's Homes [1945]. [CW 2:7:9]
Winnicott, D. W. (2017). Letter to Dr. Marjorie Franklin, October 19, 1944. [CW 2:6:12]
Winnicott, D. W. (2017). Meet to be stolen from [n.d., c. 1939–1945]. [CW 2:3:7]
Winnicott, D. W. (2017). Memorandum on corporal punishment [1945]. [CW 2:7:6]
Winnicott, D. W. (2017). Memorandum on "The relationship between clinical paediatrics and child psychology" [1943]. [CW 2:5:3]
Winnicott, D. W. (2017). Report on Q Camps [1941]. [CW 2:3:1]
Winnicott, D. W., with Bowlby, J., & Miller, E. (1939, December 16). Evacuation of small children. [CW 2:1:6]

{4}

Towards Different Objects, Other Spaces, New Integrations, 1946–1951

Vincenzo Bonaminio and Paolo Fabozzi

Hate in the Countertransference

Hate. This is the first time that a *feeling* bursts into psychoanalytic discourse with such disruptive effect on the metapsychological terrain, at a time when both theoretical and clinical thinking were predominantly taken up with the drives.[1]

This feeling emerges directly in the very title of the paper, as though Winnicott wanted from the outset to make a vehement statement of personal intent. Also groundbreaking is that this *negative* feeling is related immediately to the analyst, and this constitutes a radical challenge to the prevailing model in which transference was seen as the central configuration of psychoanalytic work, with countertransference[2] standing in the way of the analyst's engaging with the flow of the patient's free associations.

In this paper, Winnicott anticipates later developments in the concept of countertransference, taking it as a given, as an acquisition from his own clinical work. He describes this as ordinary countertransference: "The identifications and tendencies belonging to an analyst's personal experience and personal development which provide the positive setting for his analytic work and make his work different in quality from that of any other analyst" [CW 3:2:1].

Winnicott is implying a displacement of the center of gravity of psychoanalysis from the patient onto the analyst. When he gets to the heart of his argument, the reader is further unsettled by the statement that, in the case of some psychotic patients, analytic work cannot be judged as completed unless the analyst has put

[1] Winnicott's idiosyncratic and freely disrespectful way of writing in comparison with the "established" écriture of the time has been pointed out elsewhere (Bonaminio, 2005).

[2] Countertransference was yet to acquire the dignity and the official recognition that it was accorded following Paula Heimann's seminal 1950 paper "On Counter-transference."

his countertransference feelings at the disposal of the patient. His very extensive clinical work, especially with psychotic, schizoid, borderline, and other severely ill patients, is presumably the source of these revolutionary ideas.

He issues an emotional challenge to the analyst:

> This coincidence of love and hate to which I am referring is something distinct from the aggressive component complicating the primitive love impulse, and implies that in the history of the patient there was an environmental failure at the time of the first object-finding instinctual impulses.
>
> If the analyst is going to have crude feelings imputed to him he is best forewarned and so forearmed, for he must tolerate being placed in that position. Above all *he must not deny hate that really exists in himself. Hate that is justified in the present setting has to be sorted out and kept in storage and available for eventual interpretation.* [CW 3:2:1, emphasis added]

The radical suggestion that the analyst must offer something of himself to the patient was unprecedented. We cannot know Winnicott's personal motive for choosing hate with which to begin this reversal of psychoanalytic perspective, but we might speculate that it had partly to do with the transformation of the neutrality previously attributed to the analyst's position.

More significantly, perhaps, it demands a search for authenticity in the feelings of both analyst and patient, an issue that echoes through other works in Volume 3. It fleshes out a theme in Winnicott's seminal work of 1945, "Primitive Emotional Development" [CW 2:7:8], which Ogden (2001) describes as a kind of master plan from which flow all those currents of research that Winnicott would carry forward, in different directions yet with a surprising germinative unity, over the next twenty-five years. In "Ego Distortion in Terms of True and False Self" [6:1:22], he again emphasized the importance of putting something of one's self at the disposal of the patient. He continued to develop this idea, which reached its fullest elaboration in his late paper "The Use of an Object" [CW 8:2:28].

A New Semantics of Aggression

"Hate in the Countertransference" was written the year after Klein's "Notes on Some Schizoid Mechanisms" (1946). Her paper contains two strands. On the one hand, it is a synthesis and a systemization of the preceding decade's research. She describes a mind that functions and develops from a primitive paranoid-schizoid position towards a more organizing depressive position. On the other hand, it is an intuition of the theory of projective identification, perhaps her most revolutionary concept of this period. Here, Klein grasps the fact that the psychic activity of the individual is displaced onto the other, who, for the first time, is conceptualized as an object containing an inside.

This crucial transition in Kleinian theory gives primacy to the emphatically conflictual dialectic between the libidinal drives and the aggressive impulses of the child in relation to the mother's breast. Specifically, she conceptualizes the aggressive impulses of the child in terms of object relations. In a direct challenge to the Freudian concept of the death drive, Klein strips this of its conjectural implications as a biological and philosophical matrix and deflects it onto the child's inborn psychological framework. In order to express this inborn destructive impulse, the infant attacks the mother's breast, the bad breast, so as to be free of it and to maintain the relationship with the opposite pole of the split, the ideal breast.

By contrast, Winnicott does not conceptualize a primary aggression, either as an expression of the death drive or (in the more descriptive terms of academic psychology) as a reaction to frustration. He visualizes the roots of aggression as being an expression of that "primitive . . . motility potential" [CW 3:5:2] that has its origins in the first movements of the fetus within the womb. Although Winnicott does not explicitly mention the significance ascribed by the mother to these signs of life, this plays an essential role: it is the mother who will see in the infant's earliest integration either erotic potential or signs of aggressiveness.[3]

Winnicott's view of aggression is described both experientially and clinically when he introduces his concept of the fundamental developmental difference between the stages of concern and pre-concern. The aggressiveness of pre-concern is inherent in ruthless love. It embodies not an attack on the object but a potential for motility in the processes of maturation. It is only when the child is firmly anchored in the stage of concern that aggressiveness is directed against the object.

For Winnicott, there exists, therefore, an ontogenesis, a kind of natural history of aggressiveness. In states of profound narcissistic withdrawal, although aggression may appear primitive, it is never primary; it is always the result of something that the object or the environment has done to the subject. It is not that Winnicott is positing a naïve, Rousseau-esque conception of the primordial goodness of the individual ruined by society. It is that love and hate take shape within the continuous interplay between what is offered by the environment and the varyingly reactive responses of the individual.

Viewing the Child: A Radical New Perspective

At the beginning of his 1945 paper "Primitive Emotional Development" [CW 2:7:8], Winnicott makes a bold methodological statement: since he was interested in the child and the infant, he has decided to study psychosis psychoanalytically. His vision of the earliest stage of emotional development is based on his conviction

[3] It would be a mistake to imagine that Winnicott is thinking of the mother on her own in relation to the baby. Despite being the principal agent of the baby's care, she is seen as existing within a structure provided by the holding functions of the father.

that the analysis of psychotic, depressed, and hypochondriacal patients does not require a modification of Freudian technique—provided that "the transference situation inherent in such work" is taken into account.

The methodological premise of basing the study of primary development on the analyses of psychotic patients yields its greatest results in the identification and analysis of the three principal processes in emotional development: integration (starting from a condition of primary un-integration), personalization (the localization of the self in the body), and the assessment of spatial and temporal dimensions (the construction of the relationship with reality).

This conceptual organization of primary development is highly innovative, as is the proposal that integration is a slow and gradual process of construction, occurring as instinctual experiences are combined with the "technique" of maternal care. Furthermore, there is a fundamental break with earlier theorizations in Winnicott's conception and description of the relationship with external reality as a *capacity* that necessitates a slow and gradual process of construction, as well as the indispensable contribution of the maternal figure. This is the first appearance of various central Winnicottian *leitmotifs*: the establishment of an authentic relationship with external reality, the distinction and productive exchange between reality and fantasy, and the construction of the sense of being real.

In the 1945 paper, Winnicott has yet to elaborate fully the contribution of the mother's psychic functioning to the baby's development. However, the following passage allows us to understand the broader theoretical and clinical view being outlined as part of this thinking:

> In terms of baby and mother's breast . . . the baby has instinctual urges and predatory ideas. The mother has a breast and the power to produce milk, and the idea that she would like to be attacked by a hungry baby. These two phenomena do not come into relation with each other till the mother and child *live an experience together*. The mother being mature and physically able has to be the one with tolerance and understanding, so that it is she who produces a situation that may with luck result in the first tie the infant makes with an external object, an object that is external to the self from the infant's point of view. [CW 2:7:8]

With the image of a mother and baby who "*live an experience together*," Winnicott is preparing to construct a very specific situation: in presenting the baby with the breast, the mother must allow the baby to feel that he has created the experience himself.[4] The potential for this psychic function (that is also fundamental to the relationship with external reality) lies in the possibility that an *overlap* may

[4] "I think of the process as if two lines came from opposite directions, liable to come near each other. If they overlap there is a moment of *illusion*—a bit of experience which the infant can take as *either* his hallucination *or* a thing belonging to external reality" [CW 2:7:8].

be created between something that stems from the mother and something that originates from the baby's nascent psyche.

Here, we witness the gestation of other fundamental Winnicottian concepts: transitional objects and phenomena, the subjective object, the intermediate area, potential space. With the idea that the mother "would like to be attacked by a hungry baby," he introduces into the psychoanalytic field in embryonic form the point of view that considers the mother's *psychic functioning* as crucial. In broadening his focus then to include the experience of the baby who encounters the mother's experience, Winnicott calls to our attention the patient's experience (in the transference), which meets and generates effects upon the experience that the analyst has with the patient.

What unites the three situations described in "Hate in the Countertransference" [CW 3:2:1] is that the object (the mother or analyst) must face and work through reactions to "pressures" from the subject (the baby or patient). The technical implication—that the analyst must "bear strain"—opens up another unexplored field: the object's response to the subject's unconscious movements due to a tension that arises from primitive defensive processes. Winnicott explicitly establishes this crucial connection when he states that the analyst "is in the position of the mother of an infant unborn or newly born." Every detail of technique then becomes vitally important and assumes a therapeutic value for those patients "whose very early experiences have been so deficient or distorted that the analyst has to be the first in the patient's life to supply certain environmental essentials."

The Emergence of a Different View of the Relation Between Subject and Object

From the situations just described, two issues arise that profoundly change the way of approaching psychoanalysis. First, Winnicott highlights the patient's unconscious work on the analyst's unconscious and thus on his mental functioning. Second, he introduces a methodological modification: he suggests that we need to consider the functioning of the analyst's mind as a tool of psychoanalytic investigation.

There seems to be a bridge here between the 1945 essay and the one written in 1947 [CW 3:2:1]. The source of Winnicott's investigation of earliest infancy is his experience of transference situations encountered with psychotic patients. His attention to the *psychic and unconscious relationship* between mother and newborn permits him to grasp aspects of the transference–countertransference relationship, of the mental functioning of seriously ill patients, and of the origin of psychosis.

In "Hate in the Countertransference," we can see the coexistence of three levels: theoretical, clinical, and technical. At the level of theory, he offers many reasons to hypothesize the precedence of the mother's hate over that of the newborn, thereby dislodging from the model of the earliest stages of mental functioning the idea of an innate death instinct. From a clinical point of view, he implies that, in order for the psychotic patient to acquire the capacity to distinguish hate from love, he must first enter into contact with an object capable of feeling hate towards him. Technically, he is positing the coexistence of three forms of countertransference: one as a blind spot; another that constitutes the specific identity of that individual analyst; and a third, objective form that exists in reaction to the personality of that particular patient.

In this essay, it becomes evident that Winnicott's vision of psychic functioning is founded on the radical and innovative principle that the unconscious functioning of the object, as well as its transformations caused by the unconscious of the subject, must be investigated and retransformed in order that the subject may embark on a psychic transformation. The idea that he is engaged simply in magnifying the importance of the environment is clearly superficial and misleading. This is no mere introduction of the analyst's arbitrary subjectivity into the clinical situation. It involves the construction of a space that, until then, did not exist. In highlighting the phenomena created by the reciprocal action of the patient's unconscious on the unconscious of the analyst, he is maintaining that it is possible to observe such phenomena, that it is necessary to analyze them, and that it is legitimate to utilize them in understanding psychic functioning and the transformation accomplished through psychoanalysis.

This might be seen as a simple clinical deepening of a Freudian intuition. What makes it a radical turning point, however, is its proposition that the birth and development of the mind depends not only on the work of intrapsychic construction but also on unconscious *interpsychic* processes and that this is true also within the analytic relationship. This process involves not just a communication from unconscious to unconscious but (in play) the capacity for mutual unconscious modification. The unconscious of one *puts forth a demand for psychic work on the unconscious of the other*; the matter is not merely one of tolerating and containing the emotional effect of the other but of also *elaborating* what reaches the subject's unconscious from the unconscious of the object (Fabozzi, 2012). This is the intuition that Winnicott reveals in this work: the existence of a network of unconscious movements between subject and object that mark both analytic process and the development of the child's psyche. This network of unconscious movements activates the psychic activity of both analyst and mother, permitting the development of the patient's missing psychic functions and those of the neonate still *in statu nascendi*. The fruits of this theoretical-clinical position of Winnicott's will reach full maturity in his final works [CW 8:2:28; CW 9:1:15; CW 9:1:29].

Correlation Between Winnicott's Conception of Aggression and His Discovery and "Invention" of Transitional Objects and Space

In "Primitive Emotional Development" [CW 2:7:8] and "Aggression in Relation to Emotional Development" [CW: 3:5:2], Winnicott introduces a fundamental link between aggression and the initiation of a relationship with external reality, a theme that continues to represent one of his principal threads of research as he explores the functions and meanings of the transitional object.

This concept has, of course, a monumental scope. In the first place, the object coalesces from a Platonic ideal of representation to become a concrete object. The term "object" refers here to something that can be manipulated and, as such, assists in the child's progressive attribution of meanings as they take shape out of the nascent interior world. This is the starting point for his essential paradoxical vision:

> The following complex statement has to be made. The infant can employ a transitional object when the internal object is alive and real and good enough (not too persecutory). But this internal object depends for its qualities on the existence and aliveness and behaviour of the external object (breast, mother figure, general environmental care). [CW 4:2:21]

It is in this context that we can understand the revolutionary significance of the statement that the transitional object is "the first not-me possession," originally as part of the child's emotional development, but also for the patient in analysis. In these three terms, joined together in a figurative phrase, are condensed further intersecting levels of experience. "The first": the child creates a space where none existed before and that an outside observer has no capacity to grasp. "Not-me": the differentiation between "me" and "not-me" represents the integration of the ego via a kind of opposition to the fundamental unity with the mother—an awareness of that which it is not. "Possession": the pseudopod that in an inseparable entanglement of aggression and libido lays down the basis for the birth of the relationship with the object.

In an important letter to Money-Kyrle (November 27, 1952 [CW 4:1:13]), Winnicott says that he prefers the term "transitional" to "intermediate." It evokes an intrinsic dynamism, implying that both object and space are in continual movement and development. Hence, one of the principal functions of the transitional object: to act as a support for the to-ing and fro-ing between the edges of the internal and external worlds and between union and separation. Analogously, transitional space is not a fixed place but is continually recombining and restructuring itself in relation to the oscillations of the object.

Repositioning Primary Narcissism in the Context of the Early Infant–Mother Relationship

The newborn enters into a relation with the breast that was there, waiting to be discovered, and draws from it the sensation of having created it. Winnicott coins a term—subjective object—to convey this from the baby's point of view. The baby experiences the breast in terms of an absence of separateness, deriving from it an *experience* of omnipotence.

It will be clear that Winnicott's model is not a repositing of the existence of primary narcissism because the presence and contribution of the object are crucial. The mother has a natural yet complex status as the supplier of the baby's need for both nourishment and illusion, and the capacity for illusion is created by her active adaptation to her baby. At first, she will not make conscious or unconscious demands on him; she will respect his needs, emotional states, rhythms, and processes of maturation so that he may discover the environment on the basis of his own spontaneous movements.

For this, the baby needs a mother of average predictability, neither unstable, incoherent, nor subject to exaggerated mood swings. In late pregnancy and during the early weeks of the baby's life, she must be able to tolerate states of regression and complex identifications—with herself as a baby, with her own mother, and with her own child. The baby gradually establishes a relation to external reality through her gradual de-adaptation from his needs (which brings a degree of frustration) and through the baby's own discovery of a transitional object that will acquire specific functions and meanings, placing him in a particular area of reality and experience.

The transitional object constitutes the beginning of the process that will enable him to recognize the external nature of objects. It functions as a bridge: between child and mother, at those points when the mother is absent; between the subjective object and the objective object; between what is internal and what is external. It is the first external object, and it also represents the beginning of symbolism: it stands for the mother and, at the same time, for the Self of the child.

What is crucial is its material quality. The child can experience it through the senses. Its forms and deformations, its smells and new subtleties, are what first define its "not-me" nature. But for the transitional object to exist, the environment must guarantee its psychic existence. In a sense, the gaze of the observer defines the nature of the transitional object. The mother must refrain from confronting the child with the dilemma of whether its reality is internal or external and allow him or her not to answer a question that is not to be asked about the source of the transitional object (whether it was created or found).

This will enable the transitional object to remain situated in a paradoxical space, a notional psychic place hitherto unexplored by psychoanalysis. This is the intermediate area of experience, the area of illusion, of potential space (Fabozzi,

2006) that engenders a chain of developmental potentialities. Thanks to the constitution of a separateness, the child can fill up this distance by introducing an experience that symbolically allows him or her to establish a new union with the mother. Separation is thus transformed into a bond, continuity into contiguousness, distance into closeness. When the psychic and emotional prerequisites have been achieved, this leads on to developmental frustration, which can give rise to a creative gesture, a game, a movement towards the structuring of a symbol. This will "fill" and give form to the space, which is always on the point of losing and regaining its character as potential.

Winnicott's Unique Semantic of Potential

Giannakoulas and Hernandez (2001) suggest that the "limits" of potential space are constituted by four "dialectical dynamisms": the mother's movements of identification with herself and with the newborn within the primary maternal preoccupation; the paradoxical nature of the transitional object; the mother's function as a mirror, which introduces elements of similarity and difference; and the use of the object, a crucial experience in which the child destroys the object just when it is on the point of becoming real and then experiences the object's survival. There is a circularity that binds subject, object, and potential space and allows the dialectical movement between separation and union that is realized through playing and creativity.

It is perhaps too simplistic to say that the psychoanalytic process takes place within the same sort of transitional space. The space generated within the analytic relationship is not fixed but continually recreated by the reciprocal contribution of analyst and patient. Its topology is neither predictable nor able to be prescribed in any normative, abstract way. Here, the persona of the analyst comes into play. If he is capable of grasping what the patient offers, embryonically and potentially, he will facilitate and contribute to the creation of this space, an unforeseen and unforeseeable place within the analytic field.

The same conception applies to the dreamlike function of the analyst—Bion's *reverie*, an oneiric state of wakefulness (1962, p. 35), Winnicott's *unending dream* [CW 11:1], Bollas's *dreaming position of the analyst* (1997, p. 12), or Khan's *dreaming ego* (1974, p. 36). This is not a *posture* deliberately chosen by the analyst. It is created unexpectedly, something that the analyst must be capable of grasping and the patient of receiving in order to give life and form to the "play" between the two partners in the analytic relationship. This spontaneous space, continuously revealed, is the location for the communicative exchanges, both between Self and object and between the patient and himself.

It is also crucial to Winnicott's "capacity to be alone in the presence of the other" [CW 5:3:20], a concept that couples union and separateness, dependency and autonomy, both in the development of the child and in the analytic situation.

This idea revolutionizes a wide range of theories, including the whole range of separation anxieties, panic attacks, and phobias. Clinical experience shows that one of the factors underlying these forms of psychopathology, which lie within a vast spectrum, is the absence of this significant developmental step. During a panic attack, for example, the patient feels alone in facing the catastrophic threat of death; he has failed to establish the capacity to be alone in the presence of the other. Similarly, the claustro-agoraphobic patient feels lost in infinite space, like an astronaut who inadvertently severs the umbilical link to the spaceship and is left floating in the void for eternity.

For both Winnicott and Klein, these psychopathological dispositions are defenses against the earliest anxieties. Unlike Klein, Winnicott defines this "falling for ever" [CW 6:3:19] in terms of primitive agonies experienced by the infant when the environment does not fulfil its function of good-enough holding. However, it would be a misrepresentation of Winnicott's thinking to see the role of the environment as simply succeeding or failing to foster growth. In his theoretical-clinical thinking, he explores a much deeper and more complex range of psychopathology that is attributable to specific forms of excess, intrusion, unpredictability, infiltration, or colonization. When the environment, and in particular the mother's unconscious, subjects the child to these experiences, he will defend himself with well-organized, sophisticated defenses that Winnicott defines at various levels.

Authenticity and Falseness: A Unifying View

Although the papers in Volume 3 each have their own specificity, they are unified by this issue, which is both central and peculiar to Winnicott's work. "Reparation in Respect of Mother's Organized Defence Against Depression" constitutes a landmark in this line of thinking and crystallizes the nucleus of his contribution and its innovative scope. Groundbreaking in its clinical observations and remarkable for various important features, its density may account for why it has remained relatively neglected, even in the Winnicott-inspired literature.

> Early in my career a little boy came to hospital by himself and said to me "Please, Doctor, mother complains of a pain in my stomach", and this drew my attention usefully to the part mother can play. [CW 3:3:1]

With this simple anecdote, Winnicott shows the reader a new conception of the child's somatic illness as a part of a structuring relation with the mother. A few lines further on, we find the revolutionary statement:

> Probably I get a specially clear view of this problem in a children's out-patient department because such a department is really a *clinic for management of hypochondria in mothers* . . . There is no sharp dividing line between the

> frank hypochondria of a depressed woman and a mother's genuine concern for a child. [CW 3:3:1]

From a theoretical perspective, this radical assertion represents a decisive and explicit shift. Winnicott is saying that the center of gravity of psychology and psychopathology may reside not within the confines of the individual but within the other who treats the child as an extension of itself. Paraphrasing Freud's famous statement "the Ego is not master in its own house," we might say that for Winnicott the child's self is not master in its own house in as much as it is occupied and colonized by the self of the mother. So the structuring relation with the mother as environment affects both the normal development of the child and its psychopathological aspect. The role of the clinician is to judge the shift from normality to pathology.

In line with Anna Freud, Winnicott observes how an alteration in the relation of the child to his environment is organized into infantile neurosis as the result of an interiorization of the object. Anna Freud states that in judging the degree of normality or pathology in the child, it is crucial to discover whether the child's "disturbance" can be shifted through an intervention in the environment or whether it has already been absorbed into the ego, becoming a constitutive if ego-dystonic part of it.

Anna Freud, Klein, and Winnicott may use different theoretical models and idioms, but, as consummate clinicians, they are all guided by clinical practice, and they pursue what are in many respects convergent lines of thinking. However, whereas Klein's vision of pathology tends towards the extreme end of the spectrum (the infant is, so to speak, a little psychotic), Winnicott reformulates this issue in a radically different way in his essay "Paediatrics and Psychiatry" [CW 3:3:2]. Almost impudently with respect to Klein (whom he does not explicitly mention), he asserts:

> At this point I have learned to expect a misunderstanding unless deliberate care is taken to avoid it. It has often been said to me: the idea that mad people are like babies, or small children, simply isn't true. Can I make it clear that I do not suggest that the insane are behaving like infants any more than that neurotics are just like older children. Ordinary healthy children are not neurotic (though they can be) and ordinary babies are not mad.

In fact, this line of thinking originates well before 1948. It is implied, for instance, in "The Manic Defence" [CW 1:4:6]. Here, Winnicott describes the manic defense as the denial (Freud's *Verleugnung*) of internal reality and of the sensations related to depression and suspended animation. This implies a basic dissociation within the personality. He developed this idea ten years later, in 1945, through the concept of "integration and non-integration," and, in "Ego Distortion in Terms of True and False Self" [CW 6:1:22], he arrived at a final definition of "a dissociation in internal reality." This idea of a basic dissociation in personality is not the same as repression or splitting, both of which imply an ego to do the work. It forecloses the child's further development if the integration facilitated by the environment cannot be made or is blocked. Only "After integration the child starts to have a self" [CW 5:1:9].

In "Reparation in Respect of Mother's Organized Defence Against Depression" [CW 3:3:1], Winnicott refers to the "false reparation" that we meet in clinical practice. It is false because it occurs in relation not to the patient's guilt but to the external other. This theory, very radical in the context of the Kleinian ideas of the time, gives rise to his clinical discoveries concerning dissociation in connection with the false self [CW 6:1:22]. However, the central core of the configuration has a more comprehensive relevance. It is capable of explaining, along a continuum, both primitive psychopathological phenomena in the early structuring of the self and the later schizoid phenomena with which Winnicott's concept of dissociation was initially associated.

At the beginning of the 1948 paper Winnicott writes:

> This false reparation appears through the *patient's identification with the mother* and the dominating factor is not the patient's own guilt but the mother's organized defence against depression and unconscious guilt. . . . the depression of the child can be the mother's depression in reflection. The child uses the mother's depression as an escape from his or her own; this provides a false restitution and reparation in relation to the mother, and this hampers the development of a personal restitution[5] capacity . . . It will be seen that these children in extreme cases have *a task which can never be accomplished*. Their task is first *to deal with mother's mood*. If they succeed in the immediate task, they do no more than succeed in creating an atmosphere in which they can *start on their own lives*. [CW 3:3:1, emphasis added]

Here, Winnicott is starting to describe the psychic work done on behalf of the *other* within the self, through identification. The degree of this work varies, but at its most extreme it may extend to occupation of the self by the other.[6]

Close to the end of his scientific career, Winnicott concludes the journey begun with "Hate in the Countertransference." In 1967, he discusses the etiological factors proposed by his theory of emotional development, which include the "mother's capacity to adapt to the infant's needs through her healthy ability to identify with the baby" [CW 8:1:25]. He notes:

---

[5] The terms "restitution," "reparation," and "guilt" reflect the influence of the Kleinian concepts of the period with which Winnicott established a dialogue while at the same time attempting the search for an idiom of his own that would explain these clinical phenomena in a different way. The terms "reparation" and "guilt" are part of the concept of the depressive position, but the terms "restitution" and particularly "*personal* restitution" allude to the process of the development of the true self in contrast to that of false reparation and hence false analysis.

[6] The "presence" in the self of this depressed object is discussed by André Green in his paper "The Dead Mother" (1980): "[The] 'dead mother' . . . is a mother who remains alive, but who is, so to speak, psychically 'dead' in the eyes of the young child in her care" (p. 142).

> It seems necessary to add to this the concept of the mother's *unconscious* (repressed) hate of the child. Parents naturally love and hate their babies, in varying degrees. This does not do damage. At all ages, and in earliest infancy especially, the effect of the repressed death wish towards the baby is harmful, and it is beyond the baby's capacity to deal with this. At a later stage than this one that concerns us here, one can see a child all the time making efforts *in order to arrive at the starting post*—that is, to counteract the parents' unconscious wish (covered by reaction formation) that the child should be dead.

The child's effort to arrive at the starting post by managing the occupation of the potential self by the parents' unconscious hampers the development of personal capacities. This is similar to the task of the depressed child in dealing with the mother's moods in order to create an atmosphere in which he can begin a life of his own, as first described in "Reparation in Respect of Mother's Organized Defence Against Depression" [CW 3:3:1].

The Maturational Process of Integration

At the beginning, the individual is like a bubble. If the pressure from outside actively adapts to the pressure within, then the bubble is the significant thing; that is to say, the infant self. If, however, the environmental pressure is greater or less than the pressure within the bubble, then it is not the bubble that is important but the environment. The bubble adapts to the outside pressure [CW 3:4:8].

These words are taken from the analysis of a patient to whom Winnicott conveys his gratitude for having given such figurative expression to what was previously an embryonic concept of psychic life. They emphasize the role of the environmental pressure that disturbs, interferes with, or interrupts the maturational physiological processes of emotional development. The centrality of the concept of reaction runs through all of his work and is strongly related to concepts of "going on being," psychic continuity and the consequences of its interruption.

The essay "Birth Memories, Birth Trauma and Anxiety" is Winnicott's formulation of the theoretical origin of psychic life. In it, he applies the concept of "reaction" to the very earliest stages:

> There's certainly before birth the beginning of an emotional development, and it is likely that there is before birth a capacity for false and unhealthy forward movement in emotional development; in health environmental disturbances of a certain degree are valuable stimuli, but beyond a certain degree these disturbances are unhelpful in that they bring about a *reaction*. At this very early stage of development there is not sufficient ego strength for there to be a reaction without loss of identity. [CW 3:4:8]

The intuition of the phenomenon of reaction existing before birth is an exquisitely Winnicottian observation. In this essay, he also clarifies the recurring heuristic significance, for him, of the adjective "theoretical." The concept of the "theoretical first feed," for example, is a normative fiction. It is used to establish the potential frame of reference within which the business of the individual's emotional development would unfold in a state of health were there not intervening factors or environmental impingements. Depending on their intensity, such impediments may be reabsorbed into the bubble or they may compel psychic work of a reactive kind.

How does Winnicott approach the origin of psychic life? Of course, his enormous experience as a pediatrician helps him with the task of tracing the germinative seeds of psychic experience from the fetal stage onwards, but it is the analytic situation that forms the laboratory par excellence in which his hypotheses can assume substance through emotional participation with the patient. Here, he is exploring the limits of an intermediate area between physiological and psychic traumatic reactions in the light of psychic life. One can only be astonished and fascinated by the fact that many of the contemporary thematics of prenatal and neonatal psychology had already been tackled by Winnicott. What can seem like a naïve lack of inhibition in this area in fact reflects the certainty of someone with a store of observational and psychoanalytic clinical material at his disposal. It is this experience that produces his concepts of the development of the Self, the fear of breakdown, holding, handling, object-presenting, and the false self.

In "Birth Trauma, Birth Memories and Anxiety," he writes:

> Thus, in the natural process *the birth experience is an exaggerated sample of something already known to the infant*. For the time being, during birth, the infant is a reactor and the important thing is the environment; and then after birth there is a return to a state of affairs in which the important thing is the infant, whatever that means. In health the infant is prepared before birth for some environmental impingement, and already has had the experience of a natural return from reacting to a state of not having to react, which is the only state in which the self can begin to be. [CW 3:4:8]

The role of experience is a vector of growth. The progressive exchange between the environment and the fetus, then later the baby, enables the coalescing of the psychic functions of the human being. This line of thinking culminates (in Volume 3) with the extraordinary paper "Mind and Its Relation to the Psyche-Soma" [CW 3:4:20]. For Winnicott, mind is always an organized defense; it is the structural precipitate of the baby's reactions to the environment, and it sanctions the fundamental dissociation of the personality. Once the mind has been constituted, the psyche-soma loses its wholeness; the dissociation between intellect and emotions has become behavioral, and the whole range of schizoid and dissociative pathology originates from this fundamental splitting of the personality.

This essay develops the insights presented initially in "Primitive Emotional Development" and establishes the foundation for the successive elaborations of the false self and "Basis for Self in Body" [CW 9:2:12]. In this paper, he uses the expressions "false entity" and "easy identification with the environmental aspect of all relationships," which precisely evoke the processes underlying the development of the false self, and the expression "true self" makes its first appearance.

The ideas and insights of this period, 1947 to 1951, provide the foundation for the creative developments of the decades to come.

Conclusion

This third volume, which brings together many of Winnicott's fundamental papers, is a treasure trove of ideas, intuitions, clinical observations, and underlying threads. These link sketches of theory that gradually take shape and become part of a more complex corpus, continually open to changes and revisions. What strikes the reader—or at least what struck us as authors of this essay —is the inner coherence of Winnicott's thinking, his courage in carrying forward his insights, and the intellectual honesty that characterizes the whole of his work.

The essays included here constitute the source for the future germination of many themes, and they characterize that quiet genius, sometimes chaotic, that distinguishes Winnicott's unique way of working in psychoanalysis. Due to limitations of space, we have been unable to discuss some of the writings that would have taken us in different directions, but, in the end, these always relate, in one way or another, to the issues that we have highlighted.

As Winnicott himself said at the end of his clinical career, his legacy has yet to be fully understood. In "The Use of an Object" he writes:

> I cannot assume that the way in which my ideas have been developed has been followed by others, but I should like to point out there has been a sequence, and the order that there may be in the sequence belongs to the evolution of my work. [CW 8:2:28]

Our purpose has been not to guide or drive our readers—Winnicott would have wrinkled his nose at this idea—but to leave them free to find their own way, guided by their own personal feelings and inclinations. In other words, we hope to offer an object that they can create and recreate at will.

References

Bion, W. R. (1962). *Learning from experience*. London: Heinemann.

Bollas, C. (1997). *Cracking up: The work of unconscious experience*. London: Routledge.

Bonaminio, V. (2005). L'uso delle parole e la scrittura in Winnicott. *Rivista di Psicoanalisi, 50*, 259–274.

Fabozzi, P. (2006). Spazio potenziale tra vincolo e creatività. In Centro Italiano di Psicologia Analitica (Ed.), *Il vincolo* (pp. 213–226). Milan: Rafaello Cortina.

Fabozzi, P. (2012). A silent yet radical future revolution: Winnicott's innovative perspective. *Psychoanalytic Quarterly, 81*, 601–626.

Giannakoulas, A., & Hernandez, M. (2001). On the construction of potential space. In M. Bertolini, A. Giannakoulas, & M. Hernandez (Eds.), *Squiggles and spaces. Volume 1: Revisiting the work of D. W. Winnicott.* London/Philadelphia: Whurr.

Green, A. (1980). The dead mother. In *Life narcissism, death narcissism*. London: Free Association Books, trans. Andrew Weller, 2001.

Heimann, P. (1950). On counter-transference. *International Journal of Psychoanalysis, 31*, 81–84.

Khan, M. M. R. (1974). *The privacy of the self.* London: Hogarth.

Klein, M. (1946). Notes on some schizoid mechanisms. *International Journal of Psychoanalysis, 27*, 99–110.

Ogden, T. (2001). Reading Winnicott. *Psychoanalytic Quarterly, 70*, 299–323.

Winnicott, D. W. (1945). Primitive emotional development. [CW 2 7.8]

Winnicott, D. W. (1948). Paediatrics and psychiatry. [CW 3 3.2]

Winnicott, D. W. (1949). Hate in the countertransference [1947]. [CW 3 2.1]

Winnicott, D. W. (1953). Transitional objects and transitional phenomena. [CW 4 2.21]

Winnicott, D. W. (1954). Mind and its relation to the psyche-soma [1949]. [CW 3 4.20]

Winnicott, D. W. (1958). The manic defence [1935]. [CW 1 4.6]

Winnicott, D. W. (1958). Aggression in relation to emotional development [1950]. [CW3 5.2]

Winnicott, D. W. (1958). Birth memories, birth trauma and anxiety [1949]. [CW 3 4.8]

Winnicott, D. W. (1958). The capacity to be alone. [CW 5 3:20]

Winnicott, D. W. (1958). Reparation in respect of mother's organized defence against depression [1948]. [CW 3 3.1]

Winnicott, D. W. (1965). Ego distortion in terms of true and false self [1960]. [CW6 1.22]

Winnicott, D. W. (1965). Ego integration in child development. [CW 6 3.19]

Winnicott, D. W. (1965). Group influences and the maladjusted child: The school aspect [1955]. [CW 5 1.9]

Winnicott, D. W. (1968). The aetiology of infantile schizophrenia in terms of adaptive failures [1967]. [CW 8 1.25]

Winnicott, D. W. (1969). The use of an object and relating through identifications [1968]. [CW 8 2. 28]

Winnicott, D. W. (1971). Basis for self in body [1970]. [CW 9 2.12]

Winnicott, D. W. (1972). Mother's madness appearing in the clinical material as an ego-alien factor [1969]. [CW 9 1.29]

Winnicott, D. W. (1988). *Human nature.* C. Bollas, M. Davis, & R. Shepherd (Eds.), London and New York: Routledge.

Winnicott, D. W. (1989). Development of the theme of the mother's unconscious as discovered in psycho-analytic practice [1969]. [CW 9 1.15]

FIGURE 4.1 *In August 1951, Winnicott attended the Seventeenth Congress of the International Psychoanalytical Association, Amsterdam. In this photograph of attendees, Winnicott appears on the far left of the back row, second from the end.*

From the Donald Woods Winnicott Archive, in the care of the Wellcome Library, London, courtesy of the Winnicott Trust.

{5}

Reading Winnicott Slowly, 1952–1955

Dominique Scarfone

There are many ways of reading Winnicott, or, for that matter, any good author, but I am thinking here of two avowedly contrasting ways. The first and, I believe, the more common consists in probing his writings to know what his view or position is on a given topic or to find the original description of a given concept. Many examples come immediately to mind—for instance, the transitional object and transitional area, the fear of breakdown, the false self organization, holding, the squiggle, and so on. This is a very legitimate mode of enquiry, of course, and one for which the index at the end of a book is most useful.

The other way I have in mind has little use for an index and seems, at first, less productive. It requires more time and, most importantly, it requires a different attitude towards the author. It consists in reading Winnicott for Winnicott's sake; that is, not primarily in search of the "nuggets" already identified as Winnicottian ideas or concepts. It is, rather, an effort to capture the mode, the logic, the very movement of Winnicott's thinking. For this, a deliberately "naïve" way of entering his writings is necessary, by which I mean reading Winnicott after having put aside any previous knowledge of "Winnicott." It also requires reading him *slowly*, without rushing towards understanding, for, as we know, we tend to understand what is already familiar at the risk of brushing away what is really new and could possibly upset a previous way of thinking. Reading slowly sometimes implies staying long enough on a single paragraph or even a single sentence without taking anything for granted, without closing the *gestalt* too quickly. This does not amount to a religious exegesis; it is simply paying attention to what a true author has to teach us. And by "true author," I mean someone who can be trusted to go on consistently thinking from an original standpoint, someone who does not let go of his object of research until he finds something significant, something that lies as much in the *method* of thinking as in the elements of knowledge that such method obtains.

In this respect, Winnicott is a perfect example of an author who, when not approached with the proper reading method, can easily be misunderstood. Not infrequently, for instance, does one hear the question regarding Winnicott's fidelity to Freud or Klein, and one of the reasons invoked to suspect infidelity or deviance is that Winnicott was reluctant to use the traditional psychoanalytic vocabulary. This in itself is an interesting aspect, and I shall be addressing it later. But it is only part of the picture. Another important aspect is that his thinking can easily be misconstrued as merely *adding* new ideas to the psychoanalytic body of knowledge while in fact he has been *using* psychoanalytic theory in a different and original way. In what follows, I hope to illustrate this.

Keeping the Language Alive

The period in Winnicott's writing covered by Volume 4 is greatly concerned with the problem of psychosis in its relation to emotional development. It is probably no coincidence that at a time when Winnicott was writing these important papers, he also felt the need, apparently triggered by some local event, but also addressing a long-term issue, to write Melanie Klein the famous letter of November 17, 1952 [CW 4:1:12]. It is a letter that, far from dealing with petty institutional politics, gives a clear view of the nature of Winnicott's engagement with psychoanalysis as a whole. And it is most interesting that he seems highly concerned with the problem of language. Not language as a foundation of the unconscious, as Lacan was starting to propose at that very time on the other side of the Channel, but language as an indicator of creativity—of the liveliness of the mind, of the self, and indeed of psychoanalysis:

> I can see how annoying it is that when something develops in me out of my own growth and out of my analytic experience I want to put it in my own language. This is annoying because I suppose everyone wants to do the same thing, and in a scientific society one of our aims is to find a common language. This language must, however, be kept alive as there is nothing worse than a dead language.

The same issue was addressed, although from the opposite end of the argument, in a letter written fifteen months later, this time to Anna Freud [CW 4:3:7], where Winnicott expresses the fear that using a common metapsychological language may "give the appearance of a common understanding when such understanding does not exist."

These are challenging statements. As Winnicott is well aware, it is tempting to believe that, like any science, psychoanalysis should strive towards adopting a shared set of concepts and terms from which a common language should ensue, thus facilitating communication among its practitioners. One way of interpreting Winnicott's phrase would be that *at that point in time*, 1953, he felt there was no common understanding *of the same terms*. That this was not a mere question of vocabulary, however, is conspicuous in a letter to H. Ezriel of June 20, 1952. Following a presentation of Ezriel's membership paper to the British Psychoanalytic Society, a paper Winnicott deemed highly original but whose discussion he felt was unsatisfactory, he wrote:

> I think that probably there is something which the speakers . . . sensed but yet could not come to grips with, and this would probably turn out to be a real psychoanalytic difference of approach. I would suggest that the trouble is that the difference *cannot yet be clearly stated by psycho-analysts because they have not yet as a body formulated the platform from which they can talk.* (emphasis added [CW 4:1:9])

Mere vocabulary is therefore not the heart of the matter. The problem is rather of establishing a firm psychoanalytic ground on the basis of which differences can be then apprehended and thoroughly discussed. A shared vocabulary can be useful, of course, but it cannot obviate the problem that different things can be meant by different analysts using the same words. So Winnicott's search for and contribution to such a psychoanalytic platform did not follow the road of a standard vocabulary. His personal reasons for this may have been many, but one of them is openly mentioned in the form of a question, in the same letter to Anna Freud [CW 4:3:7]: "is it because of something in myself?" he asks. The answer is probably "yes," but not necessarily in the trivial sense where Winnicott would be displaying an incapacity for or a personal bent against the use of metapsychology. Considering what we now know of his way of thinking, so beautifully expressed in the letter to Klein, we can attribute more depth than Winnicott himself seems to consciously claim regarding the "something in myself" about which he wondered. The "myself" in that sentence is indeed more than a pronoun. The "self" it contains—that is, not only Winnicott's *self*, but every *self* seeking its original mode of expression—naturally resists using a standardized and impersonal terminology. In the letter to Klein, he was indeed acknowledging that his tendency to use his own language was "when something develops in [him] out of [his] own growth."

It is out of sheer fidelity, not to convention, but to his own self and to his own internal growth processes that Winnicott feels a personal language is the only possible one.

One can thereby be brought to reflect on the price that psychoanalytic theory has to pay for the sake of an author's self-respect. A cynical commentator might adopt the "I-told-you-so" attitude, remarking that he knew from the start that psychoanalysis is not a science, incapable as it is of even sharing a common set of terms, let alone concepts. This brings us back to my introductory remarks on the ways of reading Winnicott. If you think of science in the way experimentalists do, then you will find that Winnicott, or psychoanalysis in general, fails to meet its criteria. About such failure, I say thank God! I cannot imagine a psychoanalyst adopting the experimentalist's attitude and state of mind in the consulting room; which, by the way, is no laboratory. Of course, Winnicott himself noted that the consulting room is a very important, actually the main, place for us to make observations and gather experience about the human condition, but certainly not in the affectively distant way of the physicist or chemist. Even as we sometimes compare psychoanalysis to quantum physics for the reason that both acknowledge the involvement of the observer in the experiment, it is worth underlining that the involvement of psychoanalysts in the analytic situation is much deeper. For all we know, the observed fact in quantum physics may be altered by the observer, but, in psychoanalysis, not only the observed fact but *the observer himself* is changed by what is going on inside the setting. Ours is then a very special kind of science, if we really want to call our *praxis* by that name. It follows that the observer who will later be thinking and writing about his experience, and whose very person was affected by the experience, cannot recount what happened in a standardized language without leaving out a significant part thereof. Winnicott's respect and faithfulness to his own experience and to his own self not only allows but *requires* a personal language, a language that, considering the singular nature of the experience to be narrated, is all the more rigorous for its being highly personal.

Ironically, we can find, *mutatis mutandis*, a very similar attitude in Freud, albeit from a different angle. Indeed, whereas Winnicott seems to be shunning Freud's vocabulary, he is quite in tune with the Freudian spirit concerning language. Consider here a phrase of Freud's, apparently the opposite of Winnicott's stance: "one gives way first in words, and then little by little in substance too" (Freud, 1921/1955, p. 91). This is a famous sentence, certainly, which can easily be misinterpreted as meaning that, for Freud, one should cultivate a strict metapsychological *terminology*. This, however, is certainly not what Freud had in mind. The remark was meant to assert strongly his preference for explicit mention of sexual matters, by contrast to what was preferred by "educated people" who, says Freud, would rather use "the more genteel expressions of 'Eros" and "erotic." Freud is insisting on the necessity of speaking clearly and frankly without softening one's language about what one has to say. The idea is the same in Freud as in Winnicott: it is not a matter of clinging to a standard vocabulary but of saying precisely what one means to say, of staying true to one's thought without compromise, and of using the words that are felt most appropriate to the matter in hand. We know that this is precisely what Winnicott did all his life, not only in his psychoanalytic papers but in his private letters and in letters to the editors of newspapers, a number of examples of which can be found in Volume 4. We also know that Freud wrote most of the time in a plain language, using everyday words. So, whereas the vocabulary of his metapsychology became more and more strictly defined, which was unavoidable for reasons that Winnicott himself well understood ("in a scientific society one of our aims is to find a common language" [Letter to Melanie Klein, CW 4:1:12]), in the end, it is Winnicott who stays closer to Freud's spirit by not "giving way" in words for the sake of a more compliant vocabulary—compliant, that is, to the group mind that inevitably forms within psychoanalytic circles. Obviously, then, the same reasons Freud had for speaking with the appropriate words encouraged Winnicott not to always adhere to the shared language. Yet another Winnicottian paradox!

A close reading of his writings shows that, in the end, it is not so much a question of vocabulary as of *style*. After all, Winnicott did openly refer to instincts and defenses, for instance, or to Oedipus and the depressive position. But what he clearly avoided doing was to write in a desiccated, formulaic fashion that would have suggested a reverence to some leading figure in the psychoanalytic society but was liable to prevent him from thinking his own thoughts and thinking the psychoanalytic experience anew. This by no means implies that Winnicott's terms are not *rigorous*; quite the contrary: they are both conceptually sound, at least if one takes the time to examine them from up close, and, most importantly, as congruent as possible with his personal way of being and of doing psychoanalysis.

One can easily imagine how an effort to comply with a standard vocabulary could have thwarted much of his personal style, hence much of his creativity and authentic contribution. I have already hinted how his spirit was much closer to Freud's than is usually thought. For all his highly personal mode of expressing himself, Winnicott is a staunch Freudian when it comes to using theory. For here perhaps resides the secret of Winnicott's personal idiom: he *uses* Freud's acquisitions even if he is not *mimicking* Freud's mode of writing or thinking. We know how the word "use" is important in his theory, but although he will compose "The Use of an Object and Relating Through Identifications" in 1968 [CW 8:2:28] near the end of his life, the ideas contained in that important paper were clearly at work from early on and certainly during the years covered by Volume 4 of the *Collected Works*.

This essay began by referring to some of Winnicott's letters, and I cannot insist too much on the value of reading his correspondence in parallel with his main papers. The chronological order in which letters and texts are presented offers a rich opportunity for watching his ideas make their way in varied circumstances and under different guises. The letters provide the advantage of actually showing how incarnate Winnicott's theory was, how consistently he dwelled in the clinical and theoretical landscape of those years. In the letters that appear in Volume 4, he was greatly concerned with the attitude of Melanie Klein's followers while sparing Klein herself. This is not the place for deciding how right or how wrong Winnicott was in terms of facts. But in terms of the spirit he is defending (e.g., against the dogmatic attitude that was frequently encountered in those days in psychoanalytic milieus, and not only among Kleinians), I can only applaud the courage and honesty with which he addressed the issue. It is not only a question of politics, nor of concern for organizational unity within the British Psychoanalytic Society. There is clearly a sense that Winnicott's interventions are those of a scientist through and through, one who insists on the importance of keeping the field of research open and acknowledging how much we don't know rather than adopting a self-congratulatory stance towards theoretical formulations. In more than one letter of the time, Winnicott is really enjoying the challenge offered by problems that were not well understood. So much so, indeed, that finding what he deemed mistakes in a paper by a colleague was not significant as long as the problems addressed by the paper and the author's ideas were interesting. Disagreement in such a case was not a cause for quarrels but an opportunity for thinking again and eventually thinking better.

The general picture that emerges from reading the bulk of letters and papers of the period covered in Volume 4 is one in which Winnicott appears as formidably alive and in constant motion, treating patients, writing papers, discussing those of others, writing letters to medical journals and newspapers, all with a profound sense of devotion towards whatever truth can be discovered by sound psychoanalytic practice and rigorous thinking. His most significant contributions, however, can best be appreciated in the papers produced in such a lively period.

Psychosis, Regression, and the Depressive Position

Among the writings of these years, "Psychosis and Child Care" [CW 4:1:5], "The Depressive Position in Normal Emotional Development" [CW 4:3:5], and "Metapsychological and Clinical Aspects of Regression within the Psychoanalytic Set-Up" [CW 4:3:6] are, in my view, the most important, with *Holding and Interpretation* [CW 4:4:1] providing an extraordinary illustration of how the theory comes alive when confronted with practice. Winnicott shows in these writings the complex and subtle processes that his combined experience as analyst and observer of mother–infant relationships allowed him to understand.

From the very first sentences of "Psychosis and Child Care," we are invited to consider what is still today a provocative if apparently simple point of view; that is, psychosis does not reside "in" the child but concerns the child–environment set-up. This is a set-up that, in itself, supposes a very different way of positing the elements requiring the analyst's attention. Indeed, it may look at first as though Winnicott is describing the set-up from a third-person point of view, seeming simply to take notice that "there is no such thing as a baby," as the well-known quotation goes (i.e., no child without a mother, and therefore that the observational unit is the mother–infant ensemble).

The term "environment" employed in this context is already one example of a frequent misreading of Winnicott as someone who merely inserted the environment into psychoanalytic theory as an external, although, welcome complement to the more so-called insular or solipsistic Freudian take, whereas reading Winnicott's paper on "Psychoses and Child Care" [CW 4:1:5] *slowly* is to realize how much richer and more complex his contribution is. The quick, hurried reader could easily be drawn to equate "mother" with "environment" and "environment" with "external world," and obviously there are reasons for spontaneously thinking in those terms. But here lies precisely the need for reading Winnicott slowly, without rushing to what common sense suggests should be the case. For what can be missed is the more finely grained dialectical conception that Winnicott is actually putting forward. Indeed, whereas for an external observer the environment is objectively provided by the mother or whoever is in charge of childcare, Winnicott insists that an individual and its environment cannot be thought of separately: "At first the individual is not the unit. As perceived from outside the unit is an environmental–individual set-up. The outsider knows that the individual psyche can only start in a certain setting. In this setting the individual can gradually come to create a personal environment." Winnicott is thinking *simultaneously* from a third-person *and* a first-person point of view. What is more, the environment he has in mind is something ultimately *created by the individual.*

The fact is that Winnicott is a master dialectician *thinking in terms of relationships rather than isolated elements*, relationships that are at work even before (if one is forced to use a linear timeline) the partners in the relationship are clearly distinguished. So the individual–environment set-up is a relationship that preexists the birth of the individual and of the environment as *differentiated* poles of the relationship. This does not mean that the relationship is only potential. It is *actually at work* and will, in time, yield the more differentiated elements, but it would be a mistake to think of those elements as needing to "get into" a relationship. They actually *emerge* from such a relationship through the process of differentiation, and the conditions of that emergence are what make the difference between mental health and mental illness. Winnicott's way of thinking is here a most profound one, redolent of what both past masters and contemporary philosophers regard as the true state of affairs when thinking in terms of relationships.

The commonsense way of conceiving of a relationship is indeed to think first of separate elements or individuals that will then establish a relationship between them. But this view posits the individual elements as *already there*, as if by magic, and one is then entitled to ask where these terms of the relationship actually originate. This will lead the observer to positing a preexisting relational matrix, one whose individual elements must in turn be questioned about their origin, and so on . . . infinite regress ensues. The only viable solution is either to negate any relationship whatsoever, which is clearly contradicted by the facts, or to posit that the relationship has been there all the time and that it merely evolved and changed appearance: sometimes its poles were only implicit, at other times they were clearly distinguishable. This, I believe, is where Winnicott's conception of the individual–environment set-up leads. It is also the only way to go if one tries to posit *rigorously* the possibility of an object-relations theory; that is, if one tries to solve what I would call the "mystery of internalization." Although the idea of an internalized relationship seems to go without saying, I do not know of any rigorous explanation of *how* the mind proceeds to "put inside" (let alone "inside what"?) such an abstract entity as a relationship supposed to act as an effective structural element.

Thinking in terms of a relationship that has been there from the very beginning, not as a consequence but *as the origin itself*, clearly simplifies the issue and, what is more, aligns psychoanalytic thinking with the most advanced contemporary science (Bitbol, 2010). In this way of looking at a relationship, no obscure mechanics of internalization are required. It is asked of the child (and its mother) merely to evolve *within* the relationship as the latter itself changes and adjusts to their individual evolution. To go back, then, to the observational unit as the individual–environment set-up, thinking in terms of the preexisting relationship allows us to understand that the newborn baby does not *enter* a relationship with the mother; it is, rather, called upon *to be born* as an individual *out* of the relationship already at work in the undifferentiated mother–child unit.

I have previously tried to show that the same way of approaching such matters can be found in Winnicott's "The Use of an Object and Relating Through Identifications" [CW 8:2:28], this time regarding primary projection (Scarfone, 2005). In that paper, Winnicott speaks of projection at different levels of the process that is conducive to the capacity to use an object. He specifies, for instance, that, for an object to be *used*, it must be real and "not a bundle of projections," whereas, at the earlier phase of object-relating (not to be confused with true object relationship), "projection mechanisms and identifications have been operating" [CW 8:2:28]. The use of the same term "projection" can be misleading, and Winnicott is well aware of this. He therefore makes an important remark:

> As I see it, we are familiar with the change whereby projection mechanisms enable the subject to take cognizance of the object. This is not the same as claiming that the object exists for the subject because of the operation of the subject's projection mechanisms. *At first the observer uses words that seem to apply to both ideas at one and the same time, but under scrutiny we see that the two ideas are by no means identical. It is exactly here that we direct our study.* (emphasis added [CW 8:2:28])

Winnicott's study is directed at distinguishing between two wholly different states of affairs even if *the observer* uses the same word: projection. The true situation, however, requires a further effort at understanding that there can be no true projection (projection onto or into someone or something) when there is not yet an explicit relationship. Hence, I proposed speaking of "primary projection" at the phase of object-relating in contrast to true projection at the later phases. Primary projection is therefore a "projection" without a "projector" or a "recipient," if one can use such terminology. What, then, is left? Why is it possible to use the same term "projection"? Well, because *there is* in fact a relationship, but at that stage it takes the form of a "bundle of projections," a bundle that in time, retrospectively, can be thought of as a projection proper. For that moment, however, it is a relationship the terms or poles of which, at this early stage, do not yet exist as separate entities.

The same way of thinking is clearly and beautifully apparent in another of the major papers that appears in Volume 4, "Metapsychological and Clinical Aspects of Regression Within the Psycho-Analytical Set-up," where Winnicott writes: "In primary narcissism the environment is holding the individual, and at the same time the individual knows of no environment and is at one with it" [CW 4:3:6].

Winnicott is again thinking from both sides of the individual–environment set-up, at once from the observable and the not-yet-thinkable positions. And, if one is still tempted to equate "environment" with "mother" (i.e., remaining at the empirical level of observation), Winnicott's language in the paper "The Depressive Position in Normal Emotional Development" [CW 4:3:5] suggests a much more complex picture. In that paper, where holding is a major feature, the mother is more often than not said to be holding not the baby but the situation. A most important difference, in my opinion, since the situation involves the baby, the mother, and whatever is supporting the mother herself in her role as mother. Hence, the failures of environment to which Winnicott pays a great deal of attention, although most easily identifiable in the mother's doings, are in fact to be attributed to a whole situation, a situation that is called upon to evolve to a point where "the experience of the mother holding the situation becomes part of the self, becomes assimilated into the ego. In this way the actual mother gradually becomes less and less necessary. The individual acquires an internal environment."

In "Metapsychological and Clinical Aspects of Regression Within the Psycho-Analytical Set-up" [CW 4:3:6], Winnicott displays his immense talent for fluid, rigorous thinking, conjugating the theory with clinical issues in a way that is at once utterly original and yet makes us think that we somehow knew things must be so. He starts by describing three main clinical categories in which the distinctive element is whether patients operate as whole persons or not, and, if not, to what extent a personal structure is securely present. I cannot enter the minute discussion of this taxonomy, but I wish to underline the elegant way of giving useful guidelines for the clinician without reifying the strictly *human* difficulties encountered by our patients. The descriptions he makes are always intertwined with the concepts he has been developing; there is never a divorce between clinical and theoretical thinking. What is more, pathology seems to regain its original and deep meaning of "suffering" (from the Greek *pathos*), suffering because of difficulties encountered in the course of one's life and not the sense of anomaly or disorder that current psychiatric classification generally proposes. This has profound consequences for the analyst's attitude, and Winnicott takes full responsibility in that respect when, referring to one patient he is thinking about in relation to the theme of regression, he writes, "I cannot help being different from what I was before this analysis started" (p. 205). For Winnicott, the experience with this patient "has tested psycho-analysis" and elicited serious conceptual reflection on the term "regression," giving us yet another example of his rigorous theoretical stance. Whereas for him "the word regression simply means the reverse of progress," this is not the end of the story, because "on closer examination, one observes immediately *there cannot be a simple reversal of progress*" (p. 206). Once again, the fine dialectician is at work here, radically distinguishing between regression as the mere *linguistic* reverse of progress and the *actual process* of reversal. Such actual reversal cannot be simple because, for it to happen, there has to be in the individual "an organization which enables regression to occur." In other words, there has to be a sufficiently structured psychical organization to be able to undergo regression. And Winnicott immediately clarifies his thinking by stating, "It is not useful to use the word regression whenever infantile behavior appears in a case history" (p. 206). In other words, regression cannot be deduced from mere behavioral observation. You still have to establish "who" is displaying such behavior and what level of mental structure is being regressed from. One might consider that the term "regression" does not so much refer to manifest contents but to a rather complex process by which the psychical organization (which will include the environment, as we shall shortly see) is set in motion. This motion is not a simple moving backwards but a bringing to the fore, "a new opportunity for an unfreezing of the frozen situation and a chance for the environment, that is to say, the present-day environment, to make adequate though belated adaptation" (p. 208). This carries important consequences since it brings Winnicott to make an audacious statement: "It is from psychosis that a patient can make spontaneous recovery, whereas psychoneurosis makes no spontaneous recovery and the psycho-analyst is truly needed. In other words psychosis is closely related to health, in which innumerable environmental failure situations are frozen" (p. 209). Here again is an illustration of how a truly psychoanalytically informed conception of pathology runs counter to the apparently no-nonsense attitude of descriptive psychiatry, where it would go without saying that psychosis is much further from health than psychoneurosis. Winnicott's profoundly dialectical stance makes it clear that frozen situations are eventually less resistant to change than the well-organized psychoneurotic structures. He is certainly in the vanguard here, and I personally know of only one other major analyst holding a similar view, Michel de M'Uzan, one of the most respected French psychoanalysts, who considers that borderline patients are not only good candidates for psychoanalytic treatment but that they are actually more prone to psychic change through psychoanalysis than are psycho-neurotics.[1]

What both authors seem to have in common rests on the importance of one small word used by Winnicott that could go unnoticed were it not for a slow reading. The word is "fluid." When discussing the possibility for regression, Winnicott distinguishes between regression to an environmental failure situation, with the resulting defensive organization that requires analysis, and regression to a "more normal early success situation," in which regression to dependence is happening and the personal organization "is not so obvious because it has remained fluid and less defensive" (p. 208). Contrary to what psychiatric clinical intuition would uphold, organization is not automatically an asset. It all depends on whether the psychic organization is reactive and directed at playing a defensive role or whether it is a flexible, fluid organization resulting from an equally fluid relationship between individual and environment. Saying this, we must again keep in mind what environment really means: as seen earlier, environment is not

[1] Michel de M'Uzan, personal communication.

simply the "surroundings" but something like an ecological niche, where, as is well known in ecological science, the organism inhabiting the niche has a major role in defining it. What is here in Winnicott's conception of a fluid organization is a structure born from the primeval relationship "bundle," from which the terms of the more differentiated relationship evolve in a supple and mutually enriching fashion rather than creating a rigid defensive structure. Obviously, it is always a question of dosage, and there are no pure forms, but the idea is essential in understanding Winnicott's approach to psychopathology and the chances of psychoanalytic healing offered by regression.

This paper on the depressive position is in my view one of the most compelling for the illustration it provides of Winnicott's mind at work in terms of both genuine understanding of someone else's thought (in this case, Melanie Klein's) and creative elaboration on that basis. Although Winnicott gives one of the richest accounts I can think of regarding Klein's discovery in this domain, he also displays an understanding that goes well beyond the usual description, fine-tuning the concept to the point where it is no longer a concept but a whole and decisive chapter of human development, a watershed between mental health and mental illness, between being a whole person or not. This paper should be mandatory reading for anyone interested in human development, but even more so for anyone wanting to practice psychoanalysis therapeutically.

It is not a mere detail that Winnicott considers that "the term 'depressive position' is a bad name for a normal process," even though he immediately adds that "no one has been able to find a better" (p. 189). But, in fact, he does propose a much better term: *the stage of concern*. Concern is indeed the truly central affective feature of the process described under "depressive position," and a normal feature, inasmuch as it is something that must be reached in the end through the complex dynamics involved in instinctual experience, part objects and loss, whereas guilt and depression attest to the failure in doing so. A frequent misconception about the depressive position is that attaining the capacity for guilt is one of its achievements. When used in terms of pathology, that is probably true. Winnicott, however, clearly takes a different stand when he remarks that "in the concept of the depressive position in normal development there is no implication that infants normally become depressed. Depression, however common, is an illness symptom and indicates a mood, and implies unconscious complexes that could become conscious," and it is only after he has asserted the pathological nature of depression and its unconscious components that Winnicott mentions that these unconscious processes "have to do with guilt feelings" (p. 290). We therefore find ourselves facing the same mode of reasoning as that regarding psychic organization: the question is whether the development of a depressive position leads to a sense of concern, which I would correlate with the "fluidity" mentioned earlier, or is arrested to a certain extent, leaving a more rigid, defensive, and guilt-ridden structure. Obviously, here again, the process will inevitably be fraught with imperfection and incompleteness, but Winnicott's take on this is to look at the true healthy achievement of the *stage of concern*. We are thus not left with the dubious choice between persecutory anxieties or guilt: concern is rather an open-ended attitude within a process of growth that leaves guilt and anxiety on the side of defensive, pathological organization. One thing is certain: just as the depressive position has nothing to do with depression proper, concern is in no way a form of guilt. It is rather the opening up of the child's genuine care and interest for the other and belongs to the series of qualities that make for our sheer humanity: availability, hospitality, benevolence.

As to why Winnicott did not formally propose to change the name, one can easily imagine that he did not want to engage in a battle over words. We are here brought back to his relationship with psychoanalytic language. We see him at once well aware that words matter—he does indeed question "depressive position" as a misnomer—but he also seems to remain confident that the liveliness of language can be ensured by other means, notably, in this case, by comments and the actual dissection of the concept so as to prevent it becoming yet another frozen slogan.

It is also significant that in the opening paragraphs of "The Depressive Position in Normal Emotional Development" [CW 4:3:5], Winnicott establishes its relationship with the Oedipal triangulation. Here is something clearly challenging the view that presents him as other than a Freudian, if not an anti-Freudian. But if more proof of Winnicott's Freudian stance is required, what better place than the fragment of his analytic practice in *Holding and Interpretation: Fragment of an Analysis* [CW 4:4:1]. More space than is allotted for an essay would be required to underline all the moments at which Winnicott can be seen working according to the classical Freudian tenets (as in his correspondence he insists he does),[2] but let us take but one or two examples, not necessarily the most poignant ones, chosen for their being ordinary excerpts that are actually related in spite of a two-month distance.

The first is taken from the session of Monday, February 28:

ANALYST I said that these real things had not altered the fact that there is very important fantasy in the offing, and anxiety connected with it. There is the fantasy of the girls of adolescent dreams who had a penis. Perhaps the reality situation had sorted itself out according to the fantasy, so that his wife had a penis and presented a problem on that account, whereas his girl friend was being used as the girl of daydreams, who is ordinarily female.

PATIENT Here there is a difficulty in reality. There is an area of play with the girl. I need play in the real situation. Here we have a professional relationship, and the only play is through dreams and the work we do with them.

ANALYST Yes, I see that. And you feel me as reluctant to play, as you have said before in other settings. The question is, where is the penis? As there is no man rival yet, there is no one to have the penis, and you expect the girl to

---

[2] See his letter to Hannah Ries of November 27, 1953 [CW 4:2:15].

have it. In the intercourse dream, in which mother was to some extent the woman, you nearly reached the idea of a man-father. (pp. 331–332)

The second is taken from the material of Thursday, May 5:

PATIENT The alarming thing about equality is that we are then both children, and the question is, where is father? We know where we are if one of us is the father.

ANALYST You are hovering here between the idea of your relation to mother alone and your relation to father and mother as a triangle. If father is perfect, then there is nothing you can do except be perfect too, and then you and father are identified with each other. There is no clash. If on the other hand you are two human beings who are fond of mother, then there is a clash. I think you would have discovered this in your own family if it had not been for the fact that you have two daughters. A boy would have brought out this point of the rivalry between him and his father in relation to mother.

PATIENT I feel that you are introducing a big problem. I never became human. I have missed it. (p. 382)

These short excerpts show Winnicott and his patient dealing with the problems of narcissism, of identification, idealization, ego-ideal, the phallic woman fantasy, Oedipal rivalry, the role of the father, and, ultimately, the problem of truly becoming human—that is, of attaining the *stage of concern*, the depressive position where one deals with whole persons. Freud, Klein, and possibly others are all present, but the mixture is uniquely Winnicottian. This is one more reason to look at Donald Woods Winnicott as a whole person indeed.

References

Bitbol, M. (2010). *De l'intérieur du monde. Pour une philosophie et une science des relations.* Paris: Flammarion.

Freud, S. (1921/1955). Group psychology and the analysis of the ego. In *The standard edition of the complete psychological works of Sigmund Freud* (vol. XVIII, pp. 65–143). London: Hogarth and the Institute of Psychoanalysis.

Scarfone, D. (2005). Laplanche and Winnicott meet . . . and survive! In L. Caldwell (Ed.), *Sex and sexuality. Winnicottian perspectives* (pp. 33–53). London: Karnac.

Winnicott, D. W. (1969). The use of an object and relating through identifications [1968]. [CW 8:2:28]

FIGURE 5.1 *Winnicott in his mid-fifties.*

The Donald Woods Winnicott Archive, in the care of the Wellcome Library, London, courtesy of the Winnicott Trust.

FIGURE 5.2 *Winnicott with Anna Freud and Princess Marie Bonaparte, possibly around the time of the eighteenth Congress of the International Psychoanalytical Association, London, 1953.*

The Donald Woods Winnicott Archive, in the care of the Wellcome Library, London, courtesy of the Winnicott Trust.

{6}

Reaching His Peak, 1955–1959

Jennifer Johns and Marcus Johns

Volume 5 comprises both unpublished and published work, papers, and letters available to the *Collected Works* editors for the years 1955 to 1959, a period of time when Donald Winnicott was fully engaged in many aspects of his career and communicating his ideas with great enthusiasm. In 1957, he published two books addressed to ordinary parents and those with an interest in child care, *The Child and the Family* and *The Child and the Outside World*, based on the BBC broadcasts that he had been giving since before World War II. These were later to be combined as *The Child, the Family and the Outside World*. In addition, his first book for a principally psychoanalytic readership, *Collected Papers: Through Paediatrics to Psychoanalysis*, was published during this period, without the foreword by Masud Khan that accompanied subsequent editions. Consisting of papers written for different audiences but almost all engaging with the development of the individual in both normality and in departures from it, the book also underlines Winnicott's own development from pediatrician to psychoanalyst.

In 1955, Donald Winnicott was fifty-nine. His double career, as both child psychiatrist and psychoanalyst, was flourishing: as can be seen from some of the pieces in Volume 5, he was still broadcasting on radio about child development and family dynamics and accepting invitations to write for or address the many organizations that requested his contribution (see notes accompanying individual papers). His papers show his enthusiasm to contribute, and his capacity to tailor both style and content to his audiences shows the keenness to communicate his ideas and, wherever he could, to illuminate his readers and listeners on the importance of understanding the nuances of child development and their relevance in the fields of interest of each audience that he addressed. His letters show equal passion for communication and an insistence that the ideas he had first begun seriously to develop in the 1945 paper "Primitive Emotional Development" [CW 2:7:8], on the importance of understanding the very earliest phase of ego-integration and which he took so much further in different directions, were vital to the full understanding of child development at all later phases and thus to the understanding of various forms of psychopathology. It is the description in that paper of a state of primary un-integration at the beginning of life out of which the infant psyche, given an appropriate environment, can begin to integrate and individuate, and the continuation of that process towards maturity that he later elaborated from many points of view.

By the time he reached the stage in his life that includes the writings in Volume 5, Winnicott had experienced conflict and change on many levels, professional as well as personal. He had seen service in the Great War in the Royal Navy and had worked as a pediatrician in the East End of London before the introduction of those public health measures that ensure the safety of children's lives today. The book he wrote to introduce general practitioners to the newly emerging specialty of pediatrics, *Clinical Notes on Disorders of Childhood*, gives painful examples of fatal and crippling illnesses such as tuberculous meningitis and rheumatic carditis. Not until after World War II would he see the introduction of antibiotics that saved many children from such fates and widespread immunization. The universal provision of orange juice, cod-liver oil, and school milk during that war prevented the malnutrition that had been another major cause of childhood disease, and, in 1955, at the time we are considering, universal immunization against polio was added to the protection from tetanus, whooping cough, diphtheria, and smallpox already in place. Soon after, the children's hospitals no longer needed wards for children with chronic chest conditions following whooping cough or for those whose lives were dependent on an iron lung. The practice of pediatrics as a physically based medical profession was revolutionized, but Winnicott, who had eschewed holding responsibility for hospitalized children in the 1920s in order to concentrate on outpatient work, also saw other changes in pediatric practice, and his ideas about the care of young babies and children, together with their mothers, were involved in these changes. In Great Britain, the importance of the presence of the feeding mother to the survival and subsequent health of hospitalized babies had been recognized by James Spence in Newcastle some years before his *British Medical Journal* paper in 1947, and the importance of reliable and ongoing relationships to the baby's physical and psychological survival had been shown by Spitz at the New York Hospital in 1945. Prior to the publication of these studies, but in the awareness of them, when the British government at the outbreak of World War II proposed an Evacuation Scheme to remove city children from their families to protect them against anticipated bombing raids, Winnicott, together with John Bowlby and Emanuel Miller, wrote to the *British Medical Journal* in 1939 about the dangers of separating young children from their mothers, citing not only the dangers of causing acute misery but the statistical fact of an increased risk of subsequent delinquency following childhood separations. Winnicott's own subsequent wartime work in Oxford, in a hostel for evacuated children whose behavior was unacceptable to any host, informed him further about the effects of separation and provoked his thinking about antisocial behavior and delinquency. His paper

"The Antisocial Tendency" [CW 5:2:8], written in 1956, is included in Volume 5. Distinguishing between the antisocial tendency and established delinquency, he pointed out the continued presence of hope in the children he was describing for the environment to respond with understanding rather than punishment and stated,

> When there is an antisocial tendency *there has been a true deprivation* (not a simple privation); that is to say, there has been a loss of something good that has been positive in the child's experience up to a certain date, and that has been withdrawn; the withdrawal has extended over a period of time longer than that over which the child can keep the memory of the experience alive.

John Bowlby's later cooperation with James and Joyce Robertson, who filmed the reaction of children separated from their mothers in institutions during the period we are examining, led to another postwar revolution in the care of children in the hospital and persuaded hospital staff to relax their attitudes towards parental visiting and even to allow "rooming in." There was a tide of change in childcare and, despite disagreements among those responsible for the change (see Winnicott's comments on Bowlby's work in Volume 5, "On Separation Anxiety" [CW 5:4:18] and "Discussion: Grief and Mourning in Infancy by John Bowlby" [CW 5:5:17]), Winnicott's understanding of child development and the public broadcasts he made were important elements in that change.

By 1955, World War II had been over for ten years. In Britain, the period of postwar austerity, with its clothing and food rationing, had finally ended in 1954. Hundreds of thousands of demobilized troops and returned prisoners of war, not all of whom had rehabilitation programs to attend or jobs to go back to, had had to be absorbed. Marriages broke down, families disintegrated, and there was a postwar crime wave. Additionally, perceived international danger had not disappeared. Although the Korean War had ended in 1953, the Cold War and the fear of nuclear attack and annihilation continued. Young men in Britain were called up for National Service at eighteen and served in the tripartite occupation of Germany, as well as fighting in Malaya, Africa, and elsewhere. In 1956, during the period we are discussing, the Hungarian uprising and the Suez emergency were reminders of constant international tension. The French finally left South Vietnam, and US forces began to train local forces.

With this background of international strife and alongside the battles to have the health and welfare of children recognized, the British psychoanalytic world, of which Winnicott was a part, was struggling with the after-effects of its own conflicts. These had developed in relation to problems with the governance of the British Psychoanalytical Society (BPAS) but were also to do with the response of the psychoanalytic world to the new theories of Melanie Klein about the early internal psychic life of the infant. Klein deeply influenced a number of British analysts, including Winnicott; there were, however, some who believed that her stance in treating children's play in child analysis as equivalent to free association in an adult, her concepts of the depressive position and part and whole internal objects, and her earlier dating of the Oedipus complex, as well as her insistence on interpreting the negative and her emphasis on innate factors rather than environmental ones as affecting psychic development, departed too far from Freud's thought. She criticized Anna Freud's work, which advocated gaining a child's trust before interpreting and, at the beginning of a child analysis, a more educative approach. When, during the 1930s, a number of German and Austrian analysts (including eventually the Freud family) arrived in Britain fleeing Nazi persecution and were welcomed into the BPAS, the newcomers found Klein's developments of theory and their consequences for psychoanalytic technique too much of a departure from the classical approach, and fears arose of a split. As Klein continued to spell out her ideas, factions formed, and a decision to hold a series of discussion meetings was made (for a description of these controversies, see Caldwell and Taylor Robinson, Chapter 1 in this edition).

By the period of time that the papers in Volume 5 were published, a kind of uneasy stability had settled over the BPAS with the formation of three groups: followers of Anna Freud, the Kleinians, and the Middle Group (later called the Independents). The fundamental disagreement rested on how to understand the development of human beings. Winnicott argued that the infant at the beginning could not be studied as an entity alone, as a single unit, but only as part of the unit that included the caretaking elements—in most circumstances, the mother, without whom the baby would perish. This basic position is sometimes referred to by the shorthand term "There's no such thing as a baby," and its elaboration when considering the ways in which the sensitively cared-for and appropriately held infant gradually discovers its world—inside and outside; me and not-me; fantasy and reality; recognition of mother and others; and the terrifying facts of dependency and need—and develops or not towards its own unit status are reiterated and elaborated by Winnicott from different points of view in his many papers.

Members of the Middle Group in the BPAS took up his ideas and developed them with the most interest and enthusiasm, as it would seem that members of the other two groups reacted to the bitterness of the Controversial Discussions by defending their group identities and the theories that had underlain the conflict and proved reluctant to explore other points of view or sometimes even to listen to them. It seemed that each side could even refuse to accept that the other's point of view had any validity, and even those who met and enjoyed each other's company socially might privately believe that the other was "not really a psychoanalyst." Winnicott seems to have been exasperated and even hurt by these entrenched attitudes and never joined any group.

In the wider world of medical practice, there were conflicts, too. The inauguration of the National Health Service (NHS) in July 1948 had revolutionized medical practice. Although the desirability of a centrally funded medical service had been advocated regularly by the British Medical Association as early as 1911, to the extent of putting forward a plan for such a service in 1939, the system that was eventually established disappointed many doctors as being top-heavy in terms of administration, too centralized, and too vulnerable to the vagaries of politicians, and some doctors even threatened not to join. Winnicott had written to *The Times* in 1946 about the risk of turning doctors from clinicians into civil servants [CW 3:1:5] and that "medical practice is now to be subservient not to science but to politics." Despite this, he worked as a pediatrician and child psychiatrist in the new NHS until 1963, contributing clinically and by teaching the many pediatricians, child psychiatrists, and psychoanalytic colleagues who attended his clinics at Paddington Green. During the period of time (1955–1959) when he was writing the papers included in Volume 5, he was a respected authority on the development and care of children, and he lectured regularly to students at the Institute of Education and at the London School of Economics.

It is worth noting that, in some ways, Winnicott's personal life was more settled and productive that it had ever been, despite his having suffered at least three heart attacks. His thoughts on this may have been reflected in his important paper delivered to the Society for Psycho-Somatic Research at University College London in 1957, the notes for which are included in Volume 5 [CW 5:3:29]. In the notes for this presentation, "Excitement in the Aetiology of Coronary Thrombosis," he looks at both the psychology and physiology of excitement and, using the example of an increasing sexual excitement that leads to climax, he postulates that when psychological factors inhibit that ordinary process, what is reached is a complex psychophysiological state that can lead to disaster.

From 1955 onwards, Winnicott shared his life with Clare, a fellow professional with an acute interest in his work and thinking, one who had her own thriving career. His professional and publishing output flourished during this marriage, as pointed out by Kanter (2004), and his interest in the world of social work—particularly the education of social workers, Clare's specialty—is evident in Volume 5. He had reached the recognition of the general public due to his BBC broadcasts, and he was at the height of his professional career, with Presidencies of the Paediatric Section of the Royal Society of Medicine and the Association of Child Psychology and Psychiatry under his belt. Having been Physician-in-Charge of the Child Department of the London Clinic of Psychoanalysis since 1945, in 1956, he was elected President of the BPAS, a role he repeated in 1965, and he was in great demand as a speaker, speaking and writing for national and international audiences.

In addition, during the period of time under consideration, Winnicott was intensely involved in psychoanalysis, and although he continued to insist that his ideas about the earliest relationship were vital for the understanding of both normal development and its variations towards psychopathology, he also commented on the work of colleagues regularly, both by reviewing publications and commenting on papers read to the BPAS. Many of the letters in Volume 5 refer to matters concerned with the Society, and his feelings about theoretical and group differences, as well as about personalities and the internal politics of the Society, are easily discernable. Often he seemed to be making an appeal that echoes his 1946 letter to *The Times* about the dangers to medical scientific progress from political influences [CW 3:1:5], sad that the defensiveness of the groups in the Society prevented adequate discussion in Scientific Meetings and sometimes even attendance.

The letters in Volume 5 vary in tone. The comments to colleagues can be encouraging or critical, and where he disagreed strongly with something or someone, Winnicott did not pull his punches, writing his thoughts clearly and even confrontationally. Included here are his comments on papers presented by colleagues, suggestions for future programs in the BPAS's Scientific Meetings, and, the most passionate, remarks on topics that moved him particularly, such as the letter to the *British Medical Journal* on leucotomy [CW 5:2:2]. It should be held in mind that the letters available for publication in this work were largely from the selection made by Robert Rodman after lengthy discussion with Clare Winnicott some years after Winnicott's death in 1971. These were published in 1987. Others published here are available in the Winnicott Archive at the Wellcome Collection in London, but a large amount of correspondence is unavailable, currently stored in the Cornell Archive at the New York Hospital.

It seems that towards the beginning of the period 1955 to 1959, Winnicott still hoped that some fruitful communication might be possible between members of the different groups in the BPAS and that he also held the particular hope that his own ideas might be accepted by Klein and her followers. In a note attached to "The Antisocial Tendency" [CW 5:2:8], Winnicott wrote,

> In a statement in my own language of Klein's depressive position, I have tried to make clear the intimate relationship that exists between Klein's concept and Bowlby's emphasis on deprivation. Bowlby's three stages of the clinical reaction of a child of two years who goes to hospital can be given a theoretical formulation in terms of the gradual loss of hope because of the death of the internal object or introjected version of the external object that is lost. What can be further discussed is the relative importance of death of the internal object through anger and contact of "good objects" with hate products within the psyche, and ego maturity or immaturity in so far as this affects the capacity to keep alive a memory.
>
> Bowlby needs Klein's intricate statement that is built round the understanding of melancholia, and that derives from Freud and Abraham, but it is also true that psychoanalysis needs Bowlby's emphasis on deprivation, if psychoanalysis is ever to come to terms with this special subject of the antisocial tendency.

The first two letters in Volume 5, to the Kleinian analyst Roger Money-Kyrle [CW 5:1:1 and CW 5:1:6], seem to indicate that Winnicott still believed that dialogue with the Kleinians might be possible, and, although the letter to Hanna Segal written in 1955 [CW 5:1:15] does anticipate the possibility that she might be persuaded to agree that the "third area" she has spoken about might be related to his own concept of a transitional area, the letter to Joan Riviere in 1956 [CW 5:2:3] seems resigned to the fact that Klein will not accept that he can contribute anything of interest to her.

In 1957, Klein published her monograph *Envy and Gratitude*, having presented her paper "A Study of Envy and Gratitude" to the BPAS a year earlier. Winnicott's comments on the paper and his later review of her book are included in Volume 5. He found himself at odds with her conviction that "envy is an oral-sadistic and anal-sadistic expression of destructive impulses, operative from the beginning of life, and that it has a constitutional basis." Although agreeing with the ubiquity and importance of envy in the analysis of adults and children, Winnicott could not reconcile Klein's statement with his own understanding that at the beginning of life ego-integration is yet to happen, and the capacity to recognize an object as being external enough to be envied has yet to develop. For him, the clinical situation of an individual as observed in the consulting room could not be traced back directly to infancy because in infancy the individual has not yet separated out from the environment of which the mother is also a part. Study of the baby as an individual element separate from the relationship is therefore impossible. Envy and the degree of envy found in both adults and children will, according to Winnicott, be a result of what happens during the processes of ego-integration, individuation, and maturation and will inevitably carry the legacy of the actual mother's capacities to recognize, adapt to, and respond to her infant during the period when her separateness was not apparent to the future individual infant. Envy was therefore understood by Winnicott as resulting from a complex situation in which a mother satisfies the infant enough to begin to support the process of ego-integration, but, unlike the good-enough mother whose care is enough to maintain that ongoing process, her support is insufficient and a sense of deprivation results—a tantalizing mother. In the comments he wrote after Klein's first presentation of the paper to the BPAS, he even goes so far as to suggest that Klein's own concept of the depressive position is undermined by her new thinking.

The papers in Volume 5 are written for different events and audiences, and Winnicott varied his writing style according to the degree of psychological sophistication likely to be found in those reading or hearing the paper. He spoke to the general public and lay audiences in terms that could be widely understood but without condescension, as he must have spoken to the mothers in his clinic in the expectation that each would understand the other. As can be seen from some of the Notes and Fragments included in the writings, he wrote also to record his thoughts, possibly for himself, as well as to record notes for lectures, seminars, or future papers.

Winnicott's observation that, left alone to develop in a normal healthy environment, a child would become able to relate to the reality of that environment led him to study the ways that a child discovers reality and, at the same time, himself or herself. The internal and external, fantasy and reality, the existence of "me" and "not-me" are recognized together and as being different and separate. In order for a relationship between these different and separate elements to develop and be useful, Winnicott postulated in several papers and notes the question of a link, a way of bridging them, often an object important to the baby to which he attached the word "transitional." This object belongs to both and neither of the inner or outer worlds but acts as a bridge or link that connects but keeps them apart. The idea of transitional phenomena occupied him for at least twenty years and is probably the best known of his contributions as well as the most publicly accepted—most parents as well as those authorities who advise them will now recognize the need for a teddy bear or "safety blanket" that stands for the mother in her absence or is a comfort in moments of anxiety.

Although he first wrote about this phenomenon in 1951 in his paper "On Transitional Objects and Transitional Phenomena" [CW 3:6:6], presented to the BPAS in May of that year, he published a similar version in the *International Journal of Psychoanalysis* in 1953 [CW 4:2:21] and in *Collected Works: Through Paediatrics to Psycho-Analysis* [CW 5:4:24]. It was republished with slight changes in 1971 in *Playing and Reality* [CW 9:3:5]. The changes include the deletion of the second paragraph of footnote number 12, which included in the original the idea that if maternal technique were added to the concept "breast," then it would be possible for a bridge to be made between the work of Melanie Klein on an infant's early states and that of Anna Freud. It would seem that, by the later publication, Winnicott had given up such a hope. There are further thoughts about transitional phenomena in Volume 5—such as the "Letter to the *British Medical Journal* on Children's Comforters" [CW 5:1:13], the essay "First Experiments in Independence" [CW 5:1:20], the BBC broadcast "What Do We Know About Babies as Cloth Suckers?" [CW 5:2:1], and a paper presented to the Association for Child Psychology and Psychiatry in 1959 entitled "The Fate of the Transitional Object" [CW 5:5:22]—and Winnicott's repeated emphasis on the importance of the mother–baby unit and its well-being for future health led to many requests for talks and articles from those concerned with childbirth. The movement for natural childbirth had begun in 1933 with the publication of Grantly Dick-Read's first book, *Natural Childbirth*, and, despite early opposition to those ideas from the established medical hierarchy, the movement gained ground when his second book, *Childbirth Without Fear: The Principles and Practice of Natural Childbirth*, appeared in 1942. By the time that the papers published in Volume 5 were being written, there was increasing interest from midwives and some obstetricians. In 1957, the National Childbirth Trust was formed to promote this new emphasis away from routine assisted delivery involving anesthesia and forceps to a calmer, more relaxed and natural approach. This fitted very well with Winnicott's thinking about the need for a new mother to be able—and to have the necessary time and space—to relate to her baby and become the "environment mother" whose sensitivity to her baby's needs allows him or her to mature without undue impingement. This volume contains several papers directly concerned with mothers themselves, some addressed to professional colleagues such as midwives, health visitors, and others concerned with the mother's well-being, but also the 1956 paper on "Primary Maternal Preoccupation" [CW 5:2:16], written for psychoanalysts in response to a discussion on infantile neurosis in *The Psychoanalytic Study of the Child.* Addressing the state of mind and body of a mother around the time of childbirth and shortly after, this study can be seen as an essential complement to Winnicott's work on the early state of the infant. Examining the psycho-physiological conditions of the mother, whose sensitive adaptation to her baby's needs for careful, attentive holding and physical care provides the environment from which the individual can eventually emerge, he paid particular attention to the specially absorbed state of the pregnant and nursing mother, recognizing her degree of preoccupation as one that, in other circumstances, could be described as an illness.

The question of his particular interest in mothers came under consideration in the 1957 paper "The Mother's Contribution to Society" [CW 5:3:30], a postscript to his first series of BBC talks, in which he reflected on the indebtedness of each human being, including himself, to his or her mother and on problems related to the human fear of dependence. This fear, he felt, is great enough to be frequently denied, and he linked the strength of this denial to the tendency of groups to come together to find apparent safety in passivity and subjugation. As in many of his writings, this includes both the close examination of the individual psychological state and his speculations on their wider social implications. This particular line of thinking calls in and synthesizes aspects of Winnicott's experience from general medicine, pediatrics, psychiatry, developmental psychology, psychoanalytic theory and practice, social work, and the study of human nature in general.

In addition to reflecting and advising on the attitudes and effects of the various groups of health and social welfare professionals to whom he spoke, Winnicott continued his lines of thought about development and individuation. His paper "The Capacity to Be Alone" [CW 5:3:20], given to the BPAS in 1957, addresses the process of maturation from the point of view of its later stages. He described the capacity to be alone as a sophisticated state, questioning whether it is possible for an immature infant to be alone, in the sense that the as-yet-unformed ego has not yet arrived at the awareness of unit status and thus cannot appreciate aloneness, Winnicott reached the paradox that the basis of the capacity to be alone is that of being alone in the presence of another. The presence of that other, usually mother, may be at the beginning recognized by the mother and any observer, but not yet by the infant, who is temporarily protected from the threat of terror that such an awareness of vulnerability and dependence imply. It is this protection from the impingement of terror that allows continuing ego-development and eventually the ego-strength to be able to be alone in actuality.

The variety of topics that engaged Winnicott during the five years covered by Volume 5 of the *Collected Works*, the breadth of his interests, and the enthusiasm with which he communicated his thinking give a picture of a man passionately involved in life at many levels, one thoroughly convinced of his position with regard to the vital importance of understanding the earliest development of the human individual from the earliest relationship, which is at the beginning not yet a relationship. He saw this understanding as having relevance in every facet of human life, from the intimate exploration that occurs in the psychoanalytic relationship, to an understanding of human development essential for those interested in child health, welfare, and education, as well as the wider social and political worlds in which he took such a lively interest.

References

Bowlby, E. J. M. (1960). Separation anxiety. *International Journal of Psychoanalysis, 41*, 89–113.

Bowlby, E. J. M. (1960). Grief and mourning in infancy. *Psychoanalytic Study of the Child, 15*, 3–39.

Bowlby, E. J. M., Miller, E., & Winnicott, D. W. W. (1939). Letter on evacuation. *British Medical Journal, 2*, 1202.

Dick-Read, G. (1933). *Natural childbirth*. London: Pinter & Martin.

Dick-Read, G. (1942). *Childbirth without fear: The principles and practice of natural childbirth*. London: Pinter & Martin.

Kanter, J. (2004). *Face to face with children: The life and work of Clare Winnicott*. London: Karnac.

Klein, M. (1957). *Envy and gratitude*. London: Tavistock.

Klein, M. (1975). *Envy and gratitude and other works*. London: Hogarth.

Klein, M. (1975). Notes on some schizoid mechanisms. In *Envy and gratitude and other works* (pp. 1–24). London: Hogarth.

Spence, J. C. (1947). Care of children in hospital. *British Medical Journal, 1*, 125–130.

Spitz, R. A. (1945). Hospitalism: An inquiry into the genesis of psychiatric conditions in early childhood. *Psychoanalytic Study of the Child, 1*, 53–74.

Winnicott, D. W. (1931). *Clinical notes on disorders of childhood*. London: Heinemann. [CW 1:3]

Winnicott, D. W. (1945). Primitive emotional development. [CW 2:7:8]

Winnicott, D. W. (1953). On transitional objects and transitional phenomena: A study of the first not-me possession. [CW 4:2:21]

Winnicott, D. W. (1955). Letter on children's comforters. [CW 5:1:13]

Winnicott, D. W. (1956). Letter on leucotomy. [CW 5:2:2]

Winnicott, D. W. (1957). *The child and the family*. London: Tavistock.

Winnicott, D. W. (1957). *The child and the outside world*. London: Tavistock.

Winnicott, D. W. (1957). First experiments in independence [1955]. [CW 5:1:20]

Winnicott, D. W. (1957). The mother's contribution to society. [CW 5:3:30]Winnicott, D. W. (1958). The antisocial tendency [1956]. [CW 5:2:8]

Winnicott, D. W. (1958). The capacity to be alone [1957]. [CW 5:3:20]Winnicott, D. W. (1958). *Collected papers: Through paediatrics to psychoanalysis*. London: Tavistock.Winnicott, D. W. (1958). Primary maternal preoccupation [1956]. [CW 5:2:16]

Winnicott, D. W. (1964). *The child, the family and the outside world*. London: Penguin.

Winnicott, D. W. (1971). *Playing and reality*. London: Tavistock.

Winnicott, D. W. (1987). Letter to *The Times* [not published], 6 November 1946. [CW 3:1:5]
Winnicott, D. W. (1989). Discussion: Bowlby, J., "Grief and mourning in infancy" [1959]. [CW 5:5:17]
Winnicott, D. W. (1989). Excitement in the aetiology of coronary thrombosis [1957]. [CW 5:3:29]
Winnicott, D. W. (1989). The fate of the transitional object [1959]. [CW 5:5:22]
Winnicott, D. W. (1993). What do we know about babies as cloth suckers? [1956] [CW 5:2:1]
Winnicott, D. W. (2017). On "*Separation anxiety*" by J. Bowlby [1958]. [CW 5:4:18]

FIGURE 6.1 *The nineteenth Congress of the International Psychoanalytical Association, held in Geneva in 1955, where Winnicott presented "Clinical Varieties of Transference" [CW 5:1:11]. Winnicott is standing on the far right, second from the front, facing to the right.*

The Donald Woods Winnicott Archive, in the care of the Wellcome Library, London, courtesy of the Winnicott Trust.

{7}

Health

DEPENDENCE TOWARDS INDEPENDENCE, 1960–1963

Angela Joyce

Volume 6 of the *Collected Works* encompasses the last years of Donald Woods Winnicott's work within the sphere of public health. He retired from his post at Paddington Green Children's Hospital in 1961, when he was sixty-five years old. Despite this retirement, he remained very active on both the national and international stages in the field of psychoanalysis and as an analyst disseminating a set of attitudes to clinical work and to ordinary living to the helping professions and the general population. This essay aims to give the reader a general overview of what Winnicott was writing about during that time, together with a closer appraisal of key ideas that came to fruition and that led on to the final papers of the late 1960s.

The Parent–Infant Relationship

This period begins with his major contribution to the International Psychoanalytical Association (IPA) Congress in Edinburgh, "The Theory of the Parent–Infant Relationship" [CW 6:1:21], which was pre-published in the *International Journal of the Psychoanalytic Association* (*IJPA*) in 1960. The setting of that Congress is important because it reflected Winnicott's growing reputation as a psychoanalyst who was steeped in the tradition of Sigmund Freud but who also fundamentally recast critical aspects of psychoanalytic theory and practice. The ideas propounded here mark a juncture in the development of his theoretical matrix, which was to lead, over the last decade of his life, to revolutionary propositions about the nature of mental life, its development, and the implications for clinical practice.

At the IPA Congress, the panel discussion was shared by the American analyst Phyllis Greenacre (Greenacre, 1960, 1962), with whom Winnicott had been in some contact since the 1950s (Thompson, 2012). Like Winnicott, Greenacre was a children's doctor, a pediatrician who was also a psychoanalyst, a rare breed in the psychoanalytic community to this day. The panel was chaired by John Bowlby, a fellow member of the British Psychoanalytical Society, whose book *Child Care and Growth of Love* had been published in 1953 and had become an instant classic. Later, he was to achieve acclaim as the founder of what came to be termed "attachment theory." Major figures in the psychoanalytic movement at the time (Anna Freud, Masud Khan, Serge Lebovici, Daniel Lagache, Angel Garma) contributed to the discussion, and their presentations were later published in the *IJPA* in 1962.

Winnicott states at the beginning that the paper is about infancy, not about psychoanalysis. His purpose is to address what he sees as a "confusion about the relative importance of the personal and environmental influences in the development of the individual" (p. 139). This could be said to be the crux of his concerns: in infancy—that is, before language—how are the different contributions of what the baby brings and what he or she meets in the environment to be evaluated, and what are the implications of the answers for psychoanalytic practice? His view is that, in the classical theory of Sigmund Freud and in Melanie Klein's contribution, both take for granted the "double dependency" of the baby on his or her mother's care. This despite his acknowledgment that his own aphorism ("There's no such thing as a baby without taking account of maternal care") probably has its roots in Freud's paper "Formulations on the Two Principles of Mental Functioning" (Freud, 1911, p. 220) and that Klein had opened up the whole area of pre-Oedipal development in a revolutionary way (Klein, 1945). Both assumed, in his view erroneously, that the earliest situation of the newborn infant was good enough. One reading of his paper may see it as part of the ongoing dialogue with Klein in Winnicott's writing; its publication coincided with her death in September 1960. This essay will consider illustrations of this as it manifested itself during this period of Winnicott's career.

Despite its challenge to both the old and the (relatively) new in the ongoing elaboration of the psychoanalytic tradition, Winnicott immediately shows how troubling his ideas are, maybe even for himself. Before he starts on his discussion of the task in hand, he has to tell his audience that he is not going to take away individual responsibility for a person's predicament: "the patient is not helped if the analyst says: 'Your mother was not good enough' . . . 'your father seduced you' . . . 'your aunt dropped you' " (p. 139). Stating that "in infancy good and bad things happen," he begins the exposition of his theory of the central significance of maternal holding in the beginning life of the person. However, to put these things together is neither simple nor obvious, and, indeed, his use of concepts such as omnipotence and projection can sometimes be confusing because they refer to his own theoretical propositions, and Winnicott's meaning of these concepts did not always coincide with the meanings of other analysts. When he writes that, in the necessity for healthy development, everything should seem to the infant to be a projection, he is implicitly referring to "the illusion of omnipotence," for him the foundation of that healthy development. This occurs or fails to occur depending on whether the mother is able to adapt to her baby in ways that sustain this experience at the beginning of life. From the baby's point of view, this is the source of good and bad things happening. When she fails to adapt adequately—is not good enough—the baby has to take account of external reality prematurely and thus is not in the state of illusion that Winnicott insists is so crucial for the processes of primitive emotional development to be established. The use here of the concept *projection* does not imply the recognition by the infant of the mother as a separate object. Rather, it refers to the baby, out of its primary creativity, creating the world and thus its mother in this illusion of omnipotence. She will later be "found" as this capacity to recognize external reality develops over time and in good-enough circumstances. Although Winnicott does not reference Ferenczi, the links with his ideas are striking (Caldwell & Joyce, 2011; Tonnesmann, 2002). Ferenczi's interest in what he terms the stage of "hallucinatory magic omnipotence" and his emphasis on the mother's adaptations to the infant's needs to maintain that omnipotence (Ferenczi, 1913) are echoed here. It is within this tradition of psychoanalytic theories that Winnicott's account of development as arising out of a two-body relationship (later to take account of a third [father] and more) needs to be set.

The paper is an exposition of his fundamental concept of the mother's holding the baby in the stage of dependency, which enables the infant's nascent ego to begin to develop. It is that essential aspect of the environmental set-up that initially is entangled with the infant such that it is impossible to conceive of the infant without taking account of maternal care (see Scarfone's essay, Chapter 5 in this edition, for an elaboration of Winnicott's understanding of the environment). It is this that Winnicott points out that Freud recognizes but does not further investigate in his theory of primary process (hallucinatory wish-fulfillment): from the infant's point of view, the milk appears out of the need to feed; but, in reality, this assumes "the care it receives from its mother" (Freud, 1911).

Winnicott proposes that the mother's holding function facilitates the establishment of unit status (in which soma and psyche are augmented by the mind in the unity of the self; see Winnicott [CW 3:4:20]) over the course of the infant's early life. In her holding function, the mother not only attends physically to her baby's needs but in her mind imaginatively elaborates her baby's experiences. This requires her to be in the state of mind that Winnicott had written about in 1956, that of primary maternal preoccupation (see [CW 5:2:16]), a state that supports and enables the mothering person to adapt to the specificity of her baby. The idea is later extended in his writings about the mirror role of the mother [CW 8:1:38] within whose encounter with her baby the infant comes to feel known and recognized.

Winnicott references a paper written by his second wife, Clare, who had used the concept of *holding* in her 1954 paper "Casework Techniques in the Child Care Services" (Winnicott, C., 1954). Joel Kantor, who has written about her work and her influence on Donald (Kanter, 2004), claims that the concept came from her. A social worker and subsequently a psychoanalyst, Clare Winnicott explicitly focuses on what the worker/parent does with what is held; that is, the mental and psychical processes (internal work) that go into acceptance of the other person. Donald's version of that was the mother's (and the analyst's) "imaginative elaboration" of her baby.

The developmental trajectory that Winnicott sets out in this paper is of interest because he includes mention of the father, whom he is often seen as disregarding. This is probably because he is primarily interested in establishing and investigating the earliest processes of mother–infant unity (and "infant development in the holding phase") as a focus for psychoanalytic study. Here, they expand into "mother and infant living together" following which "father, mother and infant, all three living together" (p. 144). Father is not known to the baby, except perhaps as an auxiliary mother, until the establishment of separateness between mother and baby, when father as a different function can be known. It is important to realize that Winnicott is referring to maternal and paternal *functions*, for example the mother's "holding function." In a much later paper, "The Use of an Object in the Context of *Moses and Monotheism*" [CW 9:1:4], Winnicott writes about how the father, at the point of separateness, can be known as a whole object to the infant: "the baby is likely to make use of the father as a blue-print for his or her own integration when just becoming at times a unit." However, it is unclear there and in this paper whether he sees the father as instrumental in the establishment of separateness, or whether the father can only be known because of separateness between infant and mother. What is clear is that the father is given a structuring role for the baby and that this is also connected to the place of the father in the mother's mind: not only the baby's father but also her own father. In "The Use of an Object" [CW 8:2:28], where Winnicott struggles to convey his theory of how separateness is established between infant and mother, the father or paternal function is not mentioned. In psychoanalytic theory, the account of the separating function of the father derives from Lacan's development of Freud's mythical, symbolic father enunciated in *Totem and Taboo.* Lacan introduced the concept of *Le nom du Père* in *The Four Fundamental Concepts of Psychoanalysis* (1978); that is, the father who is the object of the mother's desire and as such comes between mother and baby. Winnicott was acquainted with Lacan's ideas (indeed, he had been part of the IPA visiting committee to Paris in 1953, which ultimately resulted in Lacan leaving the IPA in 1963). In Winnicott's paper "The Mirror-Role of Mother and Family in Development" [CW 8:1:38], he refers to Lacan's famous paper only to distinguish his own from Lacan's position. The place of the father in this developmental trajectory seems both necessary but also curiously passive: he has to be there in reality, but it is very unclear what he has to do. This is in great contrast to the rich account of the mother's place: she certainly is not passive but very actively adapting to, imagining, and presenting the world in small doses as she disillusions her baby in response to his or her maturational progress.

In parallel, this move from mother–infant unity to father, mother, and infant living together is Winnicott's account of a similar move from "absolute dependency," through "relative dependence," "towards independence." Despite his notion that the core of what he calls the central self is isolated in health (later to be elaborated in the paper "Communicating and Not Communicating Leading to a Study of Certain Opposites" [CW 6:4:8]; see later discussion), he insists that none of us is truly independent; in health, we reach "towards independence." Paradoxically, if the isolation at the core of the self suffers impingements, then the person (originally the infant) is exposed to the most extreme anxiety—annihilation, the very opposite of being. The holding function of the mother is to protect the infant from this, holding over time and space so that the infant's incipient ego can become established. It is in the psychopathology of these states presented in analysis (borderline psychotic patients) that Winnicott claims we can "reconstruct the dynamics of infancy and infantile dependency, and the maternal care that meets this dependence" (p. 154).

Despite his insistence at the beginning that he is writing about infancy and not psychoanalysis, he refers to the clinical consequences for patients who come to analysis with the kind of histories that result in serious psychopathology; that is, with histories that have been marked by "bad things happening." He argues for a different approach to clinical work with these kinds of patients, those he regards as "badly chosen" for classical psychoanalysis (schizophrenics and psychotics). In these circumstances, he maintains that interpretation (of the transference) becomes less important than a quality in the analyst: specifically, his or her reliability. He makes a forthright appeal for the recognition that, in some cases, the patient in analysis may for the first time be experiencing what has been taken for granted hitherto in psychoanalytic thinking: a relationship marked by the reliability of the environment now represented in the person of the analyst. This echoes the thesis advanced in his paper on regression ("Withdrawal and Regression" [CW 4:3:29]) in which he prioritizes the consistency and reliability of the analyst in working with patients who are regressed to dependency, when the earliest stages of life are reproduced in the transference. For Winnicott, neither Sigmund Freud nor Melanie Klein takes sufficient account of the early unity of the mother–baby set-up, and he believes that it alters their approach to psychoanalytic clinical work in the area of dependency.

In the discussion at the IPA Congress, Anna Freud particularly takes issue with Winnicott's assertion that psychoanalysis has neglected pre-Oedipal stages of development, citing her father's paper "Inhibitions, Symptoms and Anxiety" (Freud, S., 1926) as evidence. She disagrees that these patients need different techniques, stating instead that they cannot be treated by psychoanalysis: "where the phase of dependence has never been overcome and independence has not first been reached and then lost again, it becomes impossible to cure in analysis the state of dependency" (Freud, A., 1962). It is not that she believed that issues of dependency did not appear in psychoanalysis or that they could not be addressed (interpreted) but that, when they did, they were mediated through later development and relied on ego functioning at the level of the Oedipus complex for the cooperation of the patient in a treatment alliance. For Winnicott, the patient would then be functioning at the level of a whole person, and it was precisely those factors in the patient's early life that had prevented such development that required something different from classical technique.

"The Theory of the Parent–Infant Relationship" was addressed to a professional audience, but Winnicott made his name not just in the professional world of psychoanalysis and the health service. He was renowned uniquely at that time in Britain as a broadcaster who disseminated his ideas about children and their parents, especially mothers. In Volume 6, five BBC talks are included that also contain transcriptions of conversations between mothers, about which Winnicott then comments. His commentary certainly gives the lie to any view that he is a sentimentalist when it comes to motherhood. There is no idealizing, and motherhood is robustly recognized as being at times boring and irksome: "the care of small children can be irksome no matter how much they are loved and wanted" ("What Irks?" [CW 6:1:7]). These talks are of their time and predate the era of mothers in large numbers going to work outside the home from the 1970s onwards; nevertheless, what Winnicott chooses to explore about "what irks" is far from the usual content of parents' conscious complaints. He goes deeply and simply into the fact that, to be available to her children, a mother has to be a "free house" (p. 77) for a time; that nothing of her is sacred as her privacy is invaded (originally in her pregnancy when the baby is literally inside her body); and that she cannot defend herself successfully from this without at the same time depriving her child of some essential element—the feeling that she is accessible. It is only a limited but absolutely necessary time. And who would be a mother: "who indeed but the actual mother of children" (p. 77)? The task for the mother then becomes how she recovers her own individual status once her secrets have been plundered by her baby. Winnicott claims that the mothers who come off best are those who can surrender at the beginning: having lost everything in these terms, they later recover themselves quickly. Although his focus is on mothers, Winnicott repeatedly brings fathers in, sometimes giving an impression of them as an afterthought. But here, he emphasizes that fathers' right to say "No!" to their children can only be effective when rooted in "having been around in a friendly sort of way" (p. 84), suggesting that their function again relies on the realities of ordinary living.

The Consequences of Failures in Holding

Many of the papers written in this period (1960–1963) reflect Winnicott's ongoing amplification of the earliest relationship described in "The Theory of the Parent–Infant Relationship." Because he was increasingly not encountering the real baby and mother in his practice following his retirement from the health service but in his analytic treatment of adults, the consequences for failure at the early stages of development were of continuing interest to him. The emerging developmental process remains contingent on the quality of parental care that is provided for the young child. A paper from the end of this period, "From Dependence Towards Independence" [CW 6:4:11], charts his own journey from the psychoanalysis of the 1930s, dominated by instinct theory, to the recognition that human maturational processes develop within the context of their utter dependence on environmental provision. This puts the ego at the center of the developmental stage and, whereas ego psychology emerged in the United States and dominated psychoanalysis there for decades, Winnicott's version is different. While recognizing the processes of identification as significant in its emergence, Winnicott was far more interested in the "highly complex" adaptations made by the person mothering the baby, the "ego relatedness" that lends the infant the mother's strong ego and includes her graduated "failure," steadily presenting the world in small doses as the preconditions for the emergence of the baby's own strong ego. The corollary of this graduated process is the baby's gradual realization of dependency as the "me" and the "not-me" world become differentiated and the baby begins to notice and feel that the real, external mother is necessary in the maturational moves towards independence. This is never complete but, in health, leads to a satisfying personal existence in society. Identifications occur with parents, but Winnicott also asserts the individual's "defiantly establishing a personal identity" (p. 481).

"Ego Distortion in Terms of True and False Self" [CW 6:1:22] was written in the same year as "The Theory of the Parent–Infant Relationship," and it again refers to Greenacre, with whom Winnicott had shared the platform at the Edinburgh IPA Congress. The paper contains a set of those concepts closely associated with his name, and it contends that his treatment of borderline adult patients taught him more about early developmental processes than direct observation of infancy. This reflects an interesting tension in his writings between the celebration of what he learned from his work with thousands of mothers and babies and his pioneering psychoanalytic work with what he called "research" patients, where the "clinical infant" reconstructed is the focus. In these cases, he came into direct contact with what he regarded as the consequences of the failures of a good-enough early environment, where the infant had to endure breaks in the continuity of true self living, resulting in impingements to which he or she had to adapt. The individual is essentially compromised and lives falsely, seduced into compliance as a solution. This is the etiology of the false self, in pathology indicating a severe split, a schism in the personality whose function is to protect the true self. At its most severe, it indicates psychotic fragmentation held together by a carapace. Perhaps paradoxically, then, in this protective environment, the true self shrivels and cannot flourish. The effects associated with this attenuation are futility and despair, and suicide can be a reassertion of the true self (1959–1964). To live falsely means to live through imitation, whereas in the good-enough early environment the aliveness of the true self flourishes. Winnicott proposes a continuum that accommodates a certain falsity in health, more of a public persona, where the ability to compromise becomes an achievement, the healthy expression of an aspect of the false self that allows for social living together. He draws clinical links with these ideas and cautions against the risk of an unending analysis of the false self where this defense is never breached and the original failure situation is not relived in the transference to the psychoanalyst.

His views on healthy maturity complement these arguments as he stresses that it is necessary for individuals not to mature early, that health is "maturity at age" ("The Family and Emotional Maturity" [CW 6:1:17]). This slow process of the human being's development is not simply a theory of socialization but one that allows for iconoclastic processes of "destruction" and rebirth such that each individual can, and must, create his or her world before it is found to exist independently; this is the flourishing of the true self, the earliest expression of primary creativity.

In Health

A significant paper given first on his October 1962 lecture tour in the United States and later to the British Psychoanalytical Society (BPAS), "Communicating and Not Communicating Leading to a Study of Certain Opposites" [CW 6:4:8], evinces a familiarly idiosyncratic but necessarily complex view of a particular aspect of living healthily. In a very personal introduction, he claims the "right not to communicate" and proceeds to argue for the absolute necessity for the true self to remain unfound; that the core of the self is a true isolate. The corollary of this is that the object, to be of any use to the subject, has to be subjectively created out of need but must be found in order that the creation be realized. This is a paradox not to be solved. The problem then becomes how to live a fulfilled but internally isolated, real life without becoming insulated. Not mentioned here, but alluded to and later developed in the paper on the "Mirror-Role" [CW 8:1:38], the embryonic true self nonetheless has to be seen and recognized by the mother in order to thrive. This paradox of the isolated nascent self needing this recognition of the other (unrecognized nevertheless as other) to instate the process of the ego communicating with the emerging self and with subjectively created phenomena also cannot be solved. These processes are linked with the ideas explored in "The Capacity to Be Alone" [CW 5:3:20], where the young child, necessarily in the presence of the (m)other, can happily be in a state of noncommunication, a state very different from the distress connected with the failure to communicate. There is a profound communication that allows for isolation, but failure to communicate leads to insulation.

"In health" becomes an increasingly important concept. The person's world in health is not bland but rich and full, elaborating the diverse possibilities of what the psyche and mind can make of internal and external foundations. Ideas that he had first promulgated in the early paper "Primitive Emotional Development" [CW 2:7:8] reemerge in "Ego Integration in Child Development" [CW 6:3:19], now confirming Winnicott as that kind of analyst who can hold the unending complexity of inner and outer reality together without privileging or sacrificing one or the other. To be human is to live simultaneously in both. In good-enough healthy development, one cannot be sacrificed for the other. The true self in health contributes to holding this separation of inner from external reality. He claims his particular view of Freudian developmental theory by placing ego development at center stage. The id (the drives which, in Freudian theory, are the engine of development) only has personal meaning through the integrating processes of ego development. In privileging ego integration in this way, Winnicott subordinates the id to the ego; otherwise, instinctual life risks being not more than a "clap of thunder." The id would be truly external to the self, unable to contribute strength, and risk being an undermining, destabilizing presence. He states again most clearly that there is "no value whatever in describing babies in the earliest stages except in relation to the mother's functioning" (p. 394). Her good-enough functioning enables the baby not to fall over the brink into unthinkable anxiety.

A question about integration is posed and, here, Winnicott challenges Klein's account of the earliest neonatal functioning that places at the center anxiety derived from the death instinct. The mother in Klein's account is imbued with the projected elements of the baby's destructiveness, and the baby's inner world is built up out of the oscillation of projective and introjective processes. Bion's development of Klein privileges the mother's reverie in responding to these projective identifications, which are detoxified; the baby is thus enabled to bear them and a mental structure is created for this purpose. (Bion doesn't reference Winnicott in his theory of the container–contained but, in a letter responding to J. Wisdom's appreciation of Bion's contribution [October 26, 1964; CW 7:1:11], Winnicott complains that his own observations and ideas about the mother's active contribution to the baby's states are not recognized.) In Winnicott's view, the baby's bodily states are the stuff out of which the psyche elaborates, imaginatively, the most primitive representations of existence. These processes, in time and space, held by the mothering person, in health, are truly personal to the infant. The infant's continuity of being is confirmed in these ways, establishing his or her personal way. "I Am" emerges and, with it, the possibility of disintegration, defined as the production of chaos as a defense against and expression of absence of maternal support. In health, states of "un-integration" remain a resource, and a return to this most primitive of conditions, utterly dependent on the dependability of the environment, is possible as a haven from the "not-me world." This back-and-forth process permits a dynamic relationship of progression and regression, the possibility of return to earlier states without which the ongoing developmental pull can be too anxiety-provoking for the child. To be able to return to states of unintegration first described in "Primitive Emotional Development" [CW 2:7:8] even momentarily ultimately facilitates and supports the child's living in a real way in the world of "not-me" objects.

Winnicott was a theoretician of health, and his concerns could be said to be an extended contemplation around living, being, and feeling real, but he is renowned for his attention to the subtleties of those factors that interfere with the inherent tendency towards development and health. Although being careful not to blame parents for their shortcomings ("The Effect of Psychosis on Family Life" [CW 6:1:6])—he says that the child's illness is often caused by the parents but that "the damage was done neither wilfully nor wantonly: it just happened" (p. 66)—he nevertheless dispassionately attends to what, from the baby's perspective, might prevent the capacity to live life to the full. There are pathologies potentially present in the mother's primary maternal preoccupation, or she may never allow herself to enter what he regards as "a normal illness" ("The Relationship of a Mother to Her Baby at the Beginning" [CW 6:1:8]). In describing it thus, he was capturing the particular internal focus that a woman in her late pregnancy develops in health and continuing into the first weeks/months postnatally, for which, if not for the fact of the pregnancy, she would be regarded as ill. If she cannot enter this state, the baby risks being immersed in catastrophic anxiety: "the sense of going to pieces, the sense of falling forever, the feeling that external reality cannot be used for re-assurance, and other anxieties that are usually described as 'psychotic.'" To defend against this, the baby has to manage his premature adaptation to the external reality; one possible outcome, as we saw earlier, is the carapace of the false self, instated to protect the true self from insult.

The BBC talk on "Jealousy" [CW 6:1:4] affords Winnicott the opportunity once again to emphasize his ideas about what is healthy in development and that health is maturity at age. To be capable of jealousy is a developmental achievement, the product of the baby's dawning understanding that the mother he possesses (within a reliable environment) now has others who claim rights over her. The feeling indicates the child's capacity to be in a state of acute conflict between loving and hating, something that cannot be taken for granted at the beginning of life and only becomes possible when there is sufficient ego integration. It means that the child is aware that his love is complicated by ideas of destruction and, potentially, in health ushers in feelings of sadness and concern. The outcome of this is firmly located contingently with the way the relational environments (parents) respond to the child's experience. When jealousy becomes abnormal, Winnicott says it has gone underground and distorts the personality of the child. The child has had no real chance to be angry and aggressive in his jealousy so that he goes inside; this leads to a persistent quest for something external to make sense of a lost inner feeling. A constant theme is that health emerges provided there have been good-enough conditions at the beginning, highly predictable and adapted to the child's individual needs: the basis of morality ("The Development of the Child's Sense of Right and Wrong" [CW 6:3:4]), then, is in being the "true self." In the right environmental circumstances, where "moral codes are left lying around" ("Morals and Education" [CW 6:3:18]) in the context of loving parents (mothers and fathers), the ordinary good-enough sense of right and wrong is facilitated for the child. Thus, parents are not given the task of teaching their children to have guilt and be moral, but these are seen as predictable outcomes of a good-enough environment.

Indeed, in his view, to comply is what constitutes immorality from the point of view of the infant ("Morals and Education").

Alongside Winnicott's abiding attention to health and living fully, he returns repeatedly to the varieties of experience babies and young children have in their early years, taking an emphatically developmental view in his understanding of the etiology of mental health and illness ("Psychiatric Disorder in Terms of Infantile Maturational Processes" [CW 6:4:12]; "Psycho-neurosis in Childhood" [CW 6:2:17]; "The Mentally Ill in Your Caseload" [CW 6:4:5]; "The Psychotherapy of Character Disorders" [CW 6:4:9]). He charts the developmental stages (as opposed to ages) whose difficulties might give rise to particular psychopathology: earliest life when the processes of integration, personalization, and realization are establishing leads to psychosis; the weaning stage, when loss has to be countenanced, leads to depression or the antisocial tendency; toddlerhood and beyond, living at the level of a whole person, leads to neurosis. There is the impression that he is all the time talking to not only a psychoanalytic audience for whom these ideas would be familiar, but to the medical and psychiatric establishment whose understanding of psychopathology could veer into a simplistic, biologically based phenomenology. Although he is acute in his attention to what he sees as the "environmental" (early relational) causes of psychosis and the suffering involved for the individual as well as the family, he has a decidedly individual view as to the value of these varieties of human experience. "We are poor indeed if we are only sane" ("The Effect of Psychosis on Family Life" [CW 6:1:6]) sums up his unorthodox observation. This attitude is echoed in many of his writings, and, in the paper on "Classification" [CW 5:5:5], he observes that "the artist has an ability and the courage to be in touch with primitive processes which the psychoneurotic cannot bear to reach, and which healthy people may miss to their own impoverishment."

In "Psycho-neurosis in Childhood" [CW 6:2:17], Winnicott unusually attends to the ground more typically investigated by classical psychoanalysis: psychoneuroses, the psychopathologies of whole persons who relate to whole objects. These individuals have not experienced the impingements that he so eloquently describes. Here, the most severe intrapsychic conflicts relate to instinctual life that is felt to be part of the self, although neurotic defenses may well be used to disown the drives. In adolescence, these conditions—phobias, obsessions, inhibitions—might be chosen rather than the young person finding what Winnicott calls the "false solution." His addressing of these neurotic conditions lacks the sense of exploration evident in his writings about more primitive psychopathology, such as psychosis or the antisocial tendency. He seems almost bored by this territory, perhaps reflecting the poverty he links to sanity, despite his acknowledgment of the child's aliveness and suffering of conflicts. He focuses on neurosis and the conditions for neurotic illness, but it is as if he has to pull himself away from, tell himself that he is not attending to those other states that might mess up the clarity of nosological distinctions. Towards the end of the paper, he makes a claim that gives substance to his earlier unorthodoxy: "that *clinically* the really healthy individual is nearer to depression and to madness than to psychoneurosis. Psychoneurosis is boring. It is a relief when an individual is able to be mad . . . to flirt with the psychoses" (p. 263). It is as if he were saying that the nearer one gets to "normality," the further away one is from creativity, from aliveness. Psychosis could be said to be the psychopathology of creativity and psychoneurosis evidence of the "safety-first principle."

Implicit and explicit attitudes to conformity, compliance, sanity, falsity, living well, and health saturate Winnicott's writings. But these are also rooted in his appreciation of the potential richness or otherwise of inner reality. In his discussion of Joseph Sandler's paper to the BPAS on the "Superego" [CW 6:1:19], he takes Sandler to task about being too focused on conscious life, not paying sufficient attention to fantasy and psychic reality. Here, he also draws attention to his distinction between the mind and the psyche first promulgated in his early paper "Mind and Its Relation to Psyche-Soma" [CW 3:4:20]. The psyche is the location of the imagination and the emergent representations of somatic processes. The mind comes into being to deal with the exigencies of external reality, and it is here that the false self might be seduced into conformity with that reality. Winnicott makes an appeal for a more play-full approach to the *conceptual* field of psychoanalysis, to be distinguished from a thing in itself. Concepts can be played around with, even mucked about with, dreamed of, and played with. He charges Sandler with stripping Freud of the richness of his conceptualization of unconscious life that has its roots in nonverbalized inner reality and the core of the dream world. However, even here, Winnicott brings in the interpersonal and the fact of dependency, and the "gradual journey from dependence towards independence." The subjective quality of the child's experience of the parental figures, whether present or absent—within this reality of dependency needs met or not—colors the processes of structuralization of the superego, and, in Winnicott's view, leads back to pregenital instinctual life and also to the territory that was uniquely mapped by Melanie Klein. He asserts that it is only when emotional development in the earliest stages of the individual's life has been satisfactory that the Freudian superego can be observed, after the passing of the Oedipus complex. He claims that "a very large number of children" do not have this experience and that their superego "never becomes humanised" (pp. 129–130). He also avers that he has been a "leading figure in the movement towards a recognition of *need satisfaction* as earlier and more fundamental than wish fulfilment" (p. 130). In this forthright discussion given at a scientific meeting at the BPAS, he protests at the way classical psychoanalytic theory is presented—in his view, as an oversimplification of complex processes and not true to Freud. Additionally, the mental mechanisms that Sandler asserts are part and parcel of the structuralization of the superego (introjection, identification, imitation) are seen by Winnicott as far too presumptuous of the earlier features of the dependent relationship of the baby on the mother. He castigates Sandler for seeming to promote obedience and identification in development, for him the stuff of compliance. He incorporates defiance, which, he stresses, enables the child to assert his individuality and to feel real.

Winnicott's counterintuitive appraisal of "The Value of Depression" [CW 6:4:10] reflects his appreciation of the complexity of the mental states of which humanity is capable and also the paradox that, although the person suffers, the capacity to be depressed is valuable. To be able to be depressed implies some measure of health and development and also the risks attendant upon the loss of what has previously been taken for granted. The matter of depression was also significant in Winnicott's ongoing dialogue with Klein. He appreciated her concept of the depressive position (Klein, 1935), first developed while he was still a member of her close circle, as equal in importance in the psychoanalytic canon as Freud's Oedipus complex ("A Personal View of the Kleinian Contribution" [CW 6:3:8]). His great appreciation did not prevent him, however, from taking issue with her in many ways, as here, in her use of the term *depressive* to describe what he saw as a development in health (i.e., the capacity for concern). Indeed, one of his major contributions was a rewriting of Klein's concept of the depressive position in his own terms as the "stage of concern."

"The Development of the Capacity for Concern" [CW 6:3:11] is a paper in which he explores the processes by which the infant comes to know the difference between inner and external reality, ideas that reach fruition later in this last decade of his life in the "Use of an Object" [CW 8:2:28] papers. His account of the baby's earliest apprehension of the mother divides the so-called environment mother, who holds and handles baby, from the object mother, who is there to receive the full force of his primitive love urges, the object of his drives. Not only is this a completely different account from Klein's of the way the baby experiences himself in the world at the beginning, it is also an account of two different kinds of love. The love the baby has for the environment mother, who tenderly cares for his bodily needs, is the affectional bond that Bowlby writes about in "The Making and Breaking of Affectional Bonds" (1979) and is also described by Bethelard and Young-Bruehl in *Cherishment* (2002). It is the nonsexual, nonsublimated love that binds friendships and parents and babies. The erotic love of the drives is for the subjectively experienced "object mother" who is not afraid and who desires, indeed, to be the object of the pre-ruth attacks of the baby, devoured and enjoyed. The task of the stage of concern is for these two separately experienced subjective mothers to come together in the infant's mind as one object, thus combining the tender affectionate love with its passionate counterpart and culminating in the capacity for concern.

This is a different explanation from the splitting of Klein's theory, in which the baby projects its death-instinct–derived badness into the mother's breast, then felt to be bad and contrasted with the good, ideal breast. Such splitting is all too early for Winnicott, predicated as it is on an already established capacity to differentiate inner from outer reality, and on an entirely different conceptualization of aggression and destructiveness. The recognition of "otherness" and the capacity to use external reality was a process upon which development could founder, and this became a fundamental question for Winnicott. Its complex evolution originated from the initial illusory creation of reality by the subject, a reality that paradoxically was always there to be "found," and rested upon the continuity of the dependability of the environment provided by the good-enough mother.

The ideas in "The Development of the Capacity for Concern" contain his ongoing elaboration of his views about aggression. Although he had first written about aggression in the 1930s [CW 2:1:8], the early 1960s were significant in bringing these views together. His is a distinctive account, different from that of (later) Freud and the Kleinian development, which had privileged the vicissitudes of the death instinct (Freud, S., 1920; Klein, 1948). He locates aggression within the domain of the life instincts, initially identical to the aliveness of muscle movement and related to loving: muscle erotism. This can be compared with Freud's original theory of the drives, where the self-preservative instincts include activity and motility (Freud, S., 1915). In Winnicott's description, loving inherently comprises destructiveness (a phenomenon like Pliny's account of fire, which states that it is impossible to say whether this is inherently constructive or destructive; see "Comments on My Paper 'The Use of an Object' " [CW 8:2:38]). Taking full responsibility for the destructive aspects of loving is an ongoing acquisition throughout early development. His revision of Klein's concept of the depressive position not only emphasized the ordinariness of "concern" but located the development of its capacity in the real external relationship with the mother, whose survival of the baby's pre-ruth primitive destructiveness is fundamental to its establishment. This has nothing to do with hate; again, very different from Klein, who saw the conflict between love and hate fully present at the beginning of life, expressive of the conflict between the life and death instincts. Essential to Winnicott's description is the mother meeting and recognizing the baby's spontaneous reaching towards the "not-me" world (herself). The character of inner reality is profoundly marked by the nature of the responses of the baby's external environment, and the "surviving object" assumes an increasingly important place in Winnicott's conceptualization both of healthy development and in the psychoanalytic situation ("The Use of an Object" [CW 8:2:28]). He saw the development of the capacity for concern and guilt as achievements in health and characteristic of the life of the small child.

The themes of "The Development of the Capacity for Concern" [CW 6:3:11] and the talks he gave in many different locations linked with his interest in the antisocial tendency, which had been stimulated by his wartime experiences in the Oxford Evacuation Scheme. Although this period sees the consolidation of his views on aggression and destructiveness, most of Winnicott's work on the antisocial tendency was undertaken earlier (see Volumes 1 and 5). But, among the letters, reviews, obituaries, and talks in Volume 6, all demonstrating Winnicott's abiding interest in life as it is lived in all its myriad complexity, is the 1961 "Comments on the Report of the Committee on Punishment in Prisons and Borstals" [CW 6:2:22]. This short piece condenses much of his thinking about these phenomena: the antisocial tendency is an illness and, as such, needs treatment, not punishment; this illness is often a sophisticated defense against madness, the fear of which is ever present; hope is guarded against because of the fear of again losing what was lost; to sustain a system where the depth of the illness can be reached is not possible where institutions are organized along militaristic lines; vengeance is an unconscious motivation in punishment, and, although society needs protection, punishment is a way of enacting this revenge and cultivating a masochistic response in the individual; a deep grasp of the complex reasons behind behavior, such as delinquency or absconding, might lead to quite different treatments of the residents of prisons and borstals. His views were radical and deeply humane.

There are two papers on adolescence in Volume 6: "Adolescence: Struggling Through the Doldrums" [CW 6:2:4] and "Hospital Care Supplementing Intensive Psychotherapy in Adolescence" [CW 6:4:13]. In both, he emphasizes the young person's struggle to feel real and the unacceptability of the false solution, so that illness may feel preferable. His solution, "the passage of time," may seem simplistic, but, as with infancy, it is not merely that time passes but also that a process occurs over time that enables something to be integrated and reorganized in readiness for the immensely difficult task of being a mature adult.

A Note About Winnicott's Relationship with Melanie Klein

Winnicott was constantly in dialogue with mainstream psychoanalysis and particularly with Klein and the radical developments she brought to the field. It is of note that many of the papers reproduced here that explicitly take a different position from hers were presented in places other than the BPAS, at least initially. Klein had died at the beginning of this period (1960), and one might wonder if giving these papers away from his home ground expresses his hesitation at being so "defiant" as the Society mourned one of its most creative theoreticians. He said in one presentation, given during a lecture tour in the United States in 1962, that "in any case I found she had not included me in as a Kleinian. This did not matter to me because I was never able to follow anyone else, not even Freud. But Freud was easy to criticise because he was always critical of himself" ("A Personal View of the Kleinian Contribution" [CW 6:3:8]). This is a complex statement. It is undoubtedly true that he was not a follower of anyone, but perhaps it also both registers but plays down whatever hurt feelings he had about her exclusion of him from her circle. He saw Klein as "paying lip-service to environmental provision" (p. 335) and "temperamentally incapable" of recognizing its importance, but this did not stop him from recognizing her enormous significance in extending the interest of psychoanalysis to the pregenital era. He appreciated her as a generous teacher, but he criticized her theory of the paranoid schizoid position as being wrongly timed in that it assumed an ego functioning that requires time and experience to develop. He was vehemently opposed to her late theory of primary envy, and "The

Beginnings of a Formulation of an Appreciation and Criticism of Klein's Envy Statement" [CW 6:3:7] is a trenchant criticism of her ignoring of environmental factors.

The Clinic

In this period, Winnicott is well established in his distinctive way of being a psychoanalyst. This is not only the practice of the orthodox setting of the couch and five times a week. In "Varieties of Psychotherapy" [CW 6:2:5] and "The Aims of Psycho-analytical Treatment" [CW 6:3:2], he argues for what little need be done in the public clinic, subject as it is to the vagaries of budgets and waiting lists, in contrast to the luxury of the psychoanalytic consulting room and how much can be done there. All is dependent on a thorough psychoanalytic training with personal analysis at its heart. Such a trained analyst can do "something and do it usefully," taking into account the full complexity of human living. The parent–child paradigm is the original template for clinical work, and this can lend itself to simplistic and misleading equations. He is very clear that successful work has its roots in whatever good-enough early experience the patient has had. History and history-taking is at the heart of this clinical work, whether it is a brief encounter such as a therapeutic consultation or a full analysis: "psychoanalysis is one long, very long history taking" ("Varieties of Psychotherapy" [CW 6:2:5]). He was most concerned about the state of mind of clinicians and the need for them to bear the "great strain" of this deep work. His view was that the clinician must have higher professional standards than in private life, of punctuality, integrity, to stay alive and awake but, fundamentally, to be himself, and behave himself (p. 289). Ever attentive to the differentiations of diagnosis, Winnicott makes it clear that different kinds of patients need different things from analysis, and this idea was not always welcome in the psychoanalytic community.

Winnicott was in the process of moving into old age during this period, and retirement from his health service practice underlined this fact, despite the immense creativity of these years. He was in better health than he had been since the late 1940s (the time of his divorce, his father's death, and his marriage to Clare Britton), but leaving Paddington Green Children's Hospital was undoubtedly a wrench. Although he claimed not to be concerned that his impact on the hospital's child psychiatric provision was in danger of disappearing with him, in his memorandum of February 1961 [CW 6:2:3] he clearly regrets the way psychiatry, child and adolescent psychiatry, and pediatrics were becoming separate specialties, with high risks of splitting and fragmentation. His clinic predated the child guidance service that had begun in the 1930s (he was appointed in 1923), and he emphasizes in the memo the benefits of the integration of medicine and psychology. He describes the construction of the multidisciplinary team over the decades following his appointment and emphasizes the personal qualities of the staff members over and above their qualifications, although he does mention that the social workers appointed in the 1930s had all had personal psychoanalysis. Although Winnicott's own integration of his medical and psychoanalytic sensibilities is clear and indeed threads its way throughout all his writings, this memo suggests the precariousness of the team and its integration with the medical teams in the hospital. He wrote several papers in this period emphasizing the necessity of psychiatry, especially child and adolescent psychiatry, being linked with pediatrics and rooted in its therapeutic undertakings. In his view, this necessitated psychoanalytic knowledge and training as a central part of psychiatric training.

Among the letters and other short pieces in Volume 6 is a poem, "The Tree" [CW 6:4:14], which Winnicott wrote in November 1963 and, according to Adam Phillips (1988, and personal communication), sent to his brother-in-law James Britton. The metaphor of the tree draws on the image of Christ on the cross looking down at his weeping mother below. This poem is taken to be an account of Winnicott's experience of his own mother's depression. Rodman (1987), for instance, sees it as a deeply biographical poem and drew on Marion Milner's view. Phillips (1988) agrees with this account of Winnicott's relationship with his mother. In his view, "The Tree" was one in Winnicott's garden at his home where he did his homework in the years before he was sent to boarding school, suggesting a deep yearning for his old haunts. Whether Winnicott's mother was, in fact, depressed is uncertain. Clare Winnicott believed that the family was a happy one, giving no suggestion of his mother having been depressed. Indeed, another rather different reading of the poem is that the depression suggested is a reflection of all mothers' lived anticipation of the inevitable loss of their children, here the son on the cross, leaving to live out his personal destiny. It seems to me to be not so much a solely personal poem as one about motherhood itself and, equally, the consequences for the child of having a mother. Winnicott spent so much of his life close to mothers and was particularly attentive to the predicament of the child whose own creativity and capacity for concern could be hijacked by the depressed mother. This undermining or sabotaging of aliveness in development was of continuing interest to him, and his personal resolve to live his life authentically permeates his writing and his life as a psychoanalyst. Its derivation in his own personal history has to be allowed for, and the psychoanalytic world and the world beyond it are all the richer for what he made of it.

Conclusion

Winnicott was unusual among psychoanalysts in his energetic engagement with the psychoanalytic establishment nationally and internationally and also with wider society, including his work in the health service, and evident in the many talks he gave to varieties of organizations and groups interested in all kinds of social and psychological issues. The papers in Volume 6 reflect the consolidation of many of his seminal views elaborated over his professional lifetime: the ever-present motif of the parent–infant relationship and the evolution of dependency towards independence; the nature of aggression and its role in living with a sense of being real; the necessity for that way of living to be isolated and yet relating to others with concern from an authentic place within one's self; and what constitutes health. His frequent resorting to paradoxes reflects the necessarily complex nature of living life in this way. Life ultimately is not a problem to be resolved but is to be lived in as authentic a way as possible. That this involves contradiction and seemingly irreconcilable entities—such as being isolated but relating in the world in an uninsulated way or that, in the accomplishment of living in the world, we need first to live in an illusion and create out of it our true selves—is indeed immensely challenging. In the last ten years of Winnicott's life, these ideas were to come to fruition in ways that continue to challenge not only the views about life and living held by the psychoanalytic establishment but also those held by the wider public. They remain radical propositions that subvert any tendency to simplistic thinking.

References

Bethelard, F., & Young-Bruehl, E. (2002). *Cherishment*. New York: Free Press.

Bowlby, J. (1953). *Child care and growth of love*. Harmondsworth: Penguin.

Bowlby, J. (1979). *The making and breaking of affectional bonds*. London: Tavistock.

Caldwell, L., & Joyce, A. (2011). *Reading Winnicott*. London: New Library of Psychoanalysis/Routledge.

Ferenczi, S. (1913/1952). Stages in the development of the sense of reality. In *First contributions to psycho-analysis*. London: Hogarth.

Freud, A. (1962). The theory of the parent–infant relationship—Contributions to discussion. *International Journal of Psycho-Analysis, 43*, 224.

Freud, S. (1911). Formulations on the two principles of mental functioning. In *Standard edition* (vol. 12, pp. 213–226).

Freud, S. (1913). Totem and taboo. In *Standard edition* (vol. 13, pp. 1–161).

Freud, S. (1915). Instincts and their vicissitudes. In *Standard edition* (vol. 14).

Freud, S. (1920). Beyond the pleasure principle. In *Standard edition* (vol. 18).

Freud, S. (1926). Inhibitions, symptoms and anxiety. In *Standard edition* (vol. 20).

Greenacre, P. (1960). Considerations regarding the parent–infant relationship. *International Journal of Psycho-Analysis, 41*, 571.

Greenacre, P. (1962). The theory of the parent–infant relationship—Further remarks. *International Journal of Psycho-Analysis, 43*, 235–237.

Kanter, J. (2004). *Face to face with children: The life and work of Clare Winnicott*. London: Karnac.

Klein, M. (1935). A contribution to the psychogenesis of manic-depressive states. In *Contributions to psycho-analysis 1921–1945*. London: Hogarth/Institute of Psychoanalysis.

Klein, M. (1945). The Oedipus complex in the light of early anxieties. *International Journal of Psycho-Analysis, 26*, 11–33.

Klein, M. (1948/1970). The theory of anxiety and guilt. In *Developments in psycho-analysis*. London: Hogarth/Institute of Psychoanalysis.
Lacan, J. (1978). *The four fundamental concepts of psychoanalysis*. London: Penguin.
Phillips, A. (1988). *Winnicott*. Modern Masters Series. London: Fontana.
Rodman, R. (1987). *The spontaneous gesture*. London: Karnac.
Thompson, N. (2012). Winnicott and American analysts. In J. Abram (Ed.), *Donald Winnicott today* (pp. 386–417). London: New Library of Psychoanalysis/Routledge.
Tonnesmann, M. (2002). Early emotional development. In L. Caldwell (Ed.), *The elusive child* (pp. 45–58). London: Karnac.
Winnicott, C. (1954/1964). Casework techniques in the child care services. In *Child care and social work*. Hertfordshire: Codicote.
Winnicott, D. W. (1945). Primitive emotional development. [CW 2:7:8]
Winnicott, D. W. (1954). Mind and its relation to psyche-soma [1949]. [CW 3:4:20]
Winnicott, D. W. (1955). Metapsychological and clinical aspects of regression within the psychoanalytical set-up [1954]. [CW 4:3:6]
Winnicott, D. W. (1955). Withdrawal and regression [1954]. [CW 4:3:29]
Winnicott, D. W. (1957). Aggression [ca. 1939]. [CW 2:1:8]
Winnicott, D. W. (1958). The capacity to be alone [1957]. [CW 5:3:20]
Winnicott, D. W. (1958). *Collected papers: Through paediatrics to psycho-analysis*. London: Tavistock. [Not reprinted in this form in the *Collected Works*]
Winnicott, D. W. (1958). Primary maternal pre-occupation [1956]. [CW 5:2:16]
Winnicott, D. W. (1960). The theory of the parent–infant relationship. [CW 6:1:21]
Winnicott, D. W. (1962). Adolescence: Struggling through the doldrums [1961]. [CW 6:2:4]
Winnicott, D. W. (1963). The development of the capacity for concern [1962]. [CW 6:3:11]
Winnicott, D. W. (1963). The mentally ill in your caseload. [CW 6:4:5]
Winnicott, D. W. (1963). Morals and education [1962]. [CW 6:3:18]Winnicott, D. W. (1963). The psychotherapy of character disorders [1963]. [CW 6:4:9]
Winnicott, D. W. (1964). The value of depression [1963]. [CW 6:4:10]
Winnicott, D. W. (1965). The aims of psycho-analytical treatment [1962]. [CW 6:3:2] Winnicott D. W. (1965). Classification: Is there a psycho-analytical contribution to psychiatric classification? [1959, 1964] [CW 5:5:5]
Winnicott, D. W. (1965). Communicating and not communicating leading to a study of certain opposites [1963]. [CW 6:4:8]
Winnicott, D. W. (1965). The effect of psychosis on family life [1960]. [CW 6:1:6]
Winnicott, D. W. (1965). Ego distortion in terms of true and false self [1960]. [CW 6:1:22]
Winnicott, D. W. (1965). Ego integration in child development [1962]. [CW 6:3:19]
Winnicott, D. W. (1965). The family and emotional maturity [1960]. [CW 6:1:17]
Winnicott, D. W. (1965). *The family and individual development*. London: Tavistock. [Not reprinted in this form in the *Collected Works*]
Winnicott, D. W. (1965). From dependence towards independence in the development of the individual [1963]. [CW 6:4:11]
Winnicott, D. W. (1965). Hospital care supplementing intensive psychotherapy in adolescence [1963]. [CW 6:4:13]
Winnicott, D. W. (1965). *The maturational processes and the facilitating environment*. London: Hogarth and the Institute of Psychoanalysis. [Not reprinted in this form in the *Collected Works*]

Winnicott, D. W. (1965). A personal view of the Kleinian contribution [1962]. [CW 6:3:8]

Winnicott, D. W. (1965). Psychiatric disorder in terms of infantile maturational processes [1963]. [CW 6:4:12]Winnicott, D. W. (1965). The relationship of a mother to her baby at the beginning [1960]. [CW 6:1:8]

Winnicott, D. W. (1967). Mirror-role of mother and family in child development. [CW 8:1:38]

Winnicott, D. W. (1969). The use of an object and relating through identifications [1968]. [CW 8:2:28]

Winnicott, D. W. (1984). Comments on the report of the committee on punishment in prisons and borstals [1961]. [CW 6:2:22]

Winnicott, D. W. (1984). *Deprivation and delinquency.* Winnicott, C., Shepherd, R., & Davies, M. (Eds.). London: Tavistock. [Not reprinted in this form in the *Collected Works*]

Winnicott, D. W. (1984). Varieties of psychotherapy [1961]. [CW 6:2:5]

Winnicott, D. W. (1989). The beginnings of a formulation of an appreciation and criticism of Klein's envy statement [1962]. [CW 6:3:7]

Winnicott, D. W. (1989). Comments on J. Sandler's "On the concept of the superego." [CW 6:1:19]

Winnicott, D. W. (1989). Comments on my paper "The use of an object" [1968]. [CW 8:2:38]

Winnicott, D. W. (1989). Psycho-neurosis in childhood. [CW 6:2:17]Winnicott, D. W. (1989). The use of an object in the context of *Moses and Monotheism*. [CW 9:1:4]

Winnicott, D. W. (1993). The development of a child's sense of right and wrong [1962]. [CW 6:3:4]

Winnicott, D. W. (1993). Jealousy [1960]. [CW 6:1:4]

Winnicott, D. W. (1993). *Talking to parents*. Reading, MA: Addison-Wesley. [Not reprinted in this form in the *Collected Works*]Winnicott, D. W. (1993). What irks? [1960] [CW 6:1:7]

Winnicott, D. W. (2003). The tree [1963]. [CW 6:4:14]

Winnicott, D. W. (2017). Memorandum on organizational aspects of child care at Paddington Green Hospital [1961]. [CW 6:2:3]

Winnicott, D. W., Winnicott, C., Shepherd, R., & Davis, M. (1989). *Psychoanalytic explorations*. London: Karnac.

FIGURE 7.1 *Winnicott talking to George Packer Berry, Dean of the Harvard Medical School. On this trip to Boston, part of a month-long tour of the United States, Winnicott presented "Dependence in Infant-Care, in Child-Care, and in the Psycho-Analytic Setting" [CW 6:3:9] to the Boston Psychoanalytic Society and gave two seminars at Beth Israel Hospital, one of the teaching hospitals of Harvard Medical School. He returned to Boston five years later.*

The Donald Woods Winnicott Archive, in the care of the Wellcome Library, London, courtesy of the Winnicott Trust.

{8}

Object Presence and Absence in Psychic Development, 1964–1966

Anna Ferruta

"My Latest Brain-Child"

The writings collected in Volume 7 cover years in which the main themes that informed Winnicott's thinking were known and appreciated in England and abroad, in both the psychoanalytic world and in social and medical contexts. In this mature phase of his life, however, he did not pause to enjoy his achievements but devoted himself with even greater freedom and liveliness to exploring those aspects of his thinking that had encountered misunderstandings or trivializations and to deepening his understanding of how the mind works in the earliest stages of the birth of psychic life.

Volume 7 is characterized by a remarkable variety of topics, unified by the dialectical, often polemical quality with which the various issues are treated, and by the courageous extension of new research into increasingly primitive areas of the mind: "My latest brain-child"—that is, his latest discoveries. At the time of the Controversial Discussions (1942–1944), Winnicott, fearing that he might be assimilated into one of the conflicting positions and thus lose his personal specificity, had preferred to listen to the debates taking place in the British Psychoanalytical Society (BPAS) and then to write letters in which he expressed his viewpoint. In his mature years, however, he dealt freely and openly with the controversial aspects of psychoanalytic debate, formulating new thoughts in a clear and detailed way.

Although it is not easy to guide the reader into the complexity of a way of thinking that constantly shifts from the individual to the general, from the normal to the pathological, from the integration of fragmentary elements towards new creative constructions, I have chosen to comment on three main areas: the writings on theory, those that deal with technical issues, and those in which Winnicott's character and personality, with all its qualities and limitations, emerge.

Theoretical Dimensions: "Development Is My Special Line of Country"

Winnicott never stopped thinking that psychoanalysis after Freud could continue to progress, acquiring new territories in the understanding of the functioning of the mind. In the writings of this period, he investigated situations of breakdown with the psyche in a state of un-integration originating in the failure of an environment in holding and supporting the continuity of a sense of self; such situations may be with regard to the young child or to psychotic and borderline patients.

Significantly, Winnicott started his paper "The Psychology of Madness" [CW 7:2:18], presented to the BPAS (1965), with these words: "The practice of psychoanalysis for thirty-five years cannot but leave its mark. For me there have come about changes in my theoretical formulation, and these I have tried to state as they consolidated themselves in my mind. Often what I have discovered had been already discovered and even better stated, either by Freud himself or by other psychoanalysts or by poets and philosophers. This does not deter me from continuing to write down (and to read when a public is available) what is my latest brain-child."

He thought of his own scientific work of that period as linked to the psychic birth of the individual: "I am trying to keep nearer to the birthdate" ("The Neonate and His Mother" [CW 7:1:4]). One of his most important new interests concerns the very primitive agonies. In "The Neonate and His Mother," a paper addressed to pediatricians, he speaks about the feeling of unintegration, imagining the newborn's thoughts when his head drops during the administration of the Moro reflex test made by the doctor: "Suddenly two terrible things happened; the continuity of my going on being, which is all I have at present of personal integration, was interrupted, and it was interrupted by my having to be in two parts, a body and the head." Surprisingly, in this same paper, Winnicott also makes reference to the analytic treatment of a borderline patient who needed a prolonged regression towards dependence, whom he had subjected to the same test. "I tested what it would be like to just drop her head and see if the Moro Response would show up. Of course I knew what would happen. The patient suffered very severe mental agony. The continuity of her emotional development had stopped and she fell into an unintegrated state." For Winnicott, the analytic treatment of this patient "has provided me with the unique opportunity for watching infancy, infancy appearing in an adult."

"Fear of Breakdown" [CW 6:4:21] is the text in which he describes in theoretical terms a series of agonies (not just anxieties, he insisted) that can interrupt the continuity of being when the organization of the child's ego is too weak to face them. These agonies were lived through but were not emotionally experienced or remembered. In his opinion, the only cure was to relive the madness in the analytic setting. "In such a case any attempt on the part of the analyst to be sane or logical destroys the only route that the patient can forge back to the madness which needs to be recovered in experience because it cannot be recovered in memory. In this way the analyst has to be able to tolerate whole sessions or even periods of analysis in which logic is not applicable in any description of the transference" ("The Psychology of Madness" [CW 7:2:18]).

I wanted to quote these two papers, "The Neonate and His Mother" and "The Psychology of Madness," rather than the better-known "Fear of Breakdown" to give more evidence for Winnicott's "brain-child" at this stage of his thinking. To the pediatricians he spoke of borderline patients, and to the psychoanalysts of those very early stages of the newborn's development that preceded the ability to experience them psychically. Such stages might be seen as foreign to psychoanalytic treatment, which is a "talking cure," and his way of facing this issue is clearly counterintuitive. Winnicott was looking for a theoretical and communicative way of clarifying some crucial concepts, above all, the substantial unity-continuity of the psyche-soma, "Psychology is a gradual extension from physiology" ("The Neonate and His Mother"). His deep conviction of the developmental unity of the individual spurred him to use nontechnical terminology that would be incisive enough to grasp the dynamic and relational quality of the phenomena of psychic growth he was dealing with. Every crystallization of thought into new terminology was a hindrance he tried to avoid ("I have purposely used the term "breakdown" because it is rather vague and because it could mean various things" ["Fear of Breakdown"]). He aimed not only to differentiate himself from the medical discourse that objectifies the illness and does not pay attention to the whole patient but also to comprehend the specificity of the phenomena that block psychic growth towards the gradual integration of the self. It was this that could find a cure in psychoanalysis: "Development is my special line of country" ("This Feminism" [CW 7:1:14]).

In many of these writings, Winnicott highlights *the developmental dimension as a structuring element*. For him, the distinction between the normal and the pathological focuses on not just the quality of the defense mechanisms but particularly on the availability, for the child's ego, of suitable resources with which to face overwhelming experiences. Such resources are provided by the mind of a mother who is ready to identify completely with her child's needs. But Winnicott also pointed out that the mother's total ability to put herself in her child's shoes is possible *only because it is transitory*, necessary for a few months, after which the child begins to move towards relative dependence and finally to independence. With regard to adolescence, Winnicott also thought that awareness of the time dimension was fundamental for any therapeutic intervention: "Adolescence is the stage of becoming adult by emotional growth. . . . I have referred elsewhere to the *adolescent doldrums*, the time during which there is no immediate solution to any problem" ("Deductions Drawn from a Psychotherapeutic Interview with an Adolescent" [CW 7:1:5]).

As regards psychosis, Winnicott considered it a form of defense against primary agonies: "The basis of all learning (as well as of eating) is emptiness. But if emptiness was not experienced as such at the beginning, then it turns up as a state that is feared, yet compulsively sought after" ("Fear of Breakdown"). Analysis could then be the appropriate treatment for the patient to relive, with the analyst, those emotional states of breakdown that, in order to be psychically experienced, need an environment that allows absolute dependence.

Another issue on which Winnicott worked in dealing with the "the period immediately after birth" was the continuity between the normal and the pathological in investigating the considerable dynamic and developmental unity of the human subject. Winnicott had been impressed by this fact when, as a young student at Cambridge, he encountered the work of Darwin, a scientist interested in the continuous exchange between self-organized individuals and the environment, and one who dealt with a living world in a state of constant development. The originality of Winnicott's thought in this phase consisted in the heuristic and radical way in which he described *the formation of nonintegrated states in the child and the possibility of reaching psychoemotional and psychosomatic integration from the very beginning,* through the child's interaction with an environment that allowed him to experiment, through his own omnipotence, while feeling unreservedly rooted in his personal life experiences. For Winnicott, the function of the mother is to provide the child with an emotional environment that allows him to experience intensely a personal sense of omnipotence in the initial phase of primary narcissism; this is not a reparative or consolatory compensation for a failure. He states, "At the start the baby's ego is both feeble and powerful" ("The Importance of the Setting in Meeting Regression in Psychoanalysis" [CW 7:1:9]). The positive assessment of the experience of personal omnipotence is one of Winnicott's most significant contributions to the treatment of psychotic and borderline patients. It is an essential step in the process of integration, one in which the child has the possibility of experiencing something that belongs to him and that he does not have to project into the object, losing it, depriving himself of it, or annihilating himself. The *processes of integration start at once,* from birth, even when the child is still completely dependent: they are narcissistic elements of primary identification. Their opposite is the failure of integration, or disintegration.

Winnicott made a clear distinction between the psychic states of withdrawal and regression ("Case Notes for a Psychoanalytic Seminar: Withdrawal, Regression, Male Identification" [CW 7:2:19]). In withdrawal, the expectation is of a persecutory environment, and there is a search for pathological independence; whereas, in regression, the subject experiences positive dependence as a pathway towards independence if the mother adapts herself to her child's needs. In his work on autism in particular ("Autism" [CW 7:3:8]), Winnicott strongly argued that "it is very artificial to talk of an illness called autism." For him, autism cannot be belittled and classified as one among the other illnesses; it is, rather, the highest peak of a universal phenomenon regarding difficult relationships with other people, of there being more than one person breathing in the same environment. He states, "One of the most difficult of all these, unless it happens naturally, is simply coexistence: two people breathing together and doing nothing simply because doing is not a state of rest." It was in the mother–child relationship and in the analytic treatment that Winnicott found the tool for the retrieval of the ability for integration within the personality through a focus on making mental space available to the other person, by being interested in the manifestations of his being, rather than in his behavior or his actions.

What makes it possible for this process of integration to develop is the "ordinary devoted mother" factor, a concept amply illustrated by Winnicott in his earlier works. The new aspect evident in these writings is his dissatisfaction with how the function of psychic growth as performed by the mother is to be represented. This function allows the child to have personal experiences and to begin to integrate "in bits and pieces" an identity of his own, to say "I am":

> One can give names to these things. The main thing is covered by the word *integration*. All the bits and pieces of activity and sensation which go to form what we come to know as this particular baby begin to come together at times so that there are moments of integration in which the baby is a unit although of course a highly dependent one. We say that the mother's ego support facilitates the ego organization of the baby. Eventually the baby becomes able to assert his or her own individuality and even to feel a sense of identity. ("The Ordinary Devoted Mother" [CW 7:3:3])

Winnicott focused theoretically on this area, clarifying where necessary the ordinary devoted mother's function in fostering the child's ability to think independently: "Thinking as a Mother-Substitute, a Sitter-in" ("New Light on Children's Thinking" [CW 7:2:1]). The functions carried out by mothers, fathers, and families are extraordinary in that they are usually the ones who promote the healthy development of children. Rather than criticizing mothers or families, he strongly supported them. However, when a theory is presented, its meaning is often distorted, transformed into its opposite by issues that concern society as a whole:

> If our society delays making full acknowledgement of this dependence which is a historical fact in the initial stage of development of every individual, there must remain a block to ease and complete health, a block that comes from a fear. If there is no true recognition of the mother's part, then there must remain a vague fear of dependence. This fear will sometimes take the form of a fear of woman in general or fear of a particular woman, and at other times will take on less easily recognized forms, always including the fear of domination. (Introduction to *The Child, the Family, and the Outside World* [CW 7:1:17])

Disintegration and Dissociation

In this period, Winnicott was not only concerned to deepen his understanding of the function of integration—a turning point in psychic development facilitated by the caregivers to enable the infant to bring together subjective experiences lived in a fragmented way and in doing so to become a unique individual who can say: "I am." He was also interested in the dissociative phenomena *peculiar to* psychosomatic and borderline pathologies and in the states of disintegration that are manifested in the analysis of psychotics. Winnicott developed a rich discussion of the split represented by some rather common diseases involving somatic manifestations ("A severe disintegration threat can be hidden in a cricked neck"), and he considered psychosomatic illnesses the opposite of integration ("Psycho-Somatic Illness in Its Positive and Negative Aspects" [CW 7:1:6]). He believed that grouping certain diseases as psychosomatic only signaled that certain patients try to keep their doctors outside an emotional contact with them. In these cases, he warned the analyst against making early interpretations that could be felt by the patient as a sort of seductive intervention "which would involve an abandonment of psyche-soma and a flight into intellectual collusion." In the treatment of patients with psychosomatic symptoms, Winnicott also emphasizes that analysis is a real experience with similarities to the dream, an experience that enables the patient to "live" particular emotions rather than just recount them. The analyst's interventions have to come from a genuine emotional participation. If they remain at the level of explanatory commentary, then they simply reinforce the dissociation between psyche and soma, lining up with the intellectualized aspects of the patient.

The development of this train of thought in relation to the processes of integration led to the awareness that big dissociations often had to do with what he calls split-off male and female elements. His essay "The Split-Off Male and Female Elements to Be Found in Men and Women" [CW 7:3:2] containing the case of a male patient to whom he said "I am listening to a girl" is too well known to be quoted in detail, but what is important here is the continuity in Winnicott's thought across the papers of these two years as he felt the need to go deeper, to reach an understanding of the elements that form the basis of psychic reality and his own way of doing psychoanalysis. "I have needed to live through a deep personal experience in order to arrive at the understanding I feel I now have reached." Analysis is an emotional experience that must be shared by the analyst. If the analyst is willing to share such an experience and "sail into deep waters," then dissociated parts of the self can be reunited, as in the case of the patient with split-off male and female elements. The heuristic aspect of this concerns the very nature of the female element, which Winnicott identifies as the basis of the sense of existing: "[The child] needs a breast that is, not a breast that does" (p. 328). "The study of the pure distilled uncontaminated female element leads us to BEING, and this forms the only basis for self-discovery and a sense of existing and then on to the capacity to develop an inside, to be a container, to have a capacity to use the mechanisms of projection and introjection and to relate to the world in terms of introjection and projection" (p. 329).

This work of Winnicott's led to new research perspectives, as regards both the mechanisms of primary identification and those of dissociation, which are now studied by those authors who increasingly deal with serious pathologies, primary psychic states, and nonverbal communication. In the formation of the psychic sense of existing, aggression, "one of the two main sources of an individual's energy," plays a fundamental role. In "Roots of Aggression" [CW 7:1:18], Winnicott regarded the dimension of aggression within the framework of an individual's emotional development as crucial for the simultaneous acquisition of a sense of self and of a sense of reality. He observed that, at the beginning of development, the child comes to love and hate simultaneously and accept the contradiction. However, in this early phase, "both creation and destruction appear to happen by magic." Winnicott discusses a child's thinking functions and noticed that the child's ability to close his eyes contained the possibility of experiencing that omnipotent capacity for magical creation and destruction: "In infantile magic the world can be annihilated by a closing of the eyes and recreated by a new looking and a new phase of needing" (p. 134). This oscillation between magical creation and destruction corresponds to the alternation between moments in which me objects turn into not-me objects for the child; that is, in the shift from their being subjective phenomena to their being perceived objectively. Winnicott emphasizes the value of this dimension of aggression in establishing identity and a sense of existing. He is not interested in any kind of assessment of this behavior; rather, he insists that the baby's experience of aggression is a fundamental step in emotional development. Through his innate aggression, the baby becomes aware of being strong yet not destructive, precisely because the "not me" object has survived his "kicking out" at the world.

In this detailed analysis of a developmental emotional stage, we can fully appreciate Winnicott's mental freedom, his Darwinian interest in details, and his ability to stay in the relationship with the child or with the patient, observing and participating emotionally in what is happening as an experienced event:

> If time is allowed for maturational processes, then the infant becomes able to be destructive and becomes able to hate and to kick and to scream instead of magically annihilating the world. In this way *actual aggression is seen as an achievement.* As compared with magical destruction, aggressive ideas and behaviour take on a positive value, and hate becomes a sign of civilization, when we keep in mind the whole process of the emotional development of the individual, and especially the earliest stages.

In this same paper ("The Roots of Aggression"), Winnicott made an interesting remark that anticipates many later reflections in the development of Bionian thought on daydreaming in that he saw, in the night dream, an experience that actually took place and that allowed the subject to function in an inventive and exploratory manner within a condition of rest from the ego's defensive activities:

> Here I must make a clear distinction between dreaming and day-dreaming. The stringing together of fantasies during waking life is not what I am referring to. The essential thing about dreaming as opposed to day-dreaming is that the dreamer is asleep, and can be awakened. The dream may be forgotten, but it has been dreamed, and this is significant. (There is also the true dream that spills over into the child's waking life, but that is another story.)

Winnicott believed that dreams were an alternative to aggressive behavior: in a dream, both aggression and violence are experienced, together with bodily excitement, and that is a real experience not just an intellectual exercise. "If the dream contains too much destruction or involves too severe a threat to sacred objects, or if chaos supervenes, then the child wakes screaming." Winnicott's thoughts on the activity of dreaming as an experience that allows the dreamer to access what has not been able to be represented (because of the weakness of the ego defenses that appear in the dream) anticipate Bion's theory of the function of the dream in transforming the unrepresented beta elements into alpha elements that can then become part of the psychic life of the dreamer.

Technical Dimensions: "Consultation: It Is the Patient's Picnic"

Volume 7 of the *Collected Works* includes a number of clinical cases of consultations that are interesting both because the different relational sequences between Winnicott and his patients are described in detail and because they are often accompanied by drawings, comments, and theoretical reflections. Winnicott was increasingly convinced that a consultation with a psychoanalyst could perform a profound therapeutic function even when it was limited to a single interview. "If there is a type of case that can be helped by one or three visits to a psychoanalyst this vastly extends the social value of the analyst and helps to justify his needing to do full-scale analyses in order to learn his craft" ("The Value of the Therapeutic Consultation" [CW 7:2:22]). He then explained the reasons for this in detail. Everybody knows that the first interview in an analysis can contain material that will come forward thereafter for months and even years. Winnicott wondered about the unconscious density and depth of that first encounter, and he found in it an exquisitely psychoanalytic element that only the psychoanalyst is able to fully use. "The patient brings to the situation a certain measure of belief, or of the capacity to believe in, a helping and understanding person." This is the key element that he noticed and expanded: in a patient who comes for a consultation there is the expectation of meeting a person able to welcome his need to be welcomed, and that is what makes the encounter potentially therapeutic. Winnicott then pointed out the difference from those interviews with psychiatrists who write down the patient's case history or see the relatives first. He wanted to relate to the unconscious elements of the patient who trusts in the existence of someone who can help him; the analyst is there to give body and voice to that feeling, which is more important than any detailed information on his life history. This method contains vital elements that make it possible to assess the patient's degree of integration and ability to cope with tensions and conflicts.

In some cases, as in that of Patrick, an eleven-year-old child who suffered the loss of his father by drowning ("A Child Psychiatry Case Illustrating Delayed Reaction to Loss" [CW 7:2:23]), it was a prolonged consultation that took place in the course of a year with ten interviews with the child and four with his mother. Winnicott stated that, in order to make these brief consultations therapeutically effective, there must be a family that is sufficiently present in the background so that it can do the main work; the analyst works to activate a change in the child that will allow the family to start functioning again. With Patrick's mother, who was judged inadequate by the social services, this is exactly what happened; despite their judgment, Winnicott decided to entrust Patrick to her, suspending his school attendance so as to allow him to experience a necessary condition of regression. His mother agreed and made herself available for this transitory phase of treatment, retrieving the experience of a regressive situation that Patrick had been unable to go through in his relationship with her long before the loss of his father. "The main therapeutic provision was the way the boy's mother met his regression to dependence, and along with this there was a specific help given by myself on demand." This case is particularly interesting because it highlights two things: in the consultation, Winnicott's priority was to listen to the child's suffering rather than focus on his behavioral recovery (going back to school), and, moreover, he regarded the putting of blame on families for the child's illness as totally foreign. For him, families are an important therapeutic resource.

In other cases, like that of Ada, a girl of eight who was brought because of stealing, a single interview, made with the help of drawings, was enough to solve the problem for which she had come ("Dissociation Revealed in a Therapeutic Consultation" [CW 7:2:21]). Winnicott described the technique he followed and situated it within the psychoanalytic method, based on the dream of the analyst. "The analyst in doing this non-analytic therapy cashes in on a *dream of the analyst* that the patient may have had the night *before* this first contact, that is to say on the patient's capacity to believe in an understanding and helpful figure." With these observations and clinical examples, Winnicott provides a technical tool for extending psychoanalysis to a wider range of cases, precisely on the basis of one of the very pillars of its method: listening to the unconscious communications of a suffering patient who is looking for help from an analytically trained mind capable of activating a relationship that can unblock frozen defensive situations and activate a dynamic interaction. Winnicott did not ask for precise, detailed information, but he did put himself in a position to use and develop transference. "I saw the child without first seeing the mother who brought her. The reason for this was that I was not at this stage concerned with taking an accurate history; I was concerned with getting the patient to give herself away to me, slowly as she gained confidence in me, and deeply as she found that she could take the risk." Ada started to draw. "From now on it did not exactly matter what I said or did not say, except that I must be adapted to the child's needs and not requiring the child to adapt to my own." At a certain point, "Our work together was now hanging fire." In other words, communication between two unconscious minds in a safe environment was activated. However, Winnicott did not make interpretations; instead, he waited for the process that had been activated to expand and for the dissociated part of Ada, that acted out by stealing, to start communicating with him about a part of her that had lost intimate contact with her mother on the birth of her baby sister. Winnicott did not resort to interpretations of content; rather, he enabled a process of integration of the dissociated part by providing the child with a relational environment suitable for her needs and allowing Ada to retrieve an integrated way of functioning, not intellectually, but through the emotional experience within the session. "At the deeper layer at which the work was done it was possible for the interview to produce a result, not conscious insight, and not confession, but a true healing of a dissociation." It was indeed a psychoanalytic intervention.

The clinical cases of consultation are so numerous and interesting here that we do not regret the absence of a work of the same period, *The Piggle: An Account of the Psychoanalytic Treatment of a Little Girl (1964–1966)*, which the editors have rightly placed in the final volume (Volume 11) as a posthumous publication together with *Human Nature*, since they were notes "made" into books by others, not by Winnicott himself. The consultation method itself is a very interesting extension of the psychoanalytic method, not an aspect of applied psychoanalysis, and Winnicott practiced it even if he did not theorize it in a fully explicit manner: "The main principle is that a human setting is provided and while the therapist is free to be himself he does not distort the course of events by doing things or not doing things because of his own anxiety or guilt, or his own need to have a success. It is the patient's picnic, and even the weather is the patient's weather" ("The Value of the Therapeutic Consultation"). The psychoanalytic quality is evident in the method used in the cases described, as well as in other works contained in Volume 7, which deal with crucial technical aspects.

The Importance of the Setting in Meeting Regression in Psychoanalysis

A topic discussed by the third-year students of the Institute of Psycho-analysis at the time of this paper was that of the setting ("The Importance of the Setting in Meeting Regression in Psychoanalysis" [CW 7:1:9]). Winnicott observed that the activation of a condition of regression in analysis is an element that is only apparently simple. It is far easier for the mother to undertake since she is asked to adapt to her child's needs for a relatively short period—a few months—which is also what she wishes because she recovers her independence in the course of time. The analyst, instead, has to provide the patient with a specialized environment for a period of time that cannot be foreseen, one adapted to the patient's basic emotional needs. "In the kind of case I am talking about it is never a question of giving satisfactions in the ordinary manner of succumbing to a seduction." Winnicott gave "a very crude example" in which he himself did not maintain the necessary setting for his patient's regression: "In some patients with a certain type of diagnosis the provision and maintenance of the setting are more important than the interpretative work" (p. 86).

Another aspect of this kind of work involves the analyst's countertransference, an issue that led Winnicott to show his intolerance of those aspects of psychoanalytic language that tend to distance themselves from the relationship with the patient and are somewhat authoritarian. An element of Winnicott's personality that remained intact throughout his life and work was his intolerance for all forms of technical language that tend to hide deep individual differences under an apparent agreement. It emerges in a particularly vivid manner in the contributions in Volume 7 that are book reviews and letters, where something that he himself stated, in a famous letter to Melanie Klein (November 17, 1952 [CW 4:1:12]), is to be found. He challenges Klein to not dismiss his ideas in this letter simply as "Winnicott's illness." Klein had asked him to write a chapter for a book she was editing. Winnicott declined the invitation, explaining his reasons: he felt confronted with one of his basic personal difficulties, the relationship with the external reality shared with others, something to which he has always found it difficult to adapt. However, this same "difficulty" was the element that allowed him to understand young children and schizoid patients and to elaborate fundamental theories in relation to psychic functioning, transitional phenomena, and the split-off male and female elements.

Donald Winnicott as a Person

Many of the writings in Volume 7 consist of pieces that Winnicott was asked to write by nonpsychoanalytic agencies and associations. His interest in communicating with nonspecialized audiences continued after the end of World War II, when he had actively taken part in initiatives concerning the separation of children from their families as a result of the London bombings. In these contributions, written for pediatricians, social workers, researchers in related fields like psychosomatic medicine, and civil society associations (the Progressive League, the National Association for Mental Health, the Nursery Schools Association), one can observe Winnicott's wish to reaffirm his trust in the child's natural development, in the family as first grouping, his reliance on natural tendencies, and his ability to understand the point of view of parents who are afraid of being usurped by the therapist. At the same time, together with this welcoming availability, he consistently highlighted the centrality of unconscious factors ("The Unconscious" [CW 7:3:29]) and opposed all insistent requests for pedagogical guidelines that would thwart a live interaction with the given subject. In all these writings, one can feel Winnicott's authentic passion for the communication of psychoanalytic thinking in a clear and profound manner, without diluting or diminishing it. Indeed, in "The Unconscious," he stated that the wide acceptance of some psychoanalytic concepts had been accompanied by "a dilution of the concept of unconscious." Reading between the lines of these works, one can constantly feel the proud affirmation of a personal "I am" on Winnicott's part, in the sense of his capacity for engaging in an open dialogue without losing specificity or personalization in the concepts he communicated.

In the many reviews and letters within Volume 7 and others, Winnicott's need to feel independent in his thinking appears more evident and more complex, even when replying to unavoidable requests, as when reviewing Anna Freud's last book, clarifying an obscure concept, answering the question of an anguished mother, or attending an official ceremony like the celebration dinner for the completion of the *Standard Edition* of Freud's works. If we were to find a common feature in these different (and not always particularly special) interventions, it might be Winnicott's wish to maintain his independent way of thinking while trying to avoid seeming intolerant or detached. Some examples that could be mentioned are the review of *Memories, Dreams, and Reflections* by C. G. Jung [CW 7:1:16], which reveals Winnicott's deep oscillation and ambivalence. On the one hand, coming as he does from a Freudian standpoint, he wanted to avoid any biased critical evaluation that might appear ideological and partial. On the other, he could not avoid acknowledging the split present in Jung and his long research into the center of self. He focuses on the first chapter, a sort of autobiography of the early years of Jung's life, and comments on a dream that reflected the situation of a child in touch with a depressed mother who must set up defenses against psychosis. He concluded by making comparisons between Freud and Jung, finding them complementary to one another, as two examples of a neurotic and a psychotic organization: "they are the obverse and reverse of a coin. . . . We may well be glad that Jung and Freud separated, and that each maintained a personal integrity and lived to enrich the world exceptionally." He could not avoid adding his comment on the radical differences between Jungians and Freudians now regarding the terms *unconscious* and *self*, and, in the end, he reaffirmed the fundamental concept that is present in all the writings of this phase of his thought: "What is more important is to reach to the basic forces of individual living, and to me it is certain that if the real basis is creativeness the very next thing is destruction." This review is a very clear example of Winnicott's constant struggle between his openness in listening to the other and his need to maintain his own independence, an element that explicitly emerges in the very last lines of his review, when he observed that the book was well translated, but he objected to the translation of the term *erreichten* as *attained*, suggesting *reached* instead: "'attained' seems to imply assimilation." This shows Winnicott's great sensitivity to the alteration of the self on the part of the object.

Something similar, but with understandably greater embarrassment, happened in his review of *Normality and Pathology* by Anna Freud. After an initial tribute to her contributions and her teaching skills, Winnicott could not hide his critical amazement: "It comes as a shock when she does not mention Susan Isaacs in the context of direct observation." He then describes and clearly comments on the six chapters of the book, highlighting many interesting and controversial points. However, a question regarding the use of terms once again emphasizes his need to express his personal point of view without the risk of it being altered by any form of complacency. He lingered on the word *prestages*, which is incomprehensible for English readers unless it is hyphenated, "pre-stages," and he criticized the use of *caretaker* to indicate the child's need of a maternal figure: "the trouble is that a caretaker is something that is remote and lacking in intimacy as compared with the mother who takes care of the child." In these remarks, one can particularly grasp Winnicott's sensitivity towards words as abstract symbolizations when they distance themselves from a personal emotional experience and tend to become disembodied and depersonalized. He felt that the area of transitional phenomena is a safe anchor in relation to the personal processes of symbolization and creativity, which give a status of existence to the subjective object as well as to the subject capable of relating to someone other than himself. The subject acknowledges the existence of the object with his perceptive characteristics but, at the same time, is not impoverished or emptied by the authority of the words.

Winnicott's many letters often originated from his need to defend his personal authenticity in relation to the inevitable phenomena of divulgence and partial distortion of his thoughts. For example, he replied with care and interest to the questions about some of his terms for the Italian translations by Renata Gaddini who, together with Eugenio Gaddini, was responsible for publishing and disseminating Winnicott's works in Italy. As these letters convey, he established a relationship of deep and warm friendship and cooperation with them. On other occasions, he warned his interlocutors against interpreting his indication of the importance of the environment in the emotional development of the child as merely a sentimental invitation to look after him with love, seeing it as an undoing of his attention to the internal world (Letter to *New Society* [CW 7:1:3]); other times still, he claimed that the fact that mothers must give their full attention to children had nothing to do with their cleverness since he was not referring to women's intellectual capacity: "[That] the vast majority of women with careers do interrupt their careers for the short time required, just as they do let each new infant have a first experience of an only child, even when there are in fact other children" (Letter to *The Observer* [CW 7:1:10]). Finally, he also lost his temper with a woman reader who demanded clear pedagogical directives instead of relational theories on the functioning of the mother–child relationship: "If you want direct instruction you may find help from Benjamin Spock's *Baby and Child Care*" (Letter to Mrs. B. Knopf [CW 7:1:15]).

In his letter to John O. Wisdom [CW 7:1:11], Winnicott talked about the Bion meeting that he had been unable to attend. He appreciated Bion's moving forward from Klein's ideas: "I like the way he goes ahead on his own grooves, and I am one of those who hope for a lot from him." However, he is also eager to highlight the work that he himself did "against the terrific opposition of Melanie." In particular, Winnicott felt that there was an affinity between Bion's concept of rêverie and his own concepts of the creativity of the child and the function of the mother who "lets the baby know what is being created," but he was irritated that Bion used a term (*tantalise*) that belonged to him without making any reference to him: "I refuse to be scotomised." Once again, a word arouses Winnicott's need to claim his own position, with his own specific connotations—this time, not to reject a word that was too abstract and devoid of experience, such as "caretaker," but to reclaim a word that belonged to the context of his thinking, which was always steeped in transitionality; that is, in the passage between what is felt and what is symbolized.

He found his specificity again in a letter to Michael Fordham [CW 7:2:8], written after a clinical meeting in which he made a comment on one aspect of repetitiveness in the behavior of a child, the "pencil rolling business." He believed that it had to do, in fact, with withdrawal dynamics: "In this place dynamics is to be looked at in terms of pendulum movement. Even in stillness there is a potential pendulum movement, so that stillness alternates, as it were, from being relative to right or left. If there is no pendulum movement then there is death." Winnicott's approaches and departures in relation to the thought of other people show just this kind of pendulum movement, a searching for "his own" rhythm/period. But this oscillating pendulum movement between concepts did not seem to allow Winnicott to write books that could gather his thoughts in a more organized way, perhaps because he never felt knowledgeable enough in relation to the detail of the dynamics of the living world. Perhaps there is a parallel with Darwin, who decided to publish *Origin of Species* only when Alfred Wallace, one of his followers, wrote to him, partly anticipating the more general theoretical conclusion of his research. Fearing that his great scientific discovery about the living world might be taken away from him, Darwin then gathered his research together and rapidly published it, even though he would perhaps have liked to investigate further and better understand the dynamics of the living world. This is something that his followers went on to do, like Stephen J. Gould, with his theory of "punctuated equilibrium," modifying just those aspects that Darwin did not like, those that crystallized (in too abstract and static schemes) the phenomena of change in the relationship between the living world and its environment.

Winnicott was quite aware of this last: in a speech at the banquet held on October 8, 1966, at the Connaught Rooms, to mark the publication of the *Standard Edition of the Psychological Works of Sigmund Freud* [CW 7:3:23], he made a solemn and formal intervention as the President of the BPAS. He remarked that Freud "gave new value to inner psychic reality, and from this came a new value for things that are actual and truly external." In other words, he reaffirmed the indissoluble link between the internal world to which Freud gave the status of scientific existence and the external world, which is made real and available only by the internal world. Thus, Winnicott celebrated the English edition of Freud's works, which gave a fundamental contribution to science and culture and of which he himself was a user and a beneficiary. But he could not help making a few remarks on his own position, his difficulty in dealing with abstract constructions linked to psychic functioning, referring to the birth date issue: "In my own reading I am proud to have reached Volume 2. (Laughter) I think you are laughing because there is no Volume 1. (Laughter) But, of course, I began at the end. I like to learn that in 1896, just as I was being born, Freud was first using the term 'angst,' pointing out the implication in the word of the straight and narrow path by which we are precipitated into the brief world of our personal existence."

To deal with Winnicott's own difficulty in giving a definitive status to his wealth of thoughts, which go well beyond "the straight and narrow path by which we are precipitated into the brief world of our personal existence," the editors of these *Collected Works* mobilized and worked as a container for his wish, making Winnicott public and available. We are undoubtedly grateful to them for having performed such a Winnicottian function.

Translated by Aldo Grassi

References

Winnicott, D. W. (1964). Deductions drawn from a psychotherapeutic interview with an adolescent. [CW 7:1:5]

Winnicott, D. W. (1964). Introduction to *The child, the family, and the outside world.* [CW 7:1:17]

Winnicott, D. W. (1964, April 2). Letter to *New Society.* [CW 7:1:3]

Winnicott, D. W. (1964, October 25). Letter to *The Observer.* [CW 7:1:10]

Winnicott, D. W. (1964). The neonate and his mother. [CW 7:1:4]

Winnicott, D. W. (1964). Review: C. G. Jung, *Memories, dreams and reflections.* [CW 7:1:16]

Winnicott, D. W. (1964). Roots of aggression. [CW 7:1:18]Winnicott, D. W. (1965). A child psychiatry case illustrating delayed reaction to loss. [CW 7:2:23]

Winnicott, D. W. (1966). Dissociation revealed in a therapeutic consultation. [CW 7:2:21]

Winnicott, D. W. (1966). Psycho-somatic illness in its positive and negative aspects. [CW 7:1:6]

Winnicott, D. W. (1968). The value of the therapeutic consultation [1965]. [CW 7:2:22]

Winnicott, D. W. (1971). The split-off male and female elements to be found in men and women. (Published here as part of "Creativity and its origins.") [CW 9:3:7]

Winnicott, D. W. (1974). Fear of breakdown [c. 1963–1964]. [CW 6:4:21]

Winnicott, D. W. (1986). This feminism [1964]. [CW 7:1:14]

Winnicott, D. W. (1987). The ordinary devoted mother [1966]. [CW 7:3:3]
Winnicott, D. W. (1989). The importance of the setting in meeting regression in psychoanalysis [1964]. [CW 7:1:9]
Winnicott, D. W. (1989). New light on children's thinking [1965]. [CW 7:2:1]
Winnicott, D. W. (1989). Notes on withdrawal and regression [1965]. [CW 7:2:19]Winnicott, D. W. (1989). The psychology of madness [1965]. [CW 7:2:18]
Winnicott, D. W. (1996). Autism [1966]. [CW 7:3:8]
Winnicott, D. W. (2003). Preface to Renata Gaddini's Italian translation of *The family and individual development* [1966]. [CW 7:2:27]
Winnicott, D. W. (2017). Answers to comments on "The split-off elements male and female elements" [1968–1969]. [CW 9:1:30]
Winnicott, D. W. (2017). On the occasion of the publication of the *Standard edition* of Freud [1966]. [CW 7:3:23]
Winnicott, D. W. (2017). Review of Anna Freud: *Normality and pathology in childhood* [1965]. [CW 7:2:16]
Winnicott, D. W. (2017). The unconscious [1966]. [CW 7:3:29]

FIGURE 8.1 *Winnicott with his wife, Clare Winnicott (middle).*
The Donald Woods Winnicott Archive, in the care of the Wellcome Library, London, courtesy of the Winnicott Trust.

FIGURE 8.2 *Winnicott playing.*

The Donald Woods Winnicott Archive, in the care of the Wellcome Library, London, courtesy of the Winnicott Trust.

{9}

Communication Between Infant and Mother, Patient and Analyst

THE YEARS OF CONSOLIDATION, 1967–1968

Ann Horne

Winnicott began 1967 with a January address to the 1952 Club [CW 8:1:2];[1] he ended 1968 with his talk on "The Use of an Object and Relating Through Identifications" [CW 8:2:28] at the New York Psychoanalytic Society and Institute. Neither occasion, he felt, went well, the latter followed by his serious illness and hospitalization in New York until he and Clare, his wife, were allowed to return to London a few days before Christmas. Between these events, and amidst his later life productivity, come important papers on the emergence of the self as real, delinquency,[2] and that area in personality development critical for culture and play. His work on playing would continue through the preparation of *Playing and Reality*, but, significantly, the papers and notes on play, as we read them in Volume 8, expound his thinking on the role of the analyst and on technique, especially focusing on parallels between the analytic encounter and the interactions of the good-enough mother and her infant. This duality of purpose, indeed, is apparent in many of the other papers of this phase of work. The period begins, however, with his talk "D. W. W. on D. W. W." to the 1952 Club.

---

[1] The 1952 Club was founded in that year by Pearl King, Charles Rycroft, Armstrong Harris, and Masud Khan (Hood, 1996) as a forum for discussion for independent analysts outside the clinical meetings of the British Psychoanalytical Society, meetings that, in Rycroft's famous phrase, were more often collisions than discussions (Rycroft, 1993). They met monthly, the venue alternating around the homes of the members. Membership was (and still is) by invitation.

[2] "Delinquency as a Sign of Hope" [CW 8:1:8] elaborates the thesis of "The Anti-Social Tendency" [CW 5:2:8] to embrace stealing as the hopeful search for the object that one had and that is lost *with the addition of* the capacity for creativity, also lost, which that object brought.

Winnicott on His Theories and Influences

Addresses to the 1952 Club had not always proceeded smoothly—*vide* his letter of the following year to Adam Limentani [CW 8:2:23] dated September 27, 1968:

> Dear Limentani,
>
> I guess you found it rather a waste of time at the 1952 Club the other evening. From my point of view I did learn something in the second half, after the interval. I seem to be unable to pull it off when I visit the '52 Club which is a pity because it provides a good opportunity for an easy discussion.

On the earlier occasion in January 1967, Winnicott had been invited to speak on his theories of development, particularly in relation to other theorists. This he did, progressing chronologically through his thinking and his influences. He distributed pages of headings with much free space between to encourage his audience to jot down names of colleagues who, deduced from these headings, might have influenced him—sources that previously had remained habitually unacknowledged. These notes are fuller, even in their abbreviation, more redolent of his own development, than is the transcript of what he actually said.

He began with a statement about his inability to correlate his work with that of others—not an apology, but presented as a lack in him and a loss. In an hour and a half, he covered the debt to Freud, his concern that traditional psychoanalytic theory denied the inner life of infants,[3] engagement with Anna Freud (about whom he had been ignorant until she arrived in London), important nonanalytic influences, and his debt to Klein in the areas of inner psychic reality and the internal life of the infant, plus his objection to the institutionalization of her theories by her followers. The split with the Kleinians over his focus on environment was patently painful, as was his ensuing unacceptability as a child analyst and teacher to them and to Anna Freud. There is a good discourse on the antisocial tendency and hope—and the delightful summation: "I think that was a contribution." As he moved into adaptation and primary maternal preoccupation, he noticeably mentioned influences: he had been startled by Fairbairn's "going beyond instinctual satisfactions and frustrations to the idea of object-seeking" and his thoughts "on feeling real and feeling unreal." Klein retained a vital place for him—despite his agreeing to differ on the mother as subjective object and the importance of the early environment, and his rejection of theories built on the death instinct and envy, he had great admiration for her contribution to analytic theory:

> From my point of view people knew about inner psychic reality through Freud and they knew about fantasy and dream, but it was she who pointed out the importance of the localization of all that goes on between eating and

[3] "I thought to myself, I'm going to show that infants are ill very early, and if the theory doesn't fit it, it's just got to adjust itself. So that was that."

> defecation, and that it had to do with the inside of the body. I feel that she taught me all this without which I couldn't do the psychoanalysis of children at all.

A confession to stealing the "delusional transference concept" from Margaret Little[4] was followed by exposition of the origins of aggression in muscularity and agency. His final words perhaps tell us why this could not be a satisfying evening for him:

> I don't know whether you'd like to discuss any of this or would like to help me in a letter to try and make amends and join up with the various people all over the world who are doing work which either I've stolen or else I'm just ignoring. I don't promise to follow it all up because I know I'm just going to go on having an idea which belongs to where I am at the moment, and I can't help it.

The wish to put right encounters the undercurrent of "What is there *really* that *needs* to be put right?" The telling line may be that of stealing from his mother's handbag: Winnicott, the child of the depressed mother, seeking the lost object.

Mirroring and Becoming Real

> What does the baby see when he or she looks at the mother's face? I am suggesting that, ordinarily, what the baby sees is himself or herself. In other words the mother is looking at the baby and *what she looks like is related to what she sees there.* ("Mirror-Role of Mother and Family in Child Development" [CW 8:1:38])

This calling forth of the baby from a state of apperception to one of perception—being seen as giving rise to seeing and perceiving as a real, separate being—is the final statement from Winnicott on the body-gaze-psyche continuum. (Later, he turns to how the *object* is made real in "The Use of an Object" [CW 8:2:28].) The mother as mirror reflects back to her infant what she perceives when she sees him, "giving back to the baby the baby's own self." The reflection he sees in his mother's face is his own. When this process is absent, the infant gazing at the mother sees how *she* is feeling, not a reflection back of him, his own feeling state and being. Here, indeed, we can see the potential for the growth of a false self personality, the development of a necessarily compliant self. So the baby's sense of feeling *real* appears at the beginning, all going well in this dyadic, reciprocal relationship. As important, however—and I believe that for those who work with children and

[4] "So that's one little bit of my life where I really did get something from somebody else, almost as if I stole it out of my mother's handbag."

caregivers it matters—is our capacity to integrate this with Winnicott's earlier work on psyche and soma, to enable us to see the development that flows from experiences of holding, handling, and object relating. To "holding" and "handling" we should add the mother's use of gaze to hold and to authenticate. Importantly, we should also keep in mind the consequences not simply of an absence of this affirming gaze but also of the presence of a gaze that is corrupt, the prelude to the infant as object used to contain the adult's perverse projections (not uncommon in our clinics today) and that leads to the privileging of the body as the only source of validation of a self of a kind.

Finally, Winnicott also addresses the task of the analyst:

> This glimpse of the baby's and child's seeing the self in the mother's face, and afterwards in a mirror, gives a way of looking at analysis and at the psychotherapeutic task. Psychotherapy is not making clever and apt interpretations; by and large it is a long-term giving the patient back what the patient brings.

This parallel theme—how the good-enough analyst's engagement with the patient is akin to the good-enough mother's role with her infant—is very much one that Winnicott emphasizes in papers and talks throughout this period, and it was to emerge as one point of debate when he delivered his paper on "The Use of an Object" in New York at the end of 1968.

Before that, two further papers addressed failure in the earliest relationship, one with its focus upon the psyche and the other attending in detail to somatic communication. "Thinking and Symbol-Formation" [CW 8:2:48] seems to have been written in response to Bion's work on thinking. Winnicott claims back part of this territory, pointing to his 1949 paper "Mind and Its Relation to the Psyche-Soma" [CW 3:4:20]. Thinking, with its benign source in the infant's dealing with the mother's careful failures in adaptation, may, when faced with pathology in this process, become overvalued and split off and take over part of the mother's role—"dependence on the mind and on thinking has taken the place of reliance on the good-enough mother" ("Thinking and Symbol-Formation" [CW 8:2:48]). Intellectualization and false self personality structure are likely consequences; the roots are in maladaptive care.

"Communication Between Infant and Mother, and Mother and Infant, Compared and Contrasted" [CW 8:2:2] was given second in the Winter Lectures (January 1968), a public lecture series on psychoanalysis. It provides an affecting description of precisely what is involved in lively, nonverbal communication between mother and infant. Where "communication is in terms of mutuality in physical experience," there is the mother's movement, breathing, warm breath, smell, rocking, the sound of her heartbeat; there is playing and common ground ("the no-man's land that is each man's land"), transitional space; the uses of gaze; and the mother's provision of an anticipatory adaptation that allows an experience of omnipotence to the baby.

The links, then, to psychoanalytic practice are made—"but *essentially* it is *from* mothers and babies that we learn about the needs of psychotic patients, or patients in psychotic phases"—and the importance of the reliability of holding and handling:

> As development proceeds, and the baby has acquired an inside and an outside, then the environmental reliability becomes a belief, an introject based on the *experience of reliability* [human, not mechanically perfect] . . . The baby does not hear or register the communication, only the effects of the reliability.

This is not a perfect mother—the baby experiences the failures of ordinary day-to-day care, mended and amended by the mother who is, in his terms, reliable enough. This is one of the points that Eigen makes in writing about Winnicott as a clinical innovator—that there becomes established a "rhythm of breakdown-recovery" when analyst and patient reach the original breakdown and live through the experience together (Eigen, 2012, p. 1456). Small failures and recoveries in mothering build up just such a rhythm, internalized by the baby and serving a protective function for him while he encounters becoming real and meeting reality.

This is a delightful and important paper. It is also beautifully written. Winnicott the essayist deserves a place in the pantheon, but this paper—perhaps because it was to be given publicly—contains none of the "what does—or might—he mean here?" moments of many of his papers. It is striking in its clarity and its poetic elucidation, for the intelligent layperson, of the "place where verbalisation has no meaning"—and clear in its outline of the implications of what he terms "gross failures" of care, reliability, and adaptation for the infant:

> These gross failures of holding produce in the baby *unthinkable anxiety*—the content of such anxiety is:
> Going to pieces
> Falling for ever
> Complete isolation because of there being no means of communication
> Disunion of psyche and soma.
> These are the fruits of *privation*, environmental failure essentially unmended.

It is also the clearest statement of communication with infants at a pre-representational stage and a call to colleagues to attend to such primitive developmental needs in their patients—with all its implications for technique.

The Twenty-Fifth International Psychoanalytical Association Conference in Copenhagen, July 1967

Winnicott's second term as President of the British Psychoanalytic Society was drawing to an end. In Copenhagen, the third themed congress of the International

Psychoanalytical Association (IPA) took as its main topic "On Acting Out and Its Role in the Psychoanalytic Process." There was, however, a further symposium that was particularly close to Winnicott's heart—"On Child Analysis and Paediatrics." To this he contributed the case of Iiro, later to be part of *Therapeutic Consultations* [CW 10:1:1], a presentation illuminated by the use of squiggle drawings between analyst and child.[5] The note of this presentation in the *International Journal of Psychoanalysis* is rather dry; it opens: "Dr Winnicott gave a communication based on an inter-change of drawings obtained in what he calls a therapeutic consultation."

That it was the case of Iiro that he offered to the symposium must have gladdened Winnicott. In 1964, the Finnish Psychoanalytic Society had been accorded the status of Study Group by the IPA. The IPA Sponsoring Committee was chaired by Winnicott, its Secretary was Pearl King, and the pair traveled often to Finland. Thus, Winnicott encountered Iiro, almost ten years old, he with no English and Winnicott with no Finnish. The squiggles plus an interpreter provided the forum for a powerful exploration of identification and the need for acceptance. At the Copenhagen Congress, the Finnish Study Group was elevated to Provisional Society.[6] In 1972, a year after her husband's death, we find Clare Winnicott writing to the *International Journal of Psychoanalysis*: "I still receive letters from parents and children who do not know of his death, telling him about themselves and their progress. The Finnish child, Iiro, has recently sent a picture of himself with his new dog."

Albert Solnit's contribution to that symposium (Solnit, 1968) outlined a long-term collaboration between an analyst from the Yale Child Study Center and pediatricians involving joint interviewing, discussion, and assessment of child patients and their families and the subsequent use of the material in a larger study group of eight to ten pediatricians—an achievement that Winnicott must have envied and celebrated, being the kind of engagement that he strove hard, but in vain, to establish in the United Kingdom. Solnit's summary of the participants' subjective assessment was significant:

> The consensus was that it had enabled each to work more realistically with a small number of patients with complicated psychological problems. However, they felt that the greatest influence . . . had been to advance their effectiveness and satisfaction in the care of the majority of their patients. (Solnit 1968, p. 282)

Also present at that Congress was Professor Renata Gaddini, like Winnicott a pediatrician and psychoanalyst, and a long-time correspondent and friend whose work included the precursors of transitional objects. At this point, she was engaged—not

---

[5] "The Squiggle Game" [CW 8:2:47], in Volume 8, gives a full outline of the flow and freedom of this means of engaging his young patient.

[6] Two years later, at the Rome Congress, the Finnish Society was accepted as a Component Society of the IPA.

without publication complications—in translating into Italian Winnicott's *The Family and Individual Development*. She relates: "When people asked him whether he was a paediatrician or a psychoanalyst, I heard him say, 'I am just a doctor who is trying to help young children to get better'" (Gaddini, 2004).

A Note on Observation and Being Scientific

Among the letters written by Winnicott in 1968 is one dated March 6, to a colleague, Dr. Donald Gough [CW 8:2:7], a child psychiatrist at the Tavistock Clinic. Winnicott writes:

> I want to let you know that you have done something quite important for me in drawing attention to the interaction through the eyes which accompanies feeding in the first weeks . . . Sometime I want to use what you have shown us in this way, that in using the breast (or bottle) the baby is experimenting in exteriorizing the object, which interferes with the state of being merged in with the mother which obtains as a primary state. The interaction through the eyes seems to me to be holding on to the merging which may very likely facilitate the experiments in the exteriorization of the object.

The detailed, fine observation that Winnicott praises in Gough's filming of infants is an aspect of perception and learning that he values. He recounts to Gough how important his observation and comment on the use of gaze has been to him in his work with adult patients. That such close observation has also been of great consequence in his understanding of the psychological development of the child had been evident in his tribute to Willi Hoffer on the occasion of his seventieth birthday, a few months before Hoffer died (June 13, 1967 [CW 8:1:11]). He singles out two of Hoffer's publications, "Mouth, Hand, and Ego-Integration" (1949) and "Development of the Body Ego" (1950):

> Here Hoffer was using observations of tiny detail that he made in association with Anna Freud and her other colleagues in the Hampstead War Nursery.
>
> For me the important thing is the general fact that Hoffer was using these observations as a sure basis for theory. If observations do not fit in with theory, then theory must alter. Also Hoffer's two articles mark a change among psycho-analysts who went through a long initial phase in which it was thought that infancy could be seen through the analysis of adults or of small children, whereas, in fact, infancy can only be seen in analyses through the distorting lenses of defences organised at dates later than infancy.
>
> And later:
>
> This must surely have set a standard for much of the work that has since been done in various parts of the world. It is on close observation of

> this kind that we know we must base our ideas about object-seeking, relating to objects, excited and unexcited sensual satisfaction, exploitation of satisfaction in defence against anxiety, the beginnings of control (as compared with omnipotence, and even the experience of omnipotence through successful adaptation to need) and many other matters of vital significance.

The theme emerges again in Winnicott's March 1968 Foreword to Robert Tod's book *Disturbed Children* [CW 8:2:8], in which he states that those who work with children "need more than intuition, understanding and common sense, however valuable these qualities may be as a foundation. They need to be able to observe, to stand aside, to think things out, and to have a backbone of theory on which to hang whatever they find."

It is an approach that can be called scientific—a Winnicottian theme; its absence justified his continued criticism of the Kleinians who, like Joan Riviere (his second analyst), he saw as responsible for thwarting greater scientific effort from Melanie Klein (see "The Roots of Aggression" [CW 7:1:18]). Yet—and when was there not paradox?—he is also deeply critical of the scientific stance that excludes process and interaction, as his review of Carl Ivar Sandström's *The Psychology of Childhood and Adolescence* [CW 8:2:46] demonstrates:

> The trouble, as I see it, is that psychologists feel that it is being "scientific" when involvement is missing, and nothing is dealt with that would imply conflict, let alone unconscious conflict, or hopelessness, or value. There is nothing here to join up with your feeling that your child has an inner beauty, or a potential for destruction, or an originality that might lead either to genius or to disaster. Nothing in the book links the dilemmas that are essential in the growing-up process with the dilemma of the mentally ill adult. Things that are difficult to measure are outside "psychology."

That this had been a lifelong imperative for Winnicott is clear in his description of discovering Darwin's *Origin of Species* while at school:

> At the time I did not know why it was so important to me, but I see now that the main thing was that it showed that living things could be examined scientifically, with the corollary that gaps in knowledge and understanding need not scare me. ("Towards an Objective Study of Human Nature" [CW 2:7:11])

A similar excitement permeated his discovery of Freud:

> [A]s soon as I found Freud and the method that he gave us for investigating and for treatment, I was in line with it . . . it's an objective way of looking at things and it's for people who can go to something without preconceived notions, which, in a sense, is science. ("D. W. W. on D. W. W." [CW 8:1:2])

Playing and the Cultural Self

Winnicott's preoccupation with play and playing can be traced to his very early writing. Caldwell and Joyce (2012, p. 231) remind us of Winnicott and the child playing with the spatula ("The Observation of Infants in a Set Situation" [CW 2:3:6]) and place it and the 1942 article "Why Children Play" [CW 2:4:4] as precursors to "Transitional Objects and Transitional Phenomena" [CW 4:2:21]. In this last, we have the most memorable statement about the intermediate area of experience, between internal and external, me and not-me, "the subjective object and the object objectively perceived," and which leads us to art, to religion, and to culture. (This concept of transitional objects, Anna Freud wrote to him on October 30, 1968, "has conquered the analytic world.")

The extension of this arena—the movement from transitional experiences and phenomena to play, from playing with and trust in the object to playing alone in the presence of another, to shared playing, and to cultural experience—is one that Winnicott explores several times in the late 1960s as his preparation of *Playing and Reality* progresses. In "The Concept of a Healthy Individual" [CW 8:1:4], he outlines the three lives that healthy people live:

> 1. The life in the world, with interpersonal relationships as the key even to making use of the non-human environment.
> 2. The life of the personal (sometimes called inner) psychical reality. This is where one person is richer than another, and deeper, and more interesting when creative. It includes dreams . . .
> 3. The area of cultural experience.
>
> Cultural experience starts as play, and leads on to the whole area of man's inheritance, including the arts, the myths of history, the slow march of philosophical thought and the mysteries of mathematics, and of group management and of religion . . . [I]t starts *in the potential space between a child and the mother when experience has produced in the child a high degree of confidence in the mother*, that she will not fail to be there if suddenly needed.

And, of course, psychoanalysis takes place in that overlap, in that intermediate area of experience: "psychoanalysis has been developed as a highly specialized form of playing in the service of communication with oneself and others" ("Playing: A Theoretical Statement" [CW 8:2:15]). Winnicott continues: "The natural thing is playing, and the highly sophisticated twentieth-century phenomenon is psychoanalysis. It must be of value to the analyst to be constantly reminded not only of what is owed to Freud but also of what we owe to the natural and universal thing called playing."

"Playing: A Theoretical Statement," published in the *International Journal of Psychoanalysis* in 1968 under the title "Playing: Its Theoretical Status in the Clinical

Situation," had been read to the British Psychoanalytical Society the previous year but was then entitled "Towards a Theory of Psychotherapy: The Link with Playing." This earlier designation expresses more straightforwardly the primacy in Winnicott's mind at this time of the mother–infant relationship as a paradigm for the process between analyst and patient. It is a view of the analytic process that has become second nature to the British Independents; but, imbued with the good-enough mother–infant experience as a template for analysis, Winnicott was at the end of the year to take this style of working and thinking to New York.

America, Illness, and "The Use of an Object"

Towards the end of 1968, Winnicott undertook what was to be a last speaking tour to the United States, ending with the presentation of his paper on "The Use of an Object and Relating Through Identifications" on November 12 at the New York Psychoanalytic Society and Institute.[7] The reception accorded to his talk was said by him to have been critical; the discussants were Edith Jacobson, Samuel Ritvo, and Bernard D. Fine. Both Winnicott and Clare were already suffering from Asian flu,[8] and he may have felt unwell during his presentation; on his return to their hotel room, Winnicott's dramatic symptoms of pulmonary edema had major consequences for his heart, and, gravely ill, he was rushed to hospital, where he remained for some five weeks. His letter of November 25 to Karl and Sheila Britton [CW 8:2:33] is realistic:

> The trouble is that I have had a serious heart complication, and Clare & I both have to face up to the idea of my possible death. We can both do this. You know what I mean, and we are not morbid about it. And we can so much enjoy some more years together if I get well and get home.

On December 4 [CW 8:2:37], he is reporting to Joyce Cole, his remarkable secretary:

> Have been visited by the Hartmanns, Phyllis Greenacre, Dr & Mrs Malev, The Zetzels, Dr & Mrs Bernard Fine. I am due to walk out of the room & down the passage probably tomorrow. Sorry this is all about DWW.

---

[7] "Notes Made on the Train" [CW 7:2:6] contains the beginnings of this paper.

[8] "For the record: we would have had a fine time here had it not been for this Asian flu which I got, and Clare got from me & then we both had which made us both descend to the bottom—so that even Clare couldn't look after me when my heart went wonky. This bit of bad luck made the difference" (postscript to letter of November 25 to Karl and Sheila Britton) [CW 8:2:33]. And "I realize I have not been well for a year. I am so ashamed to have been silly enough to go to USA when not really well" (letter to Professor Renata Gaddini, January 19, 1969 [CW 9:1:5]—written from his bed). This is repeated in his letter of January 20, 1969, to Anna Freud [CW 9:1:6]: "Actually I was already ill but I think this was not noticed."

He was finally discharged on December 15, and the couple flew home on December 20.

The Use of an Object

What was so contentious—or incomprehensible—for his American audience? And so important for Winnicott? One recalls his sortie to the 1952 Club almost two years before as being somehow similar: both involved Winnicott in his later years placing his theoretical position before his peers, and both left him feeling that he had failed. Rudnytsky reports that the record of the New York discussion actually shows that "the tone of the meeting was one of spirited intellectual exchange untainted by any personal rancor" (Rudnytsky 1989, p. 340). And Reeves elegantly adds a further perspective:

> He had chosen to deliver this paper at a citadel of transatlantic ego psychology, where British "object relations theorists" were mostly viewed as theoretically eccentric if not doctrinally aberrant. (Reeves, 2007, pp. 366–367)

Robert Langs put the case in more functional terms, contrasting the shock of Winnicott's transactional relationship with his patients—available for destruction and having to survive as the patient seeks to maintain psychic homeostasis—with the more traditional US analytic practice of interpreting the neurotic projections of the patient (quoted in Kahr, 1996, p. 120).

A fortnight before giving the paper, Winnicott sent a summary to the New York Psychoanalytic Society. This comprised the concluding summary of the paper (as published in 1969) plus the following addition:

> How this usage develops naturally out of play with the object is the theme of this talk.
>
> It would help in my exposition if a reading of the following papers could be taken for granted:
>
> 1. (1966) [actually 1967—eds.] The Location of Cultural Experience, *Int. J. Psa*. 48: 3, 368–372
> 2. (1962) Hogarth Press, London, 1965. Ego Integration in Child Development (Chapter 4 in: *The Maturational Processes and the Facilitating Environment*) N.Y. I.U.P.—1965, pp. 56–63
> 3. The Capacity to be Alone. *Int. J. Psa*. 39: 5, 416–20, 1958
> 4. Playing: Its Theoretical Status in the Clinical Situation. *Int. J. Psa*. V.49, 1968—still in press. [Appendix I, CW 8:2:28]

Quite a demand, then, that his audience grasp the developmental process of his formulations and be prepared to do their homework, to give preparatory time to reading the potentially heretical!

The paper begins with comments on the making of interpretations:

> If only we can wait, the patient arrives at understanding creatively and with immense joy . . . The principle is that it is the patient and only the patient who has the answers. We may or may not enable him or her to encompass what is known or become aware of it with acceptance.

This takes us back to real-making, to the process described in "Mirror-Role of Mother and Family in Child Development" [CW 8:1:38], where the task of the analyst—following the good-enough mother who holds, handles, and presents the object—is "giving back to the patient what the patient has brought." The exhortation to his American audience is to think about the process, what happens between analyst and patient, especially in work with the borderline patient. The scene is then set for his examination of the process between mother and infant, object and self, that launches the developmental leap of the infant's recognition of a separate other rather than a subjective object. The consequence is the achievement of "object usage," arrived at, he posits, through positive destructiveness and the (real) object's survival. "Object relating," Winnicott clarifies, involves a subjective experience: the object is imbued with subjective qualities and the subject imbibes aspects of the object—both are, in small and great ways, transformed. The object, to be *used*, however, has to be real, external and facilitating, able to survive aggressive attacks—and objectively perceived. Winnicott's final amendment of Kleinian—and Freudian—theory, Adam Phillips asserts, lies in his delineation of this move from object relating to object use:

> If, in Winnicott's terms, the self is first made real through recognition, the object is first made real through aggressive destruction; and this, of course, makes experience of the object feel real to the self. (Phillips, 1988, p. 131)

This mother-object must be resilient and must survive and not retaliate.

It has been suggested that Winnicott's vulnerability to criticism of "The Use of an Object" arose from his overreaching, moving from theories of pathology to attempting a general theory of human development that he knew to be partial (Reeves, 2007). Certainly his work on *Human Nature* was ongoing, and he did say to the Association of Teachers of Mathematics in April 1968:

> I feel I must get back to my last, which is quite simply the treatment of psychiatrically ill children, and the construction of a better, more accurate, and more serviceable theory of the emotional development of the individual human being. ("*Sum*, I Am" [CW 8:2:10])

I would posit, however, that "The Use of an Object" is more straightforwardly a work that focuses on process and struggles to elucidate the "how"—that is, the growth of the capacity to abrogate the omnipotent position by coming to value the real (and thence separate) object through its fantasized destruction and its actual survival. This "how" is as much the story of the analyst and patient, their process, their "how," as it is of mother, environment, and child: the lessons are for those analysts who "do," who interpret at their patients and regard analysis as something to be "done" to another rather than a process occurring in the space between.[9] *That* message is—and was—a more difficult one to hear.

The paper, Clare Winnicott states in a letter to Eigen in 1981, gives the summation of Winnicott's theoretical position:

> [F]or Donald it was the climax of his theoretical formulations . . . his final word, his resting place. (Eigen, 2012, p. 1453)

The reception in New York (and, of course, his illness) led Winnicott to revise this paper before its publication in 1969. It would be included in *Playing and Reality* in 1971. The drama and crisis of his illness in New York have caused some commentators to impart to Winnicott's revisions a sense almost of desperation that is to my mind not at all accurate. "Comments on My Paper 'The Use of an Object'" [CW 8:2:38], written in the hospital in New York some three weeks after his collapse, presents a Winnicott sure of his ground: "my new (as I believe) principle of the capacity to use an object arrived at by the subject through the experiences involving the survival of the object," he writes, although he does concede "I realise that it is this idea of a destructive first impulse that is difficult to grasp. It is this that needs attention and discussion." Less the mark of a man who feels he has got it wrong; more one seeking to explain to those arguing from drive theory alone that "the main idea incorporated in this paper necessitates a rewriting of an important area in psycho-analytic theory," that the theory of the fusion of libidinal and aggressive drives "is not only right but is also wrong. It is at the place where it is wrong that I am trying to make a contribution." This desire to clarify—but not deny—can be found in correspondence with Robert Rodman (January 10, 1969 [CW 9:1:2]) and Anna Freud (January 20, 1969 [CW 9:1:6])—but that is another year.

Concluding Thoughts on the Analytic Process and Technique

> I do adapt quite a little to individual expectations at the very beginning. It is inhuman not to do so. ("The Aims of Psycho-Analytical Treatment" [CW 6:3:2])

As we approach Winnicott's last years and last major publications, we can see 1967 and 1968 as years of consolidation and final definition: how the infant arrives at a separate sense of self and other; the achievement of the perception of reality and

---

[9] "It will be noticed that I am talking about the making of and not about interpretations as such. It appalls me to think how much deep change I have prevented or delayed in patients *in a certain classification category* by my personal need to interpret." He is, of course, talking of "the borderline case."

the object as real; delinquency as containing hope that there might be remedy for the loss of the good object, of the reliable and resilient environment, and of the creativity that the object brought; playing, culture, and psychoanalysis. Throughout his writing—letters, reviews, talks, and articles—there flow two constant undercurrents: that theory must alter if observation challenges it to do so, and that this need not scare us (to paraphrase his words on reading Darwin) but is part of the life scientific, to be greeted with curiosity; and that the task of the analyst and his analysand is akin to that of the good-enough mother and her infant.

Much of what is perceived as Winnicott's theoretical challenge to traditional technique[10] arises from his combination of work with borderline and psychotic patients and the work on understanding the emergence of infant and object as separate. Each, he writes, has informed his thinking about the other. It is a debatable point whether he is proposing a general theory of technique, as some seem to have understood it, or more an adaptation for working with psychotic elements in the patient. Yet his approach is one I find essential in work with children who are, after all, closer to the original insult. Child psychoanalysis and psychotherapy, moreover, are themselves adaptations of classical technique:

> Modifications of technique are departures from the "normal" range of techniques applicable to neurotic children. *There is no absolute psychoanalytic technique for use with children, but rather a set of analytic principles which have to be adapted to specific cases.* Variations in technique represent appropriate specific adaptations of the basic set of analytic principles rather than deviations from standard technique. (Sandler, Kennedy, & Tyson, 1980, p. 199; emphasis added)

In this discussion with Anna Freud, Sandler et al. clarify that, like Winnicott, she was clear that adaptation does not have to mean deviation or an abandonment of analytic principles and that, in child work, it becomes a matter of course.

There is, in some of the argument around Winnicott and technique, a silent assumption that there is a standard technique. Within the parameters of working ethically, with the unconscious and in the transference–countertransference relationship, there are many possible engagements between analyst and patient. It is paradoxical that what is generally construed as a talking cure in Winnicott's writing often takes as its template a relationship that is in the main nonverbal. He does not offer this for every patient but is clear that it has a very useful and understandable role with the very traumatized and psychotically anxious patient ("The Concept of Clinical Regression Compared with that of Defence Organisation" [CW 8:1:29]). His concept of "regression to dependence" offers a helpful rethinking of defenses—and his view of the innate thrust for health and development in the individual means that it is the patient who does the work of analysis and the analyst/

[10] *Vide* Blass (2012) and the subsequent correspondence in the *International Journal of Psychoanalysis.*

mother who facilitates. Today, this is second nature for the child psychotherapist trained in either the Anna Freudian or the Independent traditions. He adds:

> We now find all these matters coming along for revival and correction to the transference relationship, matters which are not so much for interpretation as for experiencing. ("The Use of an Object in the Context of *Moses and Monotheism*," 1969 [CW 9:1:3])

For some patients, at some points, "being with" (Eigen's "living through together") is interpretation enough.

Winnicott did not think that the omnipotent analyst was a creation of parody—"there are those who fear to wait and who implant," he had written in 1963 ("Morals and Education" [CW 6:3:18]). This theme continues:

> [T]here are also analysts who in their interpretative role assume a position which is almost unassailable so that if the patient attempts to make a correction the analyst tends rather to think in terms of the patient's resistance than in terms of the possibility that the communication has been wrongly or inadequately received. ("Interpretation in Psycho-analysis" [CW 8:2:6])

For Winnicott—and for us all—psychological change continued throughout life, and ending analysis lay in the hands of the patient; omnipotence—beyond earliest infancy—was to be avoided.

Some of the issues about meaning and Winnicott's approach may—as Grolnick (1990) proposes—stem from very different constructions being put upon seemingly simple words. His public lecture presents a simple paradigm:

> All we do in successful psychoanalysis is to unhitch developmental hold-ups, and to release developmental processes and the inherited tendencies of the individual patient. ("Communication Between Infant and Mother" [CW 8:2:2])

The setting in environmental terms still comprises the reliable and facilitating environment of the psychoanalytic tradition, albeit with a theoretical base that is open to examination, criticism, and change; the shift is that the setting, in terms of the analyst's attitude, reliability, adaptation, and state of mind, is a potential, transformational one created by analyst and patient and in which the patient might—like the infant—discover the surprising and the new about himself.

References

Blass, R. B. (2012). On Winnicott's clinical innovations in the analysis of adults: Introduction to a controversy. *International Journal of Psychoanalysis, 93*(6), 1439–1448.

Caldwell, L., & Joyce, A. (2012). *Reading Winnicott.* London/New York: Routledge.

Eigen, M. (2012). On Winnicott's clinical innovations in the analysis of adults. *International Journal of Psychoanalysis, 93*(6), 1449–1459.

Gaddini, R. (2004). Thinking about Winnicott and the origins of the self. *Psychoanalysis and History, 6*, 225–235.

Grolnick, S. A. (1990). *The work and play of Winnicott*. Northvale, NJ/London: Jason Aronson.

Hoffer, W. (1949). Mouth, hand, and ego-integration. *Psychoanalytic Study of the Child, 3–4*, 49–56.

Hoffer, W. (1950). Development of the body ego. *Psychoanalytic Study of the Child, 5*, 18–23.

Hood, J. (1996/2001). The young R. D. Laing: A personal memoir and some hypotheses. In R. Steiner & J. Johns (Eds.), *Within time and beyond time: A festschrift for Pearl King*. London/New York: Karnac.

Kahr, B. (1996). *D. W. Winnicott: A biographical portrait*. London: Karnac.

Phillips, A. (1988). *Winnicott*. London: Fontana [reissued by Penguin in 2007].

Reeves, C. (2007). The mantle of Freud: Was "The use of an object" Winnicott's *Todestrieb*? *British Journal of Psychotherapy, 23*(3), 365–382.

Rudnytsky, P. (1989). Winnicott and Freud. *Psychoanalytic Study of the Child, 44*, 331–350.

Rycroft, C. (1993/2004). The last word. Reminiscences of a survivor: Psychoanalysis 1937–1993. In J. Pearson (Ed.), *Analyst of the imagination: The life and work of Charles Rycroft*. London/New York: Karnac.

Sandler, J., Kennedy, H., & Tyson, R. L. (1980). *The technique of child psychoanalysis: Discussions with Anna Freud*. London: Hogarth.

Solnit, A. J. (1968). Child analysis and paediatrics: Collaborative interests. *International Journal of Psychoanalysis, 49*, 280–285.

Winnicott, C. (1972). Letter to the editor. *International Journal of Psychoanalysis, 53*, 559–560.

Winnicott, D. W. (1941). The observation of infants in a set situation. [CW 2:3:6]

Winnicott, D. W. (1942). Why children play. [CW 2:4:4]

Winnicott, D. W. (1945). Towards an objective study of human nature. [CW 2:7:11]

Winnicott, D. W. (1953). Transitional objects and transitional phenomena. [CW 4:2:21]

Winnicott, D. W. (1954). Mind and its relation to the psyche-soma [1949]. [CW 3:4:20]

Winnicott, D. W. (1958). The antisocial tendency [1956]. [CW 5:2:8]

Winnicott, D. W. (1958). The capacity to be alone [1957]. [CW 5:3:20]

Winnicott, D. W. (1963). Morals and education [1962]. [CW 6:3:18]

Winnicott, D. W. (1964). Roots of aggression. [CW 7:1:18]

Winnicott, D. W. (1965). The aims of psycho-analytical treatment [1962]. [CW 6:3:2]

Winnicott, D. W. (1965). Ego integration in child development [1962]. [CW 6:3:19]

Winnicott, D. W. (1965). *The family and individual development*. London: Tavistock, 1965. [Not reprinted in this form in the *Collected Works*]

Winnicott, D. W. (1967). The location of cultural experience [1966]. [CW 7:3:31]

Winnicott, D. W. (1967). Mirror-role of mother and family in child development. [CW 8:1:38]

Winnicott, D. W. (1967). A tribute on the occasion of Willi Hoffer's seventieth birthday. [CW 8:1:11]

Winnicott, D. W. (1968). Communication between infant and mother, and mother and infant, compared and contrasted. [CW 8:2:2]

Winnicott, D. W. (1968). The concept of clinical regression compared with that of defence organization [1967]. [CW 8:1:29]

Winnicott, D. W. (1968). Delinquency as a sign of hope [1967]. [CW 8:1:8]

Winnicott, D. W. (1968). Foreword. In R. J. N. Tod (Ed.), *Disturbed children*. London: Longman. [CW 8:2:8]

Winnicott, D. W. (1968). Playing: A theoretical statement [1967]. [CW 8:2:15]

Winnicott, D. W. (1968). Playing: Its theoretical status in the clinical situation. Published here as "Playing: A theoretical statement." [CW 8:2:15]

Winnicott, D. W. (1968). Review: Sandström, C. I., *The psychology of childhood and adolescence*. Harmondsworth, UK: Penguin. [CW 8:2:46]

Winnicott, D. W. (1969). Notes made on the train [1956]. [CW 7:2:6]

Winnicott, D. W. (1969). The use of an object and relating through identifications [1968]. [CW 8:2:28]

Winnicott, D. W. (1971). The concept of a healthy individual [1967]. [CW 8:1:4]

Winnicott, D. W. (1971). *Playing and reality*. London: Tavistock. [Not reprinted in this form in the *Collected Works*]

Winnicott, D. W. (1971). "Iiro" *aet* 9 years 9 months. [CW 10:1:1]

Winnicott, D. W. (1984). *Sum*, I am [1968]. [CW 8:2:10]

Winnicott, D. W. (1988). *Human Nature*. [CW 11:1]

Winnicott, D. W. (1989). Comments on my paper "The use of an object" [1968]. [CW 8:2:38]

Winnicott, D. W. (1989). D. W. W. on D. W. W. [1967]. [CW 8:1:2]

Winnicott, D. W. (1989). Interpretation in psycho-analysis [1968]. [CW 8:2:6]

Winnicott, D. W. (1989). Thinking and symbol-formation [1968]. [CW 8:2:48]

Winnicott, D. W. (1989). The squiggle game [1964, 1968]. [CW 8:2:47]

FIGURE 9.1 *Winnicott listening to the American psychiatrist and psychoanalyst Ralph R. Greenson (with cigar), probably during Greenson's visit to London in the autumn of 1969.*

The Donald Woods Winnicott Archive, in the care of the Wellcome Library, London, courtesy of the Winnicott Trust.

FIGURE 9.2 *Winnicott at McLean Hospital, in Boston, with Maurice Vanderpol in 1967. The inscription reads, "In fond remembrance, Maurice Vanderpol." Vanderpol co-edited Psychotherapy in the Designed Therapeutic Milieu (1967), in which Winnicott published "The Concept of Clinical Regression Compared with that of Defence Organization" [CW 8:1:29].*

The Donald Woods Winnicott Archive, in the care of the Wellcome Library, London, courtesy of the Winnicott Trust.

{10}

Being, Creativity, and Potential Space, 1969–1971

Arne Jemstedt

In November 1968, Winnicott was invited to the New York Psychoanalytic Society, where he presented "The Use of an Object and Relating Through Identifications" [CW 8:2:28]. Although it turned out to be one of his most important and complex papers, it was not well received by his American ego psychology colleagues; they had difficulties understanding his use of the word "use" and his emphasis on destructiveness (and the object's survival of it) in the individual's discovery of an external reality outside the sphere of the subject's omnipotence.

During his visit, Winnicott fell ill with flu, which strained his heart and led to a precarious condition and a month in the intensive care unit at a New York hospital. He returned to London in December, and, after a short period of convalescence, he was again—despite his fragility—thinking, communicating, and writing. He had two more years to live; he died on January 25, 1971, in his and Clare's home. His incessant creativity and productivity during these last two years were extraordinary. Volume 9 of *The Collected Works of D. W. Winnicott* comprises his final and very valuable contributions to psychoanalysis.

The texts included in Volume 9 cover different areas, but the main theme is creativity and creative living, and this is the focus of this essay, which will survey various tracks in Winnicott's development of his ideas in this area.

Winnicott himself was exceptionally creative and one of the most original thinkers in the history of psychoanalysis since Freud. His influence continues to be powerful more than forty years after his death, as can be seen by a quick look at the PEP Psychoanalytic Literature Search: the three most read journal articles today are written by Winnicott.

What is it about Winnicott's texts that so attracts the minds of his readers? When I first came across his writings in the late 1970s, I was struck by the *living* quality in his way of writing. There was a peculiar mixture of depth, density, and lightness. Not all psychoanalytic writers have a personal style of their own. Winnicott possessed it to a high degree; you can feel his presence and his intelligence in the text.

He had both a light and distinct hand and a special ability to use ordinary words to say extraordinary things (Winnicott's writing style is discussed in the first essay of this collection).

Winnicott—who was always very much himself—insisted on the uniqueness of each individual and the right to discover, and the importance of discovering, the world in a personal, creative way. This of course also applies to psychoanalysts and to psychoanalytic theory. In a paper given to the British Psychoanalytical Society in 1948, he asks, "has due recognition been given to the need for everything to be discovered afresh by every individual analyst?" ("Reparation in Respect of Mother's Organized Defence Against Depression" [CW 3:3:1]). And in a letter to Melanie Klein in 1952, after a meeting in the Society, he points to the risk that her important work will be locked up in a dogmatic and propagandistic system: "I personally think that it is very important that your work should be restated by people discovering in their own way and presenting what they discover in their own language. It is only in this way that the language will be kept alive" [CW 4:1:12].

In his writings, Winnicott's ambition is not to teach or instruct the reader. He communicates, and you feel yourself involved in a creative and intelligent exchange that reaches and resonates in different levels of the mind, similar to the way good poetry operates. He often gives an experience of having previously known or sensed what he is expressing but of not having thought or formulated it, and yet, simultaneously, his writing gives a feeling of surprise and discovery.

One basis for this experience is Winnicott's tolerance of paradoxes, which implies an appreciation of unconscious thinking and of dream-life. A central theme in *Playing and Reality* is the paradoxical quality of the infant's transitional object: it is both created by the infant and found; its qualities come both from the inner and the outer world. In his Introduction to *Playing and Reality* [CW 9:3:4]), he writes: "I am drawing attention to the *paradox* involved in the use by the infant of what I have called the transitional object. My contribution is to ask for a paradox to be accepted and tolerated and respected, and for it not to be resolved. By flight to split-off intellectual functioning it is possible to resolve the paradox, but the price of this is the loss of the value of the paradox itself."

There is a risk that some of Winnicott's concepts ("the ordinary devoted mother," "true self") might be used in sentimental projects. Winnicott was no supporter of sentimentality. He warns against "militant sentimentalists" and states that "sentimentality is worse than useless" (letter to Scott, 1950 [CW 3:5:6]) since it "contains a denial of hate" ("Hate in the Countertransference" [CW 3:2:1] and aggression. Aggression and destructiveness are themes that run through Winnicott's writing: in his description of the ruthlessness of the primitive love impulse, in his version of Klein's depressive position, and not least in "The Use of an Object" [CW 8:2:28], where destructiveness (and the object's survival of it) creates reality.

The Creativity of Everyday Life

In "Creativity and Its Origins" [CW 9:3:7], Winnicott states: "The creativity that concerns me here is a universal. It belongs to being alive . . . The creativity that we are studying belongs to the approach of the individual to external reality." In a draft for a talk in 1970 with the title "Living Creatively," he writes: "I believe there is nothing that has to be done that cannot be done creatively, if the person is creative or has that capacity" [CW 9:2:11]. The prerequisite for this capacity is access to what he called *potential space*, the intermediate area between inner and outer reality where these two realities fertilize each other, and the question of what comes from outside and what comes from inside is kept suspended.

Not everybody has this capacity. It is—according to Winnicott—achieved through subtle processes in the infant's and child's interaction with his or her environment. But if it is there, the individual has the ability to *experience* the world creatively, be it a landscape, a theatrical or musical performance, a poem, or another individual. Attending a theatrical play is an obvious example. In the potential space between the actors on the stage and the audience, the drama of the performance and the conscious and unconscious inner worlds of the spectators overlap, engendering, if it is a good play, rich emotional experiences.

Marion Milner, who influenced Winnicott and was influenced by him, wrote extensively on psychoanalysis and art. She underlined the blurring of the boundaries between inner and outer reality in creative experiencing and borrowed a description of the "aesthetic moment" from Berenson: "In visual art the aesthetic moment is that fleeting instant, so brief as to be almost timeless, when the spectator is at one with the work of art he is looking at" (quoted in Milner, 1952, p. 97).

Reflecting on the relation between the novelist and his or her reader, Salman Rushdie (1990) formulates this interplay thus: "What is forged, in the secret act of reading, is a different kind of identity, as the reader and writer merge, through the medium of the text, to become a collective being that both writes as it reads and reads as it writes, and creates, jointly, that unique work, 'their' novel. This 'secret identity' of writer and reader is the novel form's greatest and most subversive gift."

The potential space is a third area between inner and outer, but the capacity for the kind of experiencing that belongs to it is, of course, an inner resource. There is a similarity between Winnicott's descriptions of the potential space and Wilfred Bion's (1962) term *binocular experiencing*. Bion describes the boundary between the conscious and the unconscious as a semipermeable *contact barrier* that both separates these two domains from each other and allows for a flow between them. This makes it possible to experience a situation (or a relation) simultaneously on both a conscious and an unconscious level. There is a cooperative, nonintrusive relationship between the two domains; the experience is lived through consciously and, at the same time, dreamt, giving a "stereoscopic" perspective to it. This gives depth and resonance to the experience. An analogous quality colors the experience in the potential space.

The *activity*, simple or sophisticated, that pertains to the potential space is profoundly personal. It comes from inside, sometimes from deep inside, and is spontaneous and active, not reactive. Its encounters with objects in the external reality, consciously or more intuitively chosen or found, have a quality of vital creativity, be it "a picture or a house or a garden . . . or a symphony or a sculpture" ("Creativity and Its Origins" [CW 9:3:7]). Creative *doing* takes up time and space. Creativity takes time and is dependent on the capacity to immerse oneself in a task or project, to concentrate on it, and to create in the potential space between one's imaginations and the integrity of the object or medium in one's hands.

The main focus for Winnicott is the capacity to live and experience creatively. But the same internal processes also form the basis for artistic creativity, only that the poet, the painter, the composer, and the scientist are more creatively gifted than the rest of us. They have a remarkably sensitive inner ear for conscious and unconscious associations and links and a unique capacity to transform them into artistic or scientific forms or inventions.

At the basis of this is a free-floating sensitivity to unconscious processes and perceptions—what Ehrenzweig (1967) calls "unconscious scanning." When Marion Milner poses the question "What is art?" she replies: "Can we say that it is to do with the capacity of the conscious mind to have the experience of co-operating with the unconscious depths, by means of the battle to express something with the chosen medium?" (1987, p. 215).

The source of this artistic gift will, as Freud stated in his works on Leonardo da Vinci and Dostoyevsky, remain obscure, and Winnicott, when discussing creative arts, agrees: "It is not of course that anyone will ever be able to explain the creative impulse" ("Creativity and Its Origins" [CW 9:3:7]).

Freud and Melanie Klein (and others) wrote about authors' and artists' creations, analyzing their content from a psychoanalytic perspective, discussing them in relation to the history of the artist's life. Winnicott did not do that; his focus was not on the artistic creation but on the processes behind the creation, the creative process in itself. He saw artistic creativity as a special and sophisticated version of a general human capacity for creative accomplishments and creative living.

A Creative Illusion

Before Winnicott went to New York in November 1968, Anna Freud wrote to him: "I think that your transitional object has conquered the analytic world" (Rodman, 2003, p. 323). Winnicott's theories on transitional phenomena and potential space were innovative then and now and have initiated tremendous amounts of thought, articles, and books both in and beyond the psychoanalytic world. Less thought has been given to his concept of the *subjective object*. Yet the subjective object precedes the transitional object and is a prerequisite for it. It belongs to the experiential area of the earliest phase of the infant's life and is linked to the experience of a *creative illusion* and a *benign omnipotence*.

Winnicott formulates his ideas on this subject for the first time in "Primitive Emotional Development" [CW 2:7:8]:

> I will try to describe in the simplest possible terms this phenomenon as I see it. In terms of baby and mother's breast . . . the baby has instinctual urges and predatory ideas. The mother has a breast and the power to produce milk, and the idea that she would like to be attacked by a hungry baby. These two phenomena do not come into relation with each other till the mother and the child *live an experience together*. . . . I think of the process as if two lines came from opposite directions, liable to come near each other. If they overlap there is a moment of *illusion* . . .

The mother allows the infant the illusion that the infant creates the breast that it finds. The term *illusion* generally has, also in psychoanalysis ever since Freud, negative associations: if not a delusion, it is viewed as a misperception, a piece of wishful thinking, or an illusory belief that should somehow be corrected and abandoned and maybe mourned. At the stage of the beginnings of life, Winnicott gives it a deeply positive meaning. Provided that the mother's adaptation is good enough—that is, if she presents herself in a manner and at a moment that "corresponds to the infant's capacity to create" ("Transitional Objects and Transitional Phenomena" [CW 9:3:5]—the infant not only creates the breast (which is thus a subjective object as conceived of by the infant) but creates the world.

Without this illusion, Winnicott writes in "Psychoses and Child Care," "no contact is possible between the psyche and the environment" [CW 4:1:5]. This sentence is extremely important: the experience of omnipotence is the foundation for a personal, creative relation to the world. The alternative is a reactive relation to it, one based on adaptation, where the personal impulse is absent and the vitality is lost, a relation to the world from a *false self* position. Disillusionment with loss of omnipotence and the entrance of the reality principle will follow (see below), but without this primary illusion disillusion loses its meaning.

It should be noted that there is a dual-track quality to Winnicott's theory of this early phase of life. The infant alternates between states or experiences of omnipotence, of relating to subjective objects, and states of a dawning sense of something that is not-me, especially through the experience of aggression met by resistance. "In this respect," writes Winnicott, "the baby can meet the reality principle here and there, now and then, but not everywhere all at once; that is, the baby retains areas of subjective objects along with other areas in which there is some relating to objectively perceived objects, or 'not-me' ('non-I') objects" ("Ego Integration in Child Development" [CW 6:3:19]). The infant oscillates between these two states, but the important thing is that the infant is given opportunities for the illusion of creating the object.

The Fate of the Subjective Object

In *Human Nature* Winnicott writes: "It is very important theoretically that the infant *creates* [the] object" [CW 11:4:1]. The word *theoretically* is important here. Crucial aspects of Winnicott's theories have at their base this primary creative illusion, the infant's experience of relating to subjective objects. It is possible to follow the development and vicissitudes of this kind of experiencing and to chart the fate of the subjective object. Three interrelated tracks are discernible in Winnicott's thinking:

the theory of transitional objects, intermediate area, and potential space;
the shift from relating to objects to the use of objects resulting in the discovery of external reality; and
the incommunicado center at the core of the individual where there is a silent communication with subjective objects.

"The intermediate area to which I am referring," writes Winnicott, "is the area that is allowed to the infant between primary creativity and objective perception based on reality-testing" [CW 9:3:5]. It is here that the infant intuitively selects and cathects the transitional object, with its paradoxical qualities arising both from creative illusion and from outer reality. The *potential space* is the result of a subtly increased distance between infant and mother, with experiences of separateness and the beginnings of disillusionment. One of several functions of the transitional object is to "make it possible for the individual to cope with the immense shock of loss of omnipotence."

For Winnicott, the use of the transitional object marks the beginnings of a symbolizing capacity. The child oscillates between the transitional object and the mother. The dialectics between the child, the transitional object, and the mother or between the subject, the symbol, and what it symbolizes creates inner, mental space and is a prerequisite for meaningful symbolizing processes.

The capacity to use symbols is dependent on a tolerance of distance, on the capacity to maintain a differentiation between the symbol and the symbolized, while, at the same time, a connection between them must be preserved or else the symbol loses its meaning. It is in this field of tension that the processes belonging to transitional phenomena operate, and it is from this that the capacity to play emerges and eventually the capacity to live and experience creatively.

The maintenance of the triangular space between infant, mother, and transitional object is dependent on the infant's confidence and trust in its relation to the mother or mother-figure. If the dialectic that belongs to this potential space collapses—for example, through a breakdown of the reliable relation to the mother—the vital quality of the transitional object is lost and the development of the capacity to symbolize is hampered and, with it, the capacity to play. What might happen in such an instance is that the transitional object is transformed into a fetish with a rigid quality and to which the infant defensively and obsessively clings in order to ward off catastrophic anxieties of abandonment and separation.

"The immense shock of loss of omnipotence" is pertinent also to "The Use of an Object" [CW 8:2:28]. The main idea in this profound and complex article is that the object is destroyed at the moment when it is experienced not as subjective, but as external, as objectively perceived, when it is experienced as something outside the realm of omnipotence. If the object—the real object out there—survives the destruction (and survival includes remaining intact and not retaliating), then there is a fresh discovery of the object as independent, outside the area of the subject's omnipotence, something in its own right, "not a bundle of projections."

This is the reality principle at work. It makes it possible for the infant to use and interact with real objects in the outside world and to "gain immeasurably" from it. The usual perspective on the relation between the reality principle and destruction is that the reality principle implies frustration, which evokes aggression. Winnicott turns this relation the other way around: destruction creates reality through the object's survival of the destruction. There is joy—not guilt or manic denial[1]—in the discovery of the object as real and possessing an integrity of its own and simultaneously, and this "is the price [that] has to be paid": there is a continuous destruction of the object in unconscious fantasy.

As I understand it, the end of the last sentence is related to what Winnicott describes in his extremely rich and thought-provoking paper "Communicating and Not Communicating Leading to a Study of Certain Opposites" [CW 6:4:8]. In the inner world, at the core of the personality, there is a silent communication, one that Winnicott describes as "direct" with subjective phenomena, which is "forever immune from the reality principle." "This core never communicates with the [outer] world, and the individual knows that it must never be communicated with or influenced by external reality." This is a "sacred area" that feels real and is "absolutely personal" and which must never be exploited. It is an aspect of health and "belongs to being alive." The access to this inner, non-communicating area lies hidden in the individual's capacity to be alone. It is from this fundamental aloneness that "communication naturally arises," both the kind of communication that belongs to the potential space and the communication with objectively perceived external objects, a communication that is "*explicit*, indirect and pleasurable" and "involves extremely interesting techniques, including that of language."

Winnicott's thoughts about the silent inner communication at the center of the personality have caused worries and misunderstandings among analysts, also among those who know his theories well. The thought of a center of the individual

---

[1] The survival of the object is also essential in Winnicott's version of the depressive position but from a different aspect. It is here related to the infant's development from ruthlessness to concern and to depressive anxieties about having damaged the object. The crucial element here is the object's survival of the infant's ruthlessness and *survival over time* to receive the infant's reparative gesture arising from budding guilt feelings.

that does not relate to the external world seems difficult to tolerate. Attempts have been made to explain the non-communicating part in relational terms, as a split-off part of the personality due, for instance, to a breakdown of the communication with significant objects or as a result of some other kind of trauma. This is to misunderstand Winnicott's profound thought. Tomas Tranströmer, the Swedish poet and Nobel Prize winner, understands what Winnicott is talking about and formulates it well in *The Truth Barrier* (1978; 1984, p. 27): "We become stronger through one another, but also through . . . that within us which the other can not see. Which meets only itself. The innermost paradox, the garage flower, the ventilator to the good darkness. A drink that bubbles in empty glasses . . . A pathway that grows over again behind each step. A book that can be read only in the dark."

Intrusion into this central core of the personality is for Winnicott the utmost trauma. It elicits unthinkable anxiety and protective, primitive defenses against this threat that lead to a rigid isolation of the center of the self.

The two aspects of the vicissitudes of subjective objects and phenomena that belong to object usage and to the silent core of the personality are both essential in maintaining the potential space. For Winnicott, the individual will gain immeasurably from the contributions of a world that is experienced as truly outside and that can be used for creative activities. Furthermore, the acceptance and appreciation of the externality of the outside world is essential for sustaining the overlapping balance between inner and outer reality that characterizes the potential space. If the relation to the outside world is too brittle, the inner world will collapse into reality, the distinction between symbol and symbolized will be lost, fantasies become facts, and madness threatens.[2] In the early paper from 1945 that I referred to in the beginning of this essay ("Primitive Emotional Development" [CW 2:7:8]), Winnicott makes the important proviso that "in fantasy things work by magic: there are no brakes on fantasy, and love and hate cause alarming effects. External reality has brakes on it . . . and, in fact, fantasy is only tolerable at full blast when the objective reality is appreciated well."

Inherent in the access to the "absolutely personal" silent core at the center of the personality is a connection with deep unconscious processes and thus with the creativity of dream-life and the free flow of primary processes where condensations and displacements constantly produce new internal scenarios. Winnicott writes about "the deep dreaming that is at the core of the personality" ("The Place Where We Live" [CW 8:2:1]); access to the potential space implies a contact with dreams and dreaming. "In playing," Winnicott writes, "the child manipulates external phenomena in the service of the dream and invests chosen external phenomena with dream meaning and feeling" ("Playing: A Theoretical Statement," 1968 [CW 8:2:15]). And in "Playing and Culture" [CW 8:2:9], he writes definitively:

---

[2] In Bion's terminology, this corresponds to a collapse of the contact barrier leading to an overflow of unconscious elements into the conscious mind and a breakdown of binocular experiencing.

> Undoubtedly the concept of the transitional object and of transitional phenomena brought me to my wish to study this intermediate area which has to do with living experience and which is neither dream- nor object-relating. At the same time that it is neither the one nor the other of these two it is also both. This is the essential paradox, and in my paper on transitional phenomena the most important part (in my opinion) is my claim that we need to *accept the paradox*, not to resolve it.

Drives and Creativity

For both Freud and Klein, drives are the basic source for creativity. In "Creative Writers and Day-dreaming" (1908a), Freud rather simplistically juxtaposes the fantasies of daydreaming and creative writing. Both have as their source unsatisfied wishes of an erotic or ambitious nature, only that the creative writer has a special gift in molding these fantasies into literary and poetic form that evokes aesthetic and pleasurable experiences in the reader. Freud does not bring up his concept of "sublimation" in this article, although he had introduced it already a couple of years before in "Three Essays on the Theory of Sexuality." The process of sublimation is Freud's principal theoretical tool in understanding artistic creativity, and, even though he never elaborated this concept very much, it still has an evocative quality to it that is less obvious in his article from 1908. The sexual drive, Freud writes, is endowed with a "marked characteristic of being able to displace its aim without materially diminishing its intensity. This capacity to exchange its originally sexual aim for another one, which is no longer sexual but which is psychically related to the first aim, is called the capacity for *sublimation*" (1908b, p. 187). Freud sees this variable feature of the sexual drive being transferred to nonsexual aims and objects as the basis for all cultural achievements, be it artistic, scientific, or otherwise. The artist (and the scientist) is endowed with a highly developed capacity for sublimation that combines with his or her artistic talent.

Winnicott discusses the subject of sublimation in several instances. In "The Location of Cultural Experience" [CW 7:3:31], he quotes himself from a speech at the celebration of the completion of the *Standard Edition* of Freud's work in 1966 [CW 7:3:23]: "Freud used his word 'sublimation' to point the way to a place where cultural experience is meaningful, but perhaps he did not get so far as to tell us where in the mind the cultural experience is." Regarding playing, he states that "playing needs to be studied as a subject on its own, supplementary to the concept of the sublimation of instinct" ("Playing: A Theoretical Statement" [CW 8:2:15]).

Winnicott never lost sight of the importance of drives, both libidinal and aggressive. But early on—and in this he added something new and very important to psychoanalytic theory—he emphasized those aspects of experiencing and relating to objects that are not driven by instincts and for which he used terms like *ego-needs, ego-coverage*, and *ego-relatedness*. These terms capture the subtle details in the physical and psychical relation between the infant and the mother, not least the mother's intuitive sensitivity to the infant's inner state. Winnicott calls this heightened sensitivity the primary maternal preoccupation of the "ordinary devoted mother" during the earliest phases of the infant's life.

In "Ego Distortion in Terms of True and False Self," Winnicott writes:

> It must be emphasized that in referring to the meeting of infant needs I am not referring to the satisfaction of instincts. In the area that I am examining the instincts are not yet clearly defined as internal to the infant. The instincts can be as much external as can a clap of thunder or a hit. The infant's ego is building up strength and in consequence is getting towards a state in which id-demands will be felt as part of the self, and not as environmental. [CW 6:1:22]

This building up of the infant's ego is fundamentally dependent on the mother's sensitive adaptation to the infant and her capacity to identify with her infant and to meet the infant's needs. The infant will gradually build up an internal world of imaginative elaborations of the experiences in interaction with the mother.

With time, these early imaginative elaborations will become more and more sophisticated and color the infant's relation to his or her transitional object and its extension into playing and later into the field of creative living and experiences. The richness or poorness in this area of living will rest on the qualities of the early interplay between infant and mother or mother-figure.

Coming back to the question of the relation between drives and playing, Winnicott reminds us: "Playing is inherently exciting and precarious. This characteristic derives *not* from instinctual arousal but from the precariousness that belongs to the interplay in the child's mind of that which is subjective (near-hallucination) and that which is objectively perceived (actual, or shared reality)" [CW 8:2:15].

In a sense, if one understands the libidinal drive as a primary life force, Winnicott's theories on creativity are closer to Freud than they are to Klein. In the Kleinian tradition (e.g., Segal, 1991), the source of creativity is to be found in processes inherent in the depressive position, where the infant's dawning experience of the mother as a separate, whole object gives rise to intense depressive anxieties of having damaged and lost her as a result of the infant's destructive attacks upon her and concomitant strong guilt feelings leading to an urge to repair and restore. The deep source of creativity is, in a Kleinian perspective, understood as the impulse to *re-create* an object that has been destroyed and lost by destructive impulses, at the root of which is the work of the death instinct. The aim of the creative impulse is thus to overcome the effects of destructiveness, to repair and restore.

Thus, Klein's and Winnicott's views on creativity and its origins differ considerably. Creative processes are complex and multilayered, and reparative and constructive impulses can of course color them to a greater or lesser extent, but to Winnicott the *creative spark* has an earlier and deeper source, that of the primary creative impulse and the environment's readiness to provide opportunities for its realization.

Being and Doing

In February 1966, Winnicott gave a paper at the British Psychoanalytical Society entitled "The Split-Off Male and Female Elements to Be Found in Men and Women" [CW 7:3:2]. He later included it as a subsection to "Creativity and Its Origins" [CW 9:3:7]. It can be seen as his final contribution to the issues of the subjective object and of object-relating driven or not driven by instinct. It is a complex and difficult paper. The clinical background is the analysis of a man with a split-off female element. What he discusses in the paper is not "men" and "women" but what he calls the male and female elements in both men and women. In a footnote, he excuses himself for this terminology, which had confused the discussants of his paper, but states that he has found no other suitable terms. In his "Answers to Comments" [CW 9:1:30], he says that:

> the terms "active" and "passive" are not valid in this area. Active and passive are two facets of the same thing in terms of . . . [a] consideration which goes deeper and which is more primitive. In an attempt to formulate this I found myself in the position of comparing *being* and *doing* . . . [T]he basis . . . was the separating out of the whole idea of boys and girls and men and women from *two basic principles*, those which I call male and female elements. [Emphasis added to last line]

There is an echo here of Freud's theory of the bisexuality of each individual, man and woman, and maybe also of Jung's theories on anima/animus.

The "pure female element," Winnicott writes, "relates to the breast (or to the mother) in the sense of *the baby becoming the breast (or mother), in the sense that the object is the subject.* I can see no instinct drive in this . . . *no sense of self emerges except on the basis of this relating in the sense of BEING* . . . [t]he pure female element establishes what is perhaps the simplest of all experiences, the experience of *being*" ("Creativity and Its Origins" [CW 9:3:7]). This experience presupposes a very subtle adaptation on the mother's part to give the infant the opportunity of the illusion that there is no differentiation between breast and infant; that is, the breast is a subjective object.

By contrast, the "pure male element" (in both boys and girls) is the basis of object-relating backed by instinct and drive with id-satisfaction and frustration, and it presupposes and enhances a separateness between subject and object. With it follows more complex inner processes and psychic mechanisms. The male element is related to *doing* (and passively being done to).

What Winnicott delineates is a theoretical beginning. Very soon, the male and female elements get mixed up, but what is important is that being must precede doing. At the end of the paper, he states: "After being—doing and being done to. But first, being."

What Winnicott describes here is a development and reformulation in terms of male and female elements of processes that continually have been in his focus: the early, protected going-on-being as the basis for a sense of self, the infant's ego-relatedness to the environment mother and id-relationship to the object mother and the feebleness of the infant's ego, which needs the ego coverage from the mother to have id-experiences that are felt as belonging to the infant and not as traumatic impingements. With the mother's ego support, instinctual experiences strengthen the ego; without it, they disrupt the ego ("Primary Maternal Preoccupation" [CW 5:2:16]). So, already here: ego before id, being before doing.

Winnicott's thoughts on female/male elements and being/doing go deep—beyond the issues of gender identity and gender roles—but he never elaborated his ideas except for the short "Answers to Comments" mentioned earlier. It is, however, no coincidence that Winnicott added his paper on male and female elements to "Creativity and Its Origins." At the basis of creative experiencing and creative pursuit and work is the relation to subjective objects and subjective phenomena at the central, inner core of the personality, which Winnicott here relates to "being," and, from this, creative "doing" may be accomplished in the transitional area between inner and outer reality.

Epilogue

In the summer of 1971, the Twenty-Seventh International Psychoanalytical Association Congress was to be held in Vienna, and Winnicott was due to present a paper there. The unfinished notes for the preparation of this paper from early 1971 are included in Volume 9 ("Clinical Material: Notes for Vienna Congress" [CW 9:3:12]). Winnicott was never to attend the Congress; he died on January 25.

He begins his notes with the words "I am asking for a kind of revolution in our work," and, after giving a short sketch of an analysis from several years before which somehow seems to have been in the back of his mind and brought him to write "The Use of an Object," he says about that paper that "it takes me as far as I can get." He continues: "its new feature is that it recognises the survival of the object—i.e. the world's separate existence—as a vital fact in personal emotional growth. It involves the theory of the beginning of fantasy"; that is, fantasy now being separated from the external world, which is a prerequisite of the later acquirement of a potential space.

He also briefly mentions the analytic experience with the man with a split-off female element, which is the clinical background for his paper "Split-Off Male and Female Elements," ending one of his comments on this paper by describing "the ladder (male and female elements) by which I climbed to the place where I experienced this vision."

It is remarkable and moving to see how Winnicott, up to the very end of his life and despite his physical fragility, tirelessly endeavored, led by his intelligent intuition and his experience, to search deeper and deeper into the complexities of the human psyche and into the foundation for and the obstacles to creative living.

References

Bion, W. R. (1962). *Learning from experience* In W. R. Bion, *Seven servants.* New York: Aronson, 1977.

Ehrenzweig, A. (1967). *The hidden order of art.* Los Angeles: University of California Press.

Freud, S. (1908a). Creative writers and day-dreaming. *Standard edition,* 9. London: Hogarth.

Freud, S. (1908b). "Civilized" sexual morality and modern nervous illness. *Standard edition,* 9. London: Hogarth.

Milner, M. (1952). Aspects of symbolism in comprehension of the not-self. *International Journal of Psychoanalysis,* 33, 181–194.

Milner, M. (1987). *The suppressed madness of sane men: Forty-four years of exploring psychoanalysis.* London/New York: Tavistock.

Rodman, F. R. (2003). *Winnicott: Life and work.* Cambridge, MA: Perseus.

Rushdie, S. (1990). *Is nothing sacred?* Herbert Read Memorial Lecture. New York: Granta Books.

Segal, H. (1991). *Dream, phantasy and art.* London/New York: Routledge.

Tranströmer, T. (1978). *The truth barrier.* London: Oasis, trans. 1984.

Winnicott, D. W. (1945). Primitive emotional development. [CW 2:7:8]

Winnicott. D. W. (1949). Hate in the countertransference [1947]. [CW 3:2:1]

Winnicott, D. W. (1953). Psychoses and child care [1952]. [CW 4:1:5]

Winnicott, D. W. (1953). Transitional objects and transitional phenomena [2017]. [CW 3:6:6]

Winnicott, D. W. (1958). Primary maternal preoccupation [1956]. [CW 5:2:16]

Winnicott, D. W. (1958). Reparation in respect of mother's organized defence against depression [1948]. [CW 3:3:1]

Winnicott, D. W. (1965). Communicating and not communicating leading to study of certain opposites [1963]. [CW 6:4:8]

Winnicott, D. W. (1965). Ego distortion in terms of true and false self [1960]. [CW 6:1:22]

Winnicott, D. W. (1965). Ego integration in child development [1962]. [CW 6:3:19]

Winnicott, D. W. (1967). The location of cultural experience [1966]. [CW 7:3:31]

Winnicott, D. W. (1968). Playing: A theoretical statement [1967]. [CW 8:2:15]

Winnicott, D. W. (1969). The use of an object and relating through identifications [1968]. [CW 8:2:28]

Winnicott, D. W. (1971). Creativity and its origins. [CW 9:3:7]

Winnicott, D. W. (1971). Introduction to *Playing and reality.* [CW 9:3:4]

Winnicott, D. W. (1971). The place where we live. [CW 8:2:1]

Winnicott, D. W. (1971). Transitional objects and transitional phenomena. [CW 9:3:5]

Winnicott, D. W. (1972) Answers to comments on "The split-off male and female elements to be found in men and women" [1968–1969]. [CW 9:1:30]
Winnicott, D. W. (1986). Living creatively [1970]. [CW 9:2:11]
Winnicott, D. W. (1988). *Human nature*. [CW 11:1]
Winnicott, D. W. (1989). Playing and culture [1968]. [CW 8:2:9]
Winnicott, D. W. (2013). Clinical material: Notes for Vienna Congress [1971]. [CW 9:3:12]
Winnicott, D. W. (2017). On the occasion of the publication of the *Standard edition* of Freud [1966]. [CW 7:3:23]

FIGURE 10.1 *Studio of Oscar Nemon, St James' Palace. Clare reported to F. R. Rodman (2003, p. 360) that Winnicott used to enjoy spending time in Nemon's studio on Saturday mornings, playing with clay.*

The Donald Woods Winnicott Archive, in the care of the Wellcome Library, London, courtesy of the Winnicott Trust.

FIGURE 10.2 *Oscar Nemon's studio with Nemon and his statue of Freud that Winnicott had gone to great lengths to have cast. The statue was unveiled on October 2, 1970.*

The Donald Woods Winnicott Archive, in the care of the Wellcome Library, London, courtesy of the Winnicott Trust.

FIGURE 10.3 *The Donald Woods Winnicott Archive, in the care of the Wellcome Library, London, courtesy of the Winnicott Trust.*

{11}

Expectation and Offer

THE CHALLENGE OF COMMUNICATION IN WINNICOTT'S *THERAPEUTIC CONSULTATIONS*

Marco Armellini

The first embryonic project of a volume collecting therapeutic (diagnostic) consultations with children and adolescents can be traced to some notes on the "squiggle game" written in 1964 and published in 1989 in *Psychoanalytic Explorations* ("The Squiggle Game" [CW 8:2:47]). The work contained in Volume 10 was completed in the last two years of Winnicott's life, paralleling the somewhat frantic, relentless editorial work done on the drafts of *Playing and Reality* by Winnicott and Masud Khan. After the illness he suffered in November 1968 in New York, a strong awareness of the severity of his ill health and of impending death seemed to urge the fulfilment of both older and more recent projects, selecting those he regarded as most important and sacrificing others. *Playing and Reality, Therapeutic Consultations in Child Psychiatry*, and *The Piggle* are the three volumes that, though published after his death, were completed personally and made ready for publication by Winnicott himself in the twenty-six months separating the severe illness of November 1968 from his death in January 1971. A fourth project, his autobiography (*Not Less Than Everything*), had to be left on one side.

The accomplishment of these projects may be seen as part of a process of personal integration through communication, each representing a stream within a complex pattern of development and maturation. They were also a theoretical project, with each volume representing the consolidation of Winnicott's own mature development. The shaping of these contributions never took place in isolation; Winnicott's creativity needed one or more partners who contributed to his profound need for dialogue. His gratitude to patients, students, and colleagues should not be considered a formality but a sincere acknowledgment of what he had taken from others. The reciprocity with his editor Masud M. Khan, and his scholarship and independent thinking, was the most relevant example of this attitude, but there is also the role that Winnicott assigned to Ishak Ramzy in the editing of *The Piggle* [CW 11:2:1–17]. Beyond being partners in a highly sophisticated dialogue, these friendly, noncompliant presences may be considered as "found objects" (see "Found Objects and Waifs" [CW 9:4:7]). The encounters with other "selves" was of paramount importance for Winnicott, and, although he almost never used direct or indirect quotation, he was always ready to recognize his debt to other authors ("D. W. W. on D. W. W.," read at the 1952 Club in 1967 [CW 8:1:2]).

Unlike *Playing and Reality*, the genesis of *Therapeutic Consultations in Child Psychiatry* seems less troublesome and more linear, starting from a wealth of published and unpublished clinical accounts. But the book is not just a collection of clinical vignettes; it has a strong unity and coherence. Like *The Piggle*, it cannot be considered purely as an illustration of Winnicottian technique, but it would also be totally misleading to consider these volumes as guides to the application of theory to different settings or as a demonstration of the clinical validity of theoretical concepts. There are no hierarchies, there is no "lesser God": *Therapeutic Consultations, The Piggle*, and *Playing and Reality* should be considered as different ways of communicating about integrative and maturational processes, transitional objects and transitional phenomena, the location of cultural experience, environmental provision, mirroring, object usage and object finding, identifications, and, above all, creativity and playing. Like *The Piggle, Therapeutic Consultations* represents an exploration of theoretical formulations, with a real narrative strength. The title contains two concepts—"Therapeutic Consultation" and "Child Psychiatry"—that may seem self-evident, without need of further explanation, but it is quite the contrary. Each contains an original elaboration that deserves close attention.

Child Psychiatry

When Winnicott qualified as a doctor, there were no formal specialist trainings available: specialization could be acquired by working as a consultant in a teaching hospital. He became what would later come to be called a pediatrician by working as a physician for children at Paddington Green Children's Hospital and Queen's Hospital for Children early in his medical career; both were teaching hospitals that allowed for a gradual assumption of responsibility by the trainee doctor in the care of sick children. His interest in the psychological aspects of infant and child care was nourished by his commitment to psychoanalysis, by encounters with other colleagues, and by his own study and research work. He was eager to discuss his findings and thoughts with colleagues with different views, and he voraciously read any new book on the then blossoming discipline of child psychiatry. The Proceedings of the Royal Society of Medicine testify to Winnicott's frequent contributions to the discussion of clinical reports and to his efforts to convince his colleagues of the importance of early emotional development (see Volume 1). His first book, *Clinical Notes on the Disorders of Childhood* [CW 1:3], published in 1931, reflects his systematic effort to take into account the psychological dimension of physical illness and the physical manifestations of psychological disorders.

Child psychiatry emerged in the 1920s and 1930s in Europe and the United States as the product of different cultures and experiences. Although the roots of the study of abnormal development can be traced to the accounts of eighteenth-century scholars such as Jean Itard, the foundations of child psychiatry were laid at the end of the nineteenth century by Johannes Trüper in Germany, Marcel Manheimer in France, Moritz Tramer in Switzerland, and Sante de Sanctis in Italy. During the first three decades of the twentieth century, their influence remained marginal, and the "difficult" or "nervous" child was mostly treated by either pedagogic or physical means. The child guidance movement prevailed in the United States and the United Kingdom, leading to a distorted view in which all the responsibility for the child's disorder was attributed to the environment. In England, Margaret Lowenfeld developed her own approach to child psychotherapy (play therapy) and established a psychotherapy clinic and training center in 1931. She was six years older than Winnicott, and she had also trained as a pediatrician at the Great Ormond Street Hospital for Sick Children. Her method was based more on the contemporary developmental cognitive psychology of Spearman and on the work of the English philosopher R. G. Collingwood than on psychoanalysis. She found a far more interested audience in the Jungian field (Carl Gustav Jung himself visited her, and Dora Kalff developed her sandplay technique quoted in Lowenfeld's "World Technique," 1979) than among Freudian psychoanalysts. Indeed, Winnicott was initially one of the most determined among Melanie Klein's followers in fiercely attacking Lowenfeld when she presented her work extensively at the Medical Section of the British Psychological Society in 1937. She was accused by Winnicott, as a speaker on behalf of the Kleinian group, of neglecting Klein's contribution to the knowledge of the inner world. Lowenfeld's conception of play and cultural experience was distant from Winnicott's views, but, thirty years later ("D. W. W. on D. W. W" [CW 8:1:2]), Winnicott recognized his debt to Lowenfeld and to other psychoanalytic and non-psychoanalytic thinkers for having shown him what he termed a "protest against reference to universal regression from Id satisfaction-frustration in Oedipal triangle" because the psychoanalytic theory of the time did not fit all that could be observed by those who dealt with infants and children and their mothers.

During the same years, a substantial contribution to child psychiatry was made in the United States by Leo Kanner, an Austrian émigré of Jewish-Galician origin who had studied and qualified as a medical doctor in Berlin. Kanner, who was later known for his seminal paper on autism (1943), was called by another immigrant psychiatrist, the Swiss Adolf Meyer, to direct the first academic child psychiatry department at the Johns Hopkins Hospital. Kanner published the first textbook ever of child psychiatry in 1935, in America, and the book was published in Britain and reviewed by Winnicott two years later [CW 1:4:14].

Winnicott recognized the outstanding quality of Kanner's clinical and scientific effort, his original classification of disorders, his ability to keep in mind the whole child as patient ("the latter being always reckoned as a human being with a body, an intellect, and feelings"), and his enormous experience at a remarkably young age—the book was published when he was not yet forty. Although noting the lack of reference to the psychoanalytic contribution, the quality Winnicott appreciated most was its being the fruit of a department bridging pediatrics and psychiatry. This would be stressed in all the contributions and reflections about the nature and function of child psychiatry Winnicott produced in the following decades. His position would not change: child psychiatry was *not* a subspecialty of psychiatry; rather, it was the complementary psychological half of physical pediatrics. In fact, it was worth more than half, since progress in drug treatment and scientific knowledge had made the physical component of pediatrics simpler. He repeatedly stated that child psychiatry had little to learn from adult psychiatry, which was an increasingly reductionist discipline devoted to the pharmacological treatment of diseases. "Moreover, adult psychiatry today tends to get further and further from the problems of human nature and veers towards the exploration of drug treatments, biochemistry, and the various shock therapies" (see "The Paediatric Department of Psychology" [CW 6:2:19]). For Winnicott, the psychological study of the child should always be companion to the study of bodily functions. Here, the key word, as in emotional growth, is *integration* (see "Ego Integration in Child Development" [CW 6:3:19] and *Human Nature* [CW 11:1]). Child patients need doctors who can see "diseases as things," but they also need doctors who can listen to them; recognize their feelings, moods, and anxieties; and understand communications and needs, which are frequently expressed through symptoms. The ideal would be that both functions would be accomplished by the same person (a doctor trained in dynamic psychology and aware of the emotional needs of the child), but the two should be provided by the pediatric department ("On Cardiac Neurosis in Children" [CW 7:3:16]). The pediatric department would thus be something more akin to a facilitating an *integrated* environment. Further contributions and developments on the subject can be found in the 1960s ("The Paediatric Department of Psychology"[CW 6:2:19], "The Association for Child Psychology and Psychiatry Observed as a Group Phenomenon [CW 8:1:3], and "A Link Between Paediatrics and Child Psychology: Clinical Observations" [CW 8:2:14]).

Winnicott invested time and energy in trying to communicate with "physical paediatricians"; beyond writing letters and book reviews for medical journals and participating in meetings of the Royal Society, he was often invited to speak at scientific meetings of pediatricians, where he continued to promote his views, even advocating a "tandem academic chair" for physical pediatrics and child psychiatry. In his own professional life, even when psychoanalysis of adult patients became primary, he never gave up the child psychiatric component at Paddington Green Children's Hospital or in his private practice. For him, child psychiatry was both a stance and an attitude. When speaking of his own child psychiatric work, he referred to a capacity for integrating the knowledge about bodily development and its difficulties and ailments with the ability to cope with the emotional needs of the child and to locate the diagnostic process in the relationship between the child and her human environment. Medical training was fundamental in his view because the child psychiatrist should be someone who can be trusted as a doctor, who can accept the sick or ill child as a psychosomatic unit, as a whole, and who will do as little as is needed in the given situation to produce a change.

The Therapeutic Consultation

Winnicott's professional commitment in medical practice and in psychotherapy may be characterized by the attempt to be of help in as little time and space as possible. In addition to lengthy "ordinary" psychoanalytic treatment, he always devoted a considerable part of his time to short consultations both in his private practice and in his appointment at Paddington Green Children's Hospital, a position he held for forty years, from 1923. Two qualities of the therapeutic consultation were most relevant for Winnicott: the economic challenge of a short time and limited space (with few diagnostic and therapeutic resources) and the challenge of the unexpected.

The latter was the challenge he had faced in other professional experiences that were of the utmost importance in his personal "Bildung"; these included his professional training and in his experience in the Royal Navy as a surgeon probationer when he was still a medical student, the year spent at St. Bartholomew's Hospital as a casualty officer after his medical qualification, his outpatient clinic at Paddington Green, and the work with child evacuees during World War II. In addition, there was his long analytic experience with James Strachey.

As recalled by Clare Winnicott (1989), the Paddington Green Children's Hospital clinic became a very special place where colleagues from all over the world came to visit and see him at work with children of all ages and with their mothers. There, he had the opportunity to meet thousands of mothers with their babies and children, and, over the years, his clinic turned from a strictly pediatric one to a child psychiatric space. It was a place where he could do something useful for them and their mothers in a short time; indeed, in the shortest time available. His affectionate commitment to the clinic is testified by his letter to the *British Medical Journal* [CW 3:4:19] when the Paddington Green Children's Hospital was threatened with closure.

The challenge of the unexpected has to do with one of Winnicott's most distinctive traits: his being able to tolerate gaps in his own knowledge and understanding in order to preserve the full complexity of life. He was deeply convinced that life cannot be reduced to simple mechanisms, and to study life without killing or freezing it, you have to give up any reductionist approach. This capacity to build on gaps was also a distinctive trait of Charles Darwin's contribution to scientific knowledge, and it was a model that Winnicott never ceased to admire.

The *therapeutic consultation* has very special features: it is a first interview—the child, adolescent, or adult comes in with an *expectation* that can be met and, to a certain extent, exploited in terms of what *offer* is made by (or what is "on offer from") the therapist. If the therapist is there to be met as a *subjective object*, there is an occasion to provide the necessary holding environment and reverse the developmental impasse. The expression *subjective object* was being developed by Winnicott in 1948 (see "Paediatrics and Psychiatry" [CW 3:3:2], "Primary Introduction to External Reality: The Early Stages" [CW 3:3:12], and "Environmental Needs; the Early Stages; Total Dependence and Essential Independence" [CW 3:3:13]) to describe the state of affairs that belongs to the earliest moments when the infant encounters the environment, which can be described both in terms of "illusion" on the baby's side and "reality" on the mother's. At that time, "there is an outward turning of the personality towards something" ("Environmental Needs"), something that the baby somehow expects to find outside but is not yet known and objectively perceived. If the mother comes in with her breast at the right time, she lets the baby create herself as an object that is subjective in the sense that it exists in the baby's illusion and in the reality of the mother's being there and identifying with her baby's needs. Transitional phenomena, transitional objects, and symbol formation have their origin in these processes; they will represent the solid foundation of trust that can be exploited in later life for therapeutic work. "In this role of subjective object, which rarely outlasts the first or first few interviews, the doctor has a great opportunity for being in touch with the child" (Introduction to Part 1, *Therapeutic Consultations in Child Psychiatry* [CW 10:1:Introduction]).

In order to meet the child's expectations of a "good-enough" doctor, the therapist should be ingenuous enough, flexible enough, open enough, capable of mistakes, and able to tolerate the risk of not understanding everything and also of not interpreting. What has to be avoided is omniscience and idealization. Idealization would be an obstacle to reciprocity and symmetry. The child can make use of the consultation if she lives in an average, good-enough environment. The experience of being capable of communicating in the consultation can then be brought back home, making communication and integration there again possible. It is not interpretation that is "mutative" but the experience of being able to communicate and play. Winnicott's own analytic experience with James Strachey was a model for this approach. As Winnicott recalls in his obituary to his former analyst ("Obituary: James Strachey" [CW 8:1:14]), Strachey realized that "a process develops in the patient, and . . . what transpires cannot be produced but it can be made use of." It is the process and the development that is mutative, not the interpretation. "Gradually Strachey came round to his main psycho-analytic contribution, a series of lectures in 1933 (published in the *International Journal of Psychoanalysis*, 1934) in which he formulated the concept of the mutative interpretation. Here he made explicit the principle of economic interpretation,

interpretation at the point of urgency, accurately timed, gathering together the material presented by the patient and clearly dealing with a sample of transference neurosis." In the therapeutic consultation, "the work is unlike that of psychoanalysis in that it is not done in terms of transference neurosis samples" (Comment on "Milton" [CW 10:2:12]). In psychoanalysis, the analyst has time to become a real object, to allow the transition from illusion to disillusionment. In the therapeutic interview, the therapist remains a subjective object. The child's experience of a reliable environment allows him to have confidence in the therapist's capacity to accept the communication so that frightening experiences can be relived and integrated into the child's personality.

The first therapeutic interview can be exploited because it represents, for the children and their parents, a special occasion for communicating about processes going on or having gone on elsewhere. Early experience is not *necessarily* deep experience, Winnicott warned, and the first encounter is endowed with a wealth of potential because—somewhere in the early relationship with his environment—the child has experienced being *held*, so the traumatic experience or the terrifying emotions and feelings can be relived and narrated in the consultation. Case 3, "Eliza," in Part 1 [CW 10:1:3], offers a meaningful example of how this can happen: the squiggles introduce a theme about what is inside, in the dark; the drawings become gradually endowed with emotional content, and these emotions, though terrible and aggressive, acquire a shape and can be told and given names. If the family and the school (the child's human environment) is there to be used after the consultation, then "healing" can go on; the terrifying experience, the unthinkable and unbearable feelings can be integrated into the representation of the child to himself or herself as a whole subject. The consultation can be of help if the changes produced by the therapeutic experiences can restore a healthy process within the environment. "Interpretation is minimal. Interpretation is not in itself therapeutic, but it facilitates that which is therapeutic, namely, the child's reliving of frightening experiences. With the therapist's ego support the child becomes able for the first time to assimilate these key experiences into the whole personality" ("Milton" [CW 10:2:12]). This marks a substantial difference from the Kleinian model of development and from the therapeutic process in that it is not the interpretation that heals. What matters is the role of illusion and disillusion in discovering the object and the role of the object in allowing itself to be discovered and objectively perceived through tolerating and surviving ruthless aggression. In psychoanalysis, this process occurs mostly *within* the setting, but, in the consultation, the work of disillusion cannot be done in the interviews. However, the survival of the therapist as a subjective object allows the parents to survive subsequently being discovered as objectively perceived objects.

The concept of the subjective object was further developed by Winnicott in his account of primitive emotional development (see *Human Nature* [CW 11:1:4]). The development of instinctual tension also means the development of "an expectancy, a state of affairs in which the infant is prepared to find something somewhere, not knowing what. There is no comparable expectancy in the quiet or unexcited state. At the right moment the mother offers her breast." Repeated experiences of meeting the expectancy make possible the *illusion* that the object is there to meet the need, created "by impulse out of the need." Being "good enough" means that the mother adapts herself to the emotional needs of the infant and allows the baby the illusion of creating her; that is, she allows the baby to perceive her as a *subjective object*. It is only gradually that she will be discovered as an objectively perceived object (disillusion), integrating quiet and excited states.

The subjective object is there to be met, to be hated, to be used, to be destroyed and to survive destruction, then found again within the reach of omnipotence, within the reach of the spontaneous gesture (see "Found Objects and Waifs" [CW 9:4:7]).

In the first interview with a child who has had the experience of a reliable environment, the therapist is in the position of a subjective object. This is why Winnicott insists that the child can actually *dream* about the doctor the night before the interview. From "Introduction to Part 1":

> I was struck by the frequency with which *the children had dreamed of me the night before attending*. . . . Nevertheless here I was, as I discovered to my amusement, *fitting in with a preconceived notion*. The children who had dreamed in this way were able to tell me that it was of me that they had dreamed. In language which I use now but which I had no equipment for using at that time I found myself in the role of subjective object.
>
> We can conceive this particular condition as a peculiar kind of transference, an "expectancy" transference, that facilitates creative processes, intimacy, trust and transitional experiences. (See also "Creativity and Its Origins" [CW 9:3:7].)

Another important feature of the first interview is that the therapist has no foothold or handhold to reassure her, except for her own ability to meet the child with openness and a capacity to be surprised and to surprise.

The therapist must be there to hold the child patient and be concerned about her. The frame of reference, which must be sound and consistent, is the knowledge of the developmental processes and their relationship to emotional needs and environmental provision. What has to be strengthened is the capacity of the child to trust her own environment and move forward. Parents and teachers also profit and can further boost the therapeutic gain of the consultation. Another feature of the first interview is that the therapist does not know if there will be a second one and therefore must draw as much as possible on the "here and now," while neither flooding the encounter with interpretations nor leaving a silence that can be experienced by the patient as omniscient.

THE SQUIGGLE GAME

This game gradually and naturally became part of Winnicott's first assessment interviews with children, arising from his personal habit of scribbling, doodling, and drawing. Drawing was a pleasure for him and, for him and his friends, a way of communicating with his own deepest emotions, frequently letting his hand take the lead. Sharing this process with the child patient did not arise from any deliberate plan; rather, it became a very personal way of offering an intermediate space for communicating and *playing*. Winnicott was so aware of the idiosyncratic nature of this experience that he was reluctant to communicate about it to the child because he feared that this way of interacting with the child could be seen as a technique or a diagnostic tool. Although this risk cannot be avoided—anyone trying to reproduce it mechanically will collide with a substantial obstacle: no child will go on after the very first squiggles if she feels the therapist is not enjoying the game or is not really playing. Compliance cannot fuel the game, and if there is no authentic growth of intimacy, the interest in it will quickly fade away.

The most detailed account and discussion of the Squiggle Game is to be found in the note written in 1964 and expanded and partly published in 1968:

> In regard to any technique that the consultant must be prepared to use, the basis is playing. Elsewhere I have made the statement that in my opinion psychotherapy either is performed in the overlap of the two areas of playing (that of the patient and that of the therapist), or else the treatment must be directed towards enabling the child to become able to play—that is to say, to have reason to trust the environmental provision. It has to be assumed that the therapist can play, and can enjoy playing. [CW 8:2:47]

In the Squiggle Game, it is not drawing that actually matters but *playing* and the simplicity, freedom, and openness of the setting. To ask the child patient to play, the therapist should like playing; to exploit the wealth of communication of the game, the therapist does not need to be good at drawing, but he has to *like* drawing. Winnicott would offer something to the child that seems of little apparent value—a sheet of paper, torn in two parts, to give the impression that what we are doing "is not frantically important" (ibid.), and two pencils—and the absence of rules, except for reciprocity, or an attempt to reciprocate and alternate the positions. It is the therapist's active stance, his lending himself to the game, accepting uncertainties and failures, giving meaning to the child's contribution, that keeps the game going and keeps the child's interest alive. Gradually, the child's contributions to the game acquire value because the therapist *uses* the results of the game to increase his knowledge of "what the child would like to communicate" (ibid.). For his part, the child *uses* the therapist as a whole object; that is, someone who is entirely new, who can be discovered and who can discover the child, so that he can feel *seen* from a new point of view.

The consultant offers himself as a model: he acts freely, he allows space for impulses, at the same time containing them in the setting of the game. There is space for madness, for incontinence, for unexpected forms and meanings, for all the "enrichments and complications that belong to all infants and children" ("Review: *Twins: A Study of Three Pairs of Identical Twins*" [CW 4:2:6]). The therapist brings with him his knowledge, his theories, his being able to play, even his mastery of drawing, but the most important thing is his own *integration*. In other words, the therapist is there to be *used*. The importance of whole objects as a blueprint for development was expressed by Winnicott when referring to the father's role in development: "The father may or may not have been a mother-substitute, but at some time he begins to be felt to be there in a different role, and it is here I suggest that the baby is likely to make use of the father as a blue-print for his or her own integration when just becoming at times a unit" ("The Use of an Object in the Context of *Moses and Monotheism*" [CW 9:1:4]). The integration the therapist offers "is not, I believe, a typically obsessional integration, which would contain the element of *denial of chaos*" ("The Squiggle Game" [CW 8:2:47]). We must remember that *chaos* for Winnicott is the result of an interruption in the continuity of being, the unbearable, unthinkable disturbance and disruption of his "going-on-being" (*Human Nature* CW 11:1:4]; see Chapter 6). The child can bring into the game the broken line (*chaos*) and can re-experience continuity using the therapist as a whole object. When the game succeeds, it allows the child to feel valued, to feel free to play, and to feel in no way inferior to the doctor. When the game succeeds in enabling contact to be made, in establishing a communication, the child does not feel examined by the consultant or feel as if he is being tested. The Squiggle Game is a means for establishing a transitional space between the therapist and the child rather than a tool to evaluate the child's ability.

The squiggle drawings can be satisfactory in themselves, and the satisfaction can then be shared and allow for the experience of intimacy in sharing a creation: "Often the result of a squiggle is satisfactory in itself. It is then like a 'found object,' for instance a stone or piece of old wood that a sculptor may find and set up as a kind of expression, without needing work. This appeals to lazy boys and girls, and throws light on the meaning of laziness" (see also "Found Objects and Waifs" [CW 9:4:7]).

Jan Abram usefully emphasized the relation of the Squiggle Game to the dream screen, an apparently *passim* tribute to Lewin (1949). The game does have much in common with dream work. "By 'Dream screen,' Winnicott is referring to the unconscious nature of a dream, replicating aspects of the early mother-infant relationship" (Abram, 1996, p. 309). For Winnicott, the Squiggle Game as dream screen is "a place into or onto which a dream might be dreamed" ("The Squiggle Game" [CW 8:2:47]). This means that, like the psychoanalytic session, the game does not only offer a space for transference. If the suffering child cannot dream, the Squiggle Game may restore or facilitate access to the dreaming experience. Not only do the dreams dreamed "into or onto" the squiggles reveal unconscious aspects of the primary relationship, but the unconscious processes that emerge can communicate the intense, often painful work of the imaginative elaboration of bodily functions in the holding environment of the setting. This is beautifully illustrated by the first case reported in *Therapeutic Consultations* ("'Iiro' *aet* 9 Years 9 Months" [CW 10:1:1]). But, as Abram points out, it is not only the single squiggles (the form) that have much in common with dreams, it is "how the squiggles relate to each other" (p. 308), how Winnicott's sensitive adaptation to the child's needs "keeps the ball in play" and allows the linking of squiggles. The way the sequence of squiggles develops is, in itself, a narrative where, again, the chain of squiggles depends on the contributions of both partners, linked by associations and by the generation of new associations.

THE THEORY OF INTEGRATION

Although most of the cases presented together in Volume 10 have been published before, and both the concept of therapeutic/diagnostic consultation and the "technique" of the Squiggle Game have been described on earlier occasions, *Therapeutic Consultations in Child Psychiatry* represents a major effort to offer a thorough and organized presentation of Winnicott's clinical experience, theory, and technique in a way that can be *enjoyed* by the reader. The book is conceived as a nondogmatic, unconventional teaching tool for younger generations of clinicians. The reader Winnicott has in mind is not necessarily trained in psychoanalysis, is not necessarily a child psychiatrist or psychotherapist, but is someone—teacher, social worker, psychologist, psychiatrist, pediatrician—who is professionally involved in dealing with emotional suffering and the difficulties of children and adolescents and who feels the urge not to waste "the very great confidence which children can often show" (Introduction to Part 1). The theory of emotional development of the individual and the theory of the technique of psychotherapy are not illustrated in a didactic manner; instead, they inadvertently accompany Winnicott "in exploring the unknown territory of the new case" (ibid.): "the theory that I carry around with me and that has become part of me and that I do not even have to think about in a deliberate way."

The careful study of the cases should provide an occasion for "learning by experience" and sharing the experience of the teacher, Winnicott. What is unique here is the wealth of details, so that the reader (the student, in Winnicott's words) is often in the position to "know as much as the teacher" (ibid.) about the case and can follow everything that happens in the sessions. Winnicott selected cases that would not convey a sense of "cleverness" or of magic and, therefore, unattainable understanding. And the cases that have been added to this volume further confirm this attitude. The author (Winnicott) should appear not as a virtuoso but as an experienced clinician who can show all the complexity and labor involved in reaching the children and communicating with them. Again, it is not the single interpretation that matters but the mutuality of communication established. This cannot be imitated or copied (the scene is as unique as a human being relating with another human being can be), but what can be learned is how the emotional development of the individual child shapes playing and communication between the two throughout the interview.

The theory of emotional development and the theory of the contribution of environmental provisions or failures are also evident in the structure of the book in that its three parts reflect indirectly a classification of emotional ill health according to the different qualities of the integrative processes and the consequent nature of defenses. The first part deals with cases in which the maturational process has been arrested by trauma but where a good-enough early experience and a good-enough environment can be relied on. The second part considers cases where an environmental failure adds a burden to the self or causes a distortion of self-development. Here, the early environmental failure can be described by the word *privation, impingement*, and/or *cumulative trauma*, and defenses are mostly expressed through the false self and dissociation. The third part has mostly to do with the antisocial tendency and with early deprivation.

The first part describes children for whom the consultation has helped in restoring the going-on-being, the being-at-one-with the primary object, the capacity to internalize the continuity of being and to acknowledge dependence. The case of Iiro (and the other two cases, "Matti" [CW 6:2:15] and Sakari [CW 6:2:16]) is significant, as Winnicott points out, not only because it shows how communication can develop even when language barriers occur but because it is paradigmatic of the possibility of displaying emotional conflict, strain, or difficulty if proper professional contact is available to the child. This consultation did not arise from Iiro's parents requesting it but was explicitly proposed as a teaching opportunity for the Finnish pediatric staff. Nevertheless, the sensitive management of the interview allowed a deep understanding of the complex needs and vulnerabilities of the child and of his environment. This case allows us to enjoy Winnicott's ability to keep the body present in the interview so as to allow an imaginative elaboration of bodily sensations and even of the surgery the boy had had. What Iiro needed was to be *seen*, to be loved *with*, not in spite of, his deformity. The sequence of drawings allows the child's narrative to emerge and develop through the framework offered by Winnicott. The account of the meeting with the mother completes the perspective, adding her personal experience of *her own* deformity and the way it influenced the primary relationship with Iiro, how her mirroring function could be spoiled by the presence of a shared malformation.

The second part describes children in whom there has been some obstacle to reaching the "I AM" stage, to being tolerated and accepted as someone needing to use the object and to be *ruthless* before being capable of *concern*. This kind of relative environmental failure can determine the establishment of dissociative defenses in Winnicott's theory of emotional development ("Various Types of Psycho-Therapy Material," in *Human Nature* [CW 11:1:3], see Chapter 3). Dissociation, in his view, has to do not with psychotic functioning but with the existence of parts of the self that are not communicating or not acceptable to other parts. The cases described here are more complex and might need more consultations. Their environment, too, is more complex; environmental failure may be more evident and persistent, and the parents' emotional ill health may be severe and persistent, requiring more complex casework. The psychotherapeutic interview may be part of this.

I wish to comment in detail on the case of Charles in this second section, a nine-year-old boy complaining of headaches and "thoughts" who had had unsatisfactory consultations in a child guidance clinic. "It was his mind that was troubling him and he was beginning to have ideas about his thinking apparatus. He had said that one bit of his brain was taking over the rest of him" ("Charles *aet* 9 Years" [CW 10:2:8]). He was beginning to make distressing vows that could not be achieved. I want to emphasize how Winnicott stresses the need for "useful contact." The need is not interpretative work, it is just contact. We are not offered a diagnosis of obsessive-compulsive disorder; the boy's symptoms are not read as signs of disease but are respected as the child's expression and communication of a unique developmental history, of his private suffering. We are implicitly asked not to explain, and this narrative reminds us how tyrannical the intellect can be and how the mind can be a persecutory object.

As the Squiggle Game starts, we see how the capacity to tolerate uncertainty enables a playing field to be established, a landscape in which cross-identifications can be offered for playing with and even for thinking of the child as being a girl. Since this thought belongs to Winnicott, it can be accepted or rejected without fear ("Interrelating Apart from Instinctual Drive and in Terms of Cross-identifications" [CW 9:3:8]). When Charles introduces a detailed drawing of a battlefield in which several parties are fighting and making alliances, Winnicott makes no interpretation; instead, he establishes a link between the child's description of the game and the rigid separation being kept between good and bad elements in the squiggles. Because this holding function is offered, the boy can use the drawing, consciously, as "a diagram of his mind." This is the effect of the "dogmatic" assertion that the drawing was a description of the child's mind. The asymmetry between the caring adult and the trusting child could acquire the meaning of holding and integration so that the child's mind could now be included in the process of imaginative elaboration of bodily functioning. Winnicott's "rêverie" gives the boy the opportunity to accept him as an auxiliary ego, an integrating experience that can occur only if the partner is capable of dreaming and creating links. The "tiny bit" of the brain that the boy feared, whatever it represented, was so concrete that it had acquired almost psychotic qualities. No metaphor would have been possible without Winnicott. But, by being there, he could draw a distinction between *diagram* (a necessity for the child) and *squiggle*. Squiggles about numbers ensued, so that the child could communicate how uncomfortable he felt in his position as a nine-year-old boy, and this led to Charles fantasizing about being a powerful young man. Winnicott could then ask him about dreaming, and when Charles described his dreams vividly, it also enabled him to describe an acute confusional state related to a traumatic memory. This was the "tiny bit" of his mind that had persecutory qualities and could be neither remembered nor forgotten. More interviews followed, but the first was crucial for recovery from the impasse.

The third part of *Consultations* is the most extensive, presenting nine cases (from children aged twenty-one months to adults of thirty years) with a wide range of developmental expressions that all share one feature: the antisocial act as a communication of the history of the relationship between the child (or even the adult) with his or her environment. The antisocial act emerges as an organized gesture, halfway between an unconscious urge and a sophisticated *mise en scène* of a person's developmental history. For Winnicott, the antisocial act is strongly associated with transitional phenomena, "so that the study of the one involves the study of the other" ("Lily *aet* 5 Years" [CW 10:3:19]). Here, the child who undergoes deprivation can stand the traumatic gap and the frustrations, fears, rage, and other emotions that ensue because she can rely on transitional objects and phenomena. If these are banned or disturbed, "then the child has only one way out, which is a split in the personality, with one half related to a subjective world and the other reacting on a compliance basis to the world which impinges" ("The Deprived Child and How He Can Be Compensated for Loss of Family Life" [CW 3:5:10]). The antisocial act (bedwetting, lying, stealing) is a sign of hope, an attempt to restore a satisfying state of things that was first experienced and then lost. Delinquency occurs when the secondary gains of the antisocial act become so powerful that the process is irreversible, and there is no hope that the psychotherapeutic consultation or even psychoanalytic treatment can be effective.

The theory of the antisocial tendency slowly developed in Winnicott's thought with his first reflections about the meaning of stealing to be found in a note written in the 1930s ("Delinquency: Continued" [CW 2:1:9]). Then, the experience of working as a consultant psychiatrist for the Government Evacuation Scheme had a strong impact on Winnicott, offering him a wealth of material dealing with the discontinuity of environmental provision (Abram, 1996, pp. 38–39). An early example of his awareness of these themes can be found in the letter co-authored with John Bowlby and Emanuel Miller to the *British Medical Journal* (December 16, 1939 [CW 2:1:6]). The study of transitional objects and transitional phenomena in the 1940s and 1950s, and the reconsideration of aggression, enriched Winnicott's thought and encouraged a shift towards the understanding of the developmental constellation that can be found in the antisocial tendency. There are several turning points in this process, and the exchange with other authors (mainly John Bowlby and Phyllis Greenacre, whose paper he discussed in the 1962 Edinburgh International Psychoanalytical Association Congress) strongly contributed to the reshaping of his theory of "normal" antisocial acts, here so clearly stated in the Introduction to Part 3. It was not only a matter of theoretical, intellectual understanding; Winnicott describes finding himself being able to help children for whom, previously, he could only "provide notes for a court." He became aware that the antisocial act is a sign of hope, an attempt to mend what caused the antisocial act; that is, the discontinuity of maturational processes that occurred due to a relative environmental failure: "a gap in the continuity of the child's life *from the child's point of view*" (Introduction to Part 3). "The child who is stealing is (in the initial stages) quite simply reaching back over the gap, hopeful, or not entirely hopeless, about rediscovering the lost object or the lost maternal provision, or the lost family structure" (ibid.). If this communication can be met, hope is not wasted, and the repetition of the antisocial act can stop.

Part 3 is itself a book within the book, a sort of concluding essay that can be read as a separate opus. The cases offered are diverse and provide a wide range of perspectives on the development of the antisocial tendency at different stages and in different conditions of parental contribution, consistency, and availability. We should not forget that Winnicott's theory developed side by side with those of John Bowlby and Anna Freud, with whom he had a continuous exchange. Anna Freud and Dorothy Burlingham studied the effects of trauma and deprivation while offering support to children in the Hampstead Nurseries during the war and in the postwar period (this experience was condensed in *Young Children in Wartime: A Year's Work in a Residential War Nursery, London*, for the New Era in Home and School, 1942), whereas Bowlby had published his research paper "Forty-Four Juvenile Thieves: Their Character and Home Life" in the *International Journal of Psychoanalysis* in 1944 and was thence engaged in his research on loss and separation, which would lead to the formulation of attachment theory. The milieu of John Bowlby at the Tavistock Institute also produced the research and films of James and Joyce Robertson on separations of children from their parents in hospitals and residential settings (*Young Children in Hospital*, 1958; *A Two-Year-Old Goes to Hospital*, 1953). Did they "sing the same tune" (quoting Bowlby in Hunter, 1971)? Certainly, all these authors stressed the role of the environmental factor, but Winnicott's focus was always centered on the "child's point of view." In his 1959 discussion of Bowlby's paper "Grief and Mourning in Infancy," read at a Scientific Meeting of the British Psychoanalytical Society in October 1959, Winnicott states: "I think Bowlby has omitted reference to the change-over from a relationship to a *subjective* object to a relationship to an object that is *objectively perceived*. . . . this is thrust aside by Bowlby's implication that there is a very simple object-loss phenomenon rather like the failure of a reflex because of the absence of the stimulus" ("Discussion of 'Grief and Mourning in Infancy' [CW 5:5:17]; see also Reeves, 2005).

The cases reported in Part 3 illustrate Winnicott's views while elegantly avoiding propaganda: their aim is to make learning possible. I wish to call the attention of the reader to three of them:

> The case of Cecil [CW 10:3:14] encompasses a period of fourteen years and reports six consultations, starting when the boy was aged twenty-one

months. We can see how the acting out of the antisocial tendency develops, how the symptoms "blossom," and Winnicott's careful management of this over the years.

The case of Mrs. X [CW 10:3:18], a thirty-year-old woman, is exceptional in that an interview with a parent is presented not as part of the psychotherapeutic management of a child but as a diagnostic and psychotherapeutic consultation in itself. Not only does it show the outcome of a developmental process, but it shows how persistent hope can be.

The case of Lily [CW 10:3:19], aged five years, in its astounding brevity and simplicity, illustrates how a good-enough family environment can be strained, causing the temporary loss of the capacity of providing a transitional space and actual destruction of a transitional object that the child tries to recuperate by stealing. Here, nothing had to be done but "bringing the family to recognise that they were in a state of strain and that someone needed a holiday."

A remark in this last case history can be read as a sort of clinical testament of Donald Winnicott: "Unfortunately I can look back on a time when as an ardent psycho-analyst, pleased with having learned the technique of the treatment of an individual, I would have referred this child for analytic treatment, and perhaps would have missed the more important thing, which was rehabilitation of the family." This statement provides a vivid example of how *Therapeutic Consultations* is the fruit of an extraordinary maturity, one that never repudiates the components that have made up its author's own personal trajectory: pediatrics and psychoanalysis *in primis*.

Therapeutic Consultations in Child Psychiatry has much to offer to the contemporary reader in addition to the opportunity to encounter Donald Woods Winnicott in a lively and thoughtful discourse with his patients. Four decades from publication have not altered the richness and freshness of this book. Indeed, the reader who is aware of what has been added by research in psychoanalysis, in infant development, or in the clinical applications of attachment theory will be fascinated by the many implications that can still be found here. Psychoanalysts from distant traditions have found these accounts surprisingly familiar, and I think that any reader interested in human nature can learn much from these pages, if only by allowing herself enough curiosity and humility, the very qualities that Donald Winnicott exemplified when writing them.

Acknowledgment

This essay is dedicated to Andreas Giannakoulas who never ceases to teach me to listen to the unspoken.

References

Abram, J. (1996). *The language of Winnicott: A dictionary of Winnicott's use of words.* London: Karnac.

Bowlby, J. (1944). Forty-four juvenile thieves; their character and home life. *International Journal of Psychoanalysis, 25*, 19–52.

Bowlby, J. (1960). Grief and mourning in infancy and early childhood. In *The Psycho-Analytic Study of the Child, 15*. London: Imago.

Freud, A., & Burlingham, D. (1942). *Young children in wartime: A year's work in a residential war nursery.* London: Allen and Unwin, for New Era in Home and School.

Hunter, V. (1971). John Bowlby: An interview. *Psychoanalytic Review, 78*, 159–175.

Issroff, J., with Reeves, C., & Hauptman, B. (2005). *Donald Winnicott and John Bowlby: Personal and professional perspectives.* London: Karnac.

Lewin, Bertram D. (1949). Sleep, the mouth and the dream screen. *Psychoanalytic Quarterly, 15*(4), 419–34.

Lowenfeld, M. (1979). *The world technique.* London/Boston: Allen & Unwin/.Institute of Child Psychology.

Kanner, L. (1935). *Child psychiatry.* Springfield, Charles C. Thomas. First British edition (1937), London: Bailliere, Tindall and Cox.

Kanner, L. (1943). Autistic disturbances of affective contact. *The Nervous Child, 2*, 217–250.

Reeves, C. (2005). Singing the same tune? Bowlby and Winnicott on deprivation and delinquency. In J. Issroff, *Donald Winnicott and John Bowlby: Personal and professional perspectives* (pp. 71–100). London, Karnac, 2005.

Robertson, J. (1953). *A two-year-old goes to hospital.* 16-mm film. London: Tavistock Institute of Human Relations.

Robertson, J. (1958). *Young children in hospital.* London: Tavistock.

Strachey, J. (1934). The nature of the therapeutic action of psychoanalysis. *International Journal of Psychoanalysis, 15*, 127–159.

Winnicott, D. W. (1931). *Clinical notes on the disorders of childhood.* London: Heinnemann. [CW 1:3]

Winnicott, D. W. (1938). Review: *Child Psychiatry* by Leo Kanner. [CW 1:4:14]

Winnicott, D. W. (1939, December 16). Letter to *British Medical Journal*, "Evacuation of small children" (with J. Bowlby & E. Miller). [CW 2:1:6]

Winnicott, D. W. (1948). Paediatrics and psychiatry. [CW 3:3:2]

Winnicott, D. W. (1949, September 24). Letter to *British Medical Journal*, "Paddington Green Children's Hospital." [CW 3:4:19]

Winnicott, D. W. (1953). Review: *Twins: A study of three pairs of identical twins* by Dorothy Burlingham. [CW 4:2:6]

Winnicott, D. W. (1961). The paediatric department of psychology. [CW 6:2:19]

Winnicott, D. W. (1965). The deprived child and how he can be compensated for loss of family life [1950]. [CW 3:5:10]

Winnicott, D. W. (1965). Ego integration in child development [1962]. [CW 6:3:19]

Winnicott, D. W. (1968). "Eliza" *aet* 7½ years. [CW 10:1:3]

Winnicott, D. W. (1968). The squiggle game. [CW 8:2:47]

Winnicott, D. W. (1969). A link between paediatrics and child psychology: Clinical observations [1968]. [CW 8:2:14]

Winnicott, D. W. (1969). Obituary: Strachey, James. [CW 8:1:14]
Winnicott, D. W. (1971). "Bob" *aet* 6 years. [CW 10:1:4]
Winnicott, D. W. (1971). "Cecil" *aet* 21 months at first consultation. [CW 10:3:14]
Winnicott, D. W. (1971). "Charles" *aet* 9 years. [CW 10:2:8]
Winnicott, D. W. (1971). Creativity and its origins. [CW 9:3:7]
Winnicott, D. W. (1971). "Iiro" *aet* 9 years 9 months, Case 1. [CW 10:1:1]
Winnicott, D. W. (1971). Interrelating apart from instinctual drive and in terms of cross-identifications. [CW 9:3:8]
Winnicott, D. W. (1971). "Lily" *aet* 5 years. [CW 10:3:19]
Winnicott, D. W. (1971). "Milton" *aet* 8 years. [CW 10:2:12]
Winnicott, D. W. (1971). "Mrs X" *aet* 30 years. [CW 10:3:18]
Winnicott, D. W. (1971). *Playing and reality.* London: Tavistock.
Winnicott, D. W. (1971). *Therapeutic consultations in child psychiatry.* [CW 10:1]
Winnicott, D. W. (1988). *Human nature.* [CW 11:1]
Winnicott, D. W. (1989). Discussion of John Bowlby's "Grief and mourning in infancy" [1959]. [CW 5:5:17]
Winnicott, D. W. (1989). D. W. W. on D. W. W. [1967] [CW 8:1:2]
Winnicott, D. W. (1989). The use of an object in the context of *Moses and Monotheism* [1969]. [CW 9:1:4]
Winnicott, D. W. (1996). The Association for Child Psychology and Psychiatry observed as a group phenomenon [1967]. [CW 8:1:3]
Winnicott, D. W. (1996). Environmental needs; the early stages; total dependence and essential independence. [1948]. [CW 3:3:13]
Winnicott, D. W. (1996). On cardiac neurosis in children [1966]. [CW 7:3:16]
Winnicott, D. W. (1996). Primary introduction to external reality: The early stages [1948]. [CW 3:3:12]Winnicott, D. W. (2017). Delinquency: Continued [ca. 1930s]. [CW 2:1:9]
Winnicott, D. W. (2017). Found objects and waifs. [CW 9:4:7]
Winnicott, D. W. (2017). "Matti," *aet* 12 years: A therapeutic consultation [1961]. [CW 6:2:15]
Winnicott, D. W. (2017). Not less than everything [extracts] [c. 1968–1971]. [CW 9:3:11]
Winnicott, D. W. (2017). Sakari: A therapeutic consultation [1961]. [CW 6:2:16]

{12}

Winnicott and the Primacy of Life

Steven Groarke

The two works that make up Volume 12 exemplify the original nature of Donald Winnicott's contribution to psychoanalysis, although both *The Piggle* and *Human Nature* remained unfinished at the time of his death in 1971. The account of his analysis of Gabrielle ("Piggle") was published in 1977 by the Hogarth Press and in a paperback edition by Penguin Books in 1980. It includes the typescripts of all sixteen sessions, verbatim excerpts of what was said, letters from and to the parents, and Winnicott's occasional working notes, comments, and marginalia. Winnicott suggested in his introduction that the comments were kept to a minimum, allowing readers to form their own views of the case as the basis for a useful discussion. This seems a wise suggestion, and we shall hold to the same principle in our introductory remarks on *The Piggle*.

Although it offers an intimate portrait of the analytic couple in his own words, *The Piggle* was not prepared for publication by Winnicott. The typewritten notes of the case were edited by Ishak Ramzy under the auspices of the Winnicott Publications Committee. Similarly, an incomplete typescript of *Human Nature*, together with two synopses of the book, edited by Christopher Bollas, Madeleine Davis, and Ray Shepherd, was published posthumously in 1988 by Free Association Books. Strictly speaking, neither of these books was written by Winnicott, although this does not in any way diminish their importance.

The circumstances that led to the writing of *Human Nature* are in themselves significant. The typescript is based on notes from the university lecturing regularly undertaken by Winnicott over a period of almost forty years from the mid-1930s until his death. His indebtedness to Susan Isaacs, who invited him to lecture on Human Growth and Development at the Institute of Education, may be singled out for special mention. From the late 1940s, he continued to lecture to social work students, teachers of young children, nurses, magistrates, and parents. Thoroughly at home in the company of non-analysts, the classroom seems to have been a further occasion for Winnicott's highly original and creative way of communicating, and we should keep the pedagogic context in mind when reading *Human Nature*. Although, in many ways, the least didactic of thinkers, there are nonetheless "lessons" that Winnicott sought to bring home in this single attempt at a treatise.

Human Nature was an unrealized *summa*, however. This is evident if one compares the two synopses of the book (found in the appendix in Volume 12). Synopsis I (in five parts) is dated August 1954, and we know that the first draft of the book was begun and completed in the summer of that year. Synopsis II (in three parts) is dated circa 1967, and the degree to which it differs from the first synopsis is indicative of the ongoing revisions Winnicott made to the manuscript until the time of his death. The existing typescript compares roughly with the first three parts of the first synopsis, starting with a preliminary statement on the study of human nature from a developmental standpoint (Part I). The developmental argument is further underpinned by a psychosomatic framework that, as we shall see, grounds Winnicott's thinking throughout and distinguishes it from classical Freudian theory. The manuscript then follows the tripartite structure set out in the first synopsis: interpersonal relationships (Part II, § A), formation of the self (Part II, § B), and primitive emotional development (Part II, § C). Some of the contents of Part III, most notably "Study of Sequences," are not elaborated under the same headings but incorporated elsewhere in the book. Nevertheless, there are notable divergences between the book and the first synopsis. The book does not discuss, for instance, transitional objects and transitional phenomena (Part III) under a separate heading; nor does it include any discussion of deprivation and delinquency (Part IV) or post-Oedipal maturation (Part V). Where these ideas are embedded in *Human Nature*, we shall endeavor in the course of our essay to draw them out. This is particularly important in the case of transitional phenomena and potential space, ideas that occupy the center of Winnicott's thinking.

We might reasonably suppose that the second synopsis is a revision of the first. While this remains conjecture on our part (the editors of the 1988 edition are of the same opinion), it is useful when considering the trajectory of Winnicott's thought. If we assume, then, that the discriminations of the synopses are doctrinal, the following points become particularly significant. First, Winnicott retains the psychosomatic framework as the basis for his understanding of human life. Second, the psychosomatic framework is accorded primacy over Freudian instinct theory; illusion precedes *Trieb*. Third, Winnicott emphasizes the environmental factor while at the same time postulating the constitutive nature of individual creativity. We shall elaborate on the theoretical implications of these points later.

A Psychosomatic Frame of Reference

Winnicott went on revising the typescript of *Human Nature* over a period of almost twenty years and, although it remained unfinished at the time of his death, it is the only example we have of a theoretical overview of his ideas. In spite of the fact that it remained a work in progress, it is the fullest statement available of where Winnicott got to on the way to where he was going. It may be described, to borrow a paradoxical phrase from Hopkins (2013, p. 795) that Winnicott would surely have appreciated, as "work done by being broken off undone." And although it was conceived in the form of a treatise, addressing the central themes of human nature and emotional development formally and systematically, the book remains a deeply personal statement. Winnicott was at his most creative when using clinical thinking in freely associative and spontaneous ways. As readers, we enjoy and are surprised by *his* enjoyment, the way he seemed to surprise himself in what he had to say. Nevertheless, aware of the ambitious task he had set himself, Winnicott sought to place the study of human nature in a rigorous framework of his own making. The results are simultaneously measured and startlingly original. He adopts a meticulous method in tracing the psychology of early childhood back to the most primitive human experiences and, in doing so, formulates a new conception of health based on the criterion of maturity.

We shall come back to his principal idea that health is more than a relative absence of disease. As for the basic frame of reference, Winnicott was not a speculative thinker; that is to say, he was not a philosopher. In keeping with a tradition of clinical realism in English psychoanalysis, he acknowledged that understanding extends only as far as one's experience allows. As an empirical thinker rather than an empiricist, his writings are based on a professional life in pediatrics and psychoanalysis. Although he made a point of describing a trajectory through pediatrics to psychoanalysis, suggesting a movement from one to the other, the fact is that he applied himself to these two professions in tandem. In doing so, he held consistently to the basic assumption that "physical" and "mental" are not opposed phenomena. The idea that psyche forms a vital unity with the body is at the center of his thinking.

Winnicott continued to practice medicine throughout his working life, and his outpatient clinic at Paddington Green Children's Hospital was essential for the development of his thinking. Although specializing in child psychiatry, he states in his introduction to *Human Nature* that he never left general pediatrics. We cannot overestimate the significance of this claim. Winnicott learned to do analysis as a pediatrician. His move towards specialization on the "psychological side" originates in pediatrics; hence, a psychosomatic frame of reference that eschews the division into physical and psychological medicine. In this context, child analysis became an integral part of his clinical practice, and Anna Freud's appreciation of his work became increasingly important to him, although initially the most influential analytic figure (other than Freud) was Melanie Klein. Winnicott remained enthusiastic about Klein's work throughout the 1930s, acknowledging that without her notion of the "internal world" he could not have gotten started with his own work in the psychoanalysis of children.

Although the relationship between Winnicott and leading members of the Kleinian group became increasingly disputatious, Klein's lasting influence on

Winnicott's thinking is borne out especially in Part III of *Human Nature*, which includes a discussion of their respective evaluations of inner psychic change. He was clearly indebted to Klein's revision of Freud from the standpoint of the object, and, in turn, she respected her debt to Winnicott. Unlike Klein, however, he sought to emphasize the element that comes from outside, the infant's dependence on the actual mother (prior to introjection-projection) for its healthy development. For Winnicott, psychical space itself requires a framing structure, and his insistence on the irreducibility of the early environment as the matrix of transference gave notice of two incommensurable forms of clinical thinking. The fundamental divergence in theory and practice to which this gave rise remains part of the legacy of the British school of psychoanalysis.

Winnicott was elected as a member of the British Psychoanalytical Society in 1935 and qualified as a child analyst in the following year. Around the same time, he began a four-year analysis with the Kleinian analyst Joan Riviere that ended in 1941. The scene was now set for the consolidation of the analytic work that forms the basis of his thinking, and he describes how his practice developed with a large number of cases in his outpatient clinic, innumerable short psychotherapies, and the provision of therapeutic management. In terms of management, Winnicott ("D. W. W. on D. W. W." [CW 8:1:2]) makes the point that initially he avoided having "antisocial children" in his clinic because of their disruptive impact.

Based on his work with evacuated children in Oxfordshire during World War II, however, he went on to elaborate a decisive link between deprivation and delinquency, which culminated in his theory of the "antisocial tendency." The treatment of delinquent children constitutes a major part of the new field in psychoanalysis brought about by his work. Starting from a Freudian perspective, he came to understand the "antisocial act" of the delinquent child, the child who steals something from mother's purse or goes out and steals a book from the school library, in terms of what he called "the moment of hope." This introduced an entirely new way of understanding the difficulties of "difficult children" along psychoanalytic lines. The understanding of helplessness (*Hilflosigkeit*) itself takes a new turn in Winnicott, the validity of which is a matter for genuine discussion. Why should we understand antisocial action as an expression of hope? Are there good grounds for making this claim? For Winnicott, the hope consists in an unconscious communication where the child reaches beyond feelings of deprivation, trying to reclaim whatever it is he believes has been lost and to which he feels entitled. The consequences of this construction are far-reaching. Indeed, that there is no account of this new understanding of unconscious communication in *Human Nature*—antisocial behavior, environmental failure, and the link between deprivation and delinquency are referred to only in Synopsis I (Part IV)—demonstrates the extent to which the book is unfinished and incomplete.

In addition to the treatment of difficult children, Winnicott augmented the Freudian field through the analysis of non-neurotic structures in adult patients, including borderline states and the delusional transference as well as manic depressives. In applying himself to the problem of emotional contact in cases of severe disturbance, Winnicott acknowledged the methodological advances made by Margaret Little. He took over and developed the idea that, in analytic work with adults of psychotic type, the ego becomes accessible to transference interpretation only insofar as reality is "presented undeniably and inescapably so that contact with it cannot be refused" (Little, 1986, p. 85). Winnicott reckoned that working in this way with patients who were threatened with a failure of life rather than an intrapsychic neurotic conflict taught him more than any other kind of therapeutic work. The estimation is telling. While the direct clinical observation of infants remained a mainstay of his work, nonetheless, Winnicott was clear that the analysis of young children tells us more about infants than we learn from infant observation. Moreover, he maintained that we learn more about the earliest phenomena of human life from adults deeply regressed in the course of analytic treatment than from either infant observation or the psychoanalysis of young children. Whereas the sexuality of children is, in principle at least, an observable phenomenon, infantile psychic functioning is a construct of analytic regression, a phenomenon of the immemorial past rather than a psychological fact. This is another way of saying that developmental psychology is an elaboration based on clinical psychoanalysis.

The decisive impact that clinical work with the more psychotic type of adult patient had on Winnicott's thinking was evident in a series of papers published after World War II. Most notably, the combined ontological and therapeutic reach of "Primitive Emotional Development" [CW 2:7:8] extends throughout his entire work. His preoccupation with the question of health culminates in *Human Nature* but is evident from the beginning, with respect to a lively infant experiencing the "illusion of omnipotence" in the care of an emotionally mature, reliable, and physically available mother. At the same time, the 1945 paper anticipates Winnicott's innovative approach to the repetition compulsion in the analytic situation as a phenomenon of environmental failure. In terms of "transference difficulties that belong to an essential lack of true relation to external reality" [CW 2:7:8], he identifies dissociative processes that are manifest regressively in the analysis of psychotic and borderline states. In this respect, the paper reorients the treatment of these difficulties as unconscious reenactments of blank, unresolved pain. It also anticipates the fundamental claim that, insofar as they are retained in illness, primitive emotional states may be seen as regressive replications of real deficiencies in the earliest relationship.

The Analytic Encounter

Winnicott's treatment of Gabrielle ("Piggle") forms an integral part of his innovations in clinical practice. The analysis extended over two and a half years, from 1964 to 1966; the patient was two years five months old when the treatment began and five years two months at the time of the sixteenth and final consultation.

The mother contacted Winnicott in January 1964 when the child was two years four months old, describing a lifeless state in which Gabrielle was disinclined to play during the day and subject to anxieties ("worries") that kept her awake at night. In her initial letters, the mother refers to the birth of a sister when Gabrielle was twenty-one months old, alludes to a state of depersonalization ("she hardly even admits to being herself"), and describes the fantasies that most troubled the child. The latter consisted of a "black mummy" who lived in the Piggle's tummy, who came at night to claim her "yams" (breasts), and who sometimes put the Piggle into the toilet. In the fantasy, the "black mummy" could be contacted by telephone but was often ill and difficult to make better. In an earlier configuration of the patient's fantasy, the "black mummy" and the "black daddy" were yoked together in a "babacar," which at other times contained only the solitary figure of a man. It seems she experienced the "babacar" as a kind of space rather than an object, marking the contours of a particular interior environment. The mother also reported the occasional appearance of "black Piggle" among the child's fantasies.

A detailed reconstruction of the treatment is not undertaken here, allowing readers instead to encounter the clinical material relatively unencumbered. However, the case does provide valuable insight into Winnicott's views about the analytic task and the aims of therapeutic treatment. In a paper presented to the British Psychoanalytical Society two years before the start of Gabrielle's analysis, "The Aims of Psycho-Analytical Treatment" [CW 6:3:2], he had clarified some important technical issues. Most notably, the paper includes proposed modifications to the so-called standard type of analysis, towards which Winnicott claims he was invariably maneuvering in his practice in general. Briefly, by "standard analysis" he meant "communicating with the patient from the position in which the transference neurosis (or psychosis) puts me. . . . Most of what I do is of the nature of a verbalization of that which the patient brings for me to use today" [CW 6:3:2].

It is important not to lose sight of Winnicott's emphasis on verbalization and the function of speech in the analytic setting, although typically he renders "standard analysis" itself in his own idiom. He claims that he made transference interpretations, first to let the patient know that he was not all-knowing but could be off the mark or quite simply wrong and second to facilitate growth and integration by linking secondary and primary processes, transforming affect into forms of representation through the mobilization of associative forces. The first point confirms the importance of the analyst *not* understanding what the patient has yet to make available for understanding. It is not a question of analysts showing their patients what they know. On the contrary, in Gabrielle's case, Winnicott adds the following comment at the end of the third consultation: "Only she knew the answers, and when she could encompass the meaning of the fears she would make it possible for me to understand too." The distinction between "unknowable" and "unthinkable" is crucial for Winnicott's therapeutic model and represents his mature view of the transference, expressed in "The Use of an Object" [CW 8:2:28] in terms of the analyst's capacity to wait, allowing the patient to arrive at understanding creatively. The biblical exhortation to wait patiently (Ps. 37:7) and quietly (Lam. 3:26), and indeed to make positive use of the silence, underwrites a view of therapy in which understanding itself is considered an act of faith. Complementary to which, the second point draws attention to the symbolization of analytic speech under the conditions of the analytic encounter. Winnicott makes a case for the work of representation on clinical grounds, where interpretation itself is seen as part of the frame for psychical space.

At the same time, he argues that "modified analysis" is required where certain patterns of disturbance are manifest in the diagnostic picture. These patterns are treated as special cases and include, for example, the fear of breakdown; a successfully entrenched false self; an antisocial tendency; dissociation between inner psychic reality and cultural life; and the overwhelming presence of a psychotic parental figure. What is to be done in these circumstances? Essentially, Winnicott concludes, "I change over into being a psycho-analyst who is meeting the needs, or trying to meet the needs, of that special case" ("The Aims of Psycho-Analytical Treatment" [CW 6:3:2]). The setting is used, accordingly, as a potential space in which the process of internalization is seen as more important than the analysis of internalized phenomena. Winnicott puts the matter succinctly in a final proposal: "If our aim continues to be to verbalize the nascent conscious in terms of the transference, then we are practising analysis; if not, then we are analysts practising something else that we deem to be appropriate to the occasion" [CW 6:3:2]. It seems Winnicott was not reluctant to do "something else" when necessary, adapting the technique to the patient rather than the patient to the technique.

He subscribed to this view on the proviso that, even when it comes to the treatment of non-neurotic modes of functioning and of regressed patients, there is always a question of weighing the use of interpretation and holding as the main therapeutic agents of psychoanalysis. In other words, there is no suggestion of holding taking the place of interpretation, a basic misunderstanding that may be found among Winnicott's detractors and advocates alike. The formation of an analytic object, which presupposes the communication of inchoate object relations, represents *a reach for meaning* through symbolization of one kind or another. André Green (1975) presents his seminal reading of Winnicott along these lines. Allowing for modifications to the setting, the therapeutic action of psychoanalysis rests on the function of representation, and Winnicott is perfectly clear that he was "all the time manoeuvring into a position for standard analysis" ("The Aims of Psycho-Analytical Treatment" [CW 6:3:2]). This challenges the view of him as a maverick or revolutionary thinker and puts his clinical innovations and technical modifications into perspective.

Clinically, Winnicott was a genuinely independent thinker, with roots in the Freudian–Kleinian tradition of British psychoanalysis. Once again, what he meant by the standard type of analysis was communicating with the patient in the transference, which is not to say that he advocated relentless interpretations *of* the transference. The innovative move was allowing the analyst, while communicating in this way, to assume certain characteristics of a subjective analytic object for the patient, or to *play out* a transitional experience through the analytic encounter. The enabling use of playacting as symbolization may be seen as part of what Winnicott meant by holding, allowing patients time to find words for both intrasubjective and intersubjective experiences. Where things do not go into words, or where words actually fail us, the game is useful in allowing for silence without an atmosphere of recrimination. Silence isn't interpreted automatically as an attack on the analyst or the analysis. The use of play as an inclusive form of make-believe, including the enactment of the "greedy Winnicott baby" in *The Piggle* (cf. "Second Consultation" [CW 11:2:3]), is based on the idea of a maturational line of object-relations—namely, from subjectively perceived objects through transitional objects to objects that exist outside the subjective world or the area of omnipotence. As we shall see when we turn to his theory of the primitive phases of development, Winnicott identified this perceptual shift from subjective to objective alongside a related shift from absolute dependence to growing maturity.

In reading *The Piggle*, we appreciate the extent to which Winnicott established enjoyment and playing as conditions for analytic treatment. It was the "play role" that he judged the most valuable of the various roles Gabrielle attributed to him in the course of the treatment. And he saw it as a matter of principle that "the analyst always allows the enjoyment to become established before the content of the play is used for interpretation" (cf. "Thirteenth Consultation" [CW 11:2:14]). This is not an argument for play as something *instead of* interpretation; the point is that play provides a relational context in which interpretations can be used in meaningful ways. This principle guides us in our reading of *The Piggle* on two counts. First, Winnicott ("Playing: A Theoretical Statement" [CW 8:2:15]) saw play as the "universal" phenomenon and treated psychoanalysis as a specific formation of play. Second, he envisaged the analyst facilitating the patient's use of play as the framework of analysis and, where necessary, "bringing the patient from a state of not being able to play into a state of being able to play" [CW 8:2:15].

On both counts, the principle of two people playing together, modeled on the mother and baby living an experience together, safeguards the essential process of free association from the imposition of extraneous or gratuitous interpretation. It is only when the game is played and enjoyed that the reach for meaning comes spontaneously from the life of the child. This applies both to the earliest environment and, by analogy, to the analytic setting; to the primary maternal frame, as well as to the transitional field of the transference. Winnicott was intent on demonstrating that it is living that gives life meaning and, at the same time, that playing is not a prelude to the real thing but a way of constantly keeping things alive and real. In this case, playing constitutes the *frame* that sustains the viability of transference (Parsons, 2000, p. 136). Winnicott established this threefold schema as the basis of his technique, combining the provision of a setting, including the internal setting in the analyst's mind, with the transference and countertransference.

Life Itself

Let us now turn to the main theoretical contributions of *Human Nature.* Winnicott reshaped the basic exercise of psychoanalysis by finding out for himself what he could do with it. This meant working as a psychoanalyst, if not always doing standard analysis, while at the same time enabling the innate tendency in patients towards healthy development. He was concerned first and foremost with the development of life coming into itself as health, the manifestation of felt life in its self-growth. But how did he picture the healthy individual? What did it mean for Winnicott to be on good terms with life? What kind of life did he assume a healthy person is able to live? And, where treatment is called for, how might we live fuller, more meaningful lives? He relied neither on biology nor on medicine for answers to these questions. While he saw health, life, and the body as inextricably linked, he judged physical pediatrics alone as an inadequate understanding of the latter. He approached patients neither as physiological problems to be resolved nor as mere objects of knowledge. Instead, he looked beyond both physiology and science for the meaning of the body as the basis of human experience. The biological aspect of growth, therefore, was accorded only limited value in his psychoanalytic studies of human nature, which focused instead on the emotional condition of human beings through an articulation of physical and psychological experience.

Winnicott reformulated the criterion of health in terms of maturity rather than the absence of disease. Accordingly, *Human Nature* may be seen as a treatise of human health, the basic argument of which was summed up in a talk Winnicott gave to the Royal Medico-Psychological Association, Psychotherapy and Social Psychiatry Section, contemporaneous with the second synopsis: "Perhaps at one time psychoanalysts did tend *to think of health in terms of the absence of psychoneurotic disorder*, but this is no longer true" ("The Concept of a Healthy Individual" [CW 8:1:4], emphasis in the original). In this respect, Winnicott made a decisive contribution to a shift in twentieth-century thought by maintaining that maturity is health and health is maturity, the implication being that health depends on "the maturity that belongs to the age of the individual" [CW 8:1:4]. The criterion of maturity places the central Winnicottian preoccupation with health in a temporal frame, although of course the historicity of the psyche remains irreducible to the temporal order of conventional history. Nor are maturational processes explicable in terms of the standardized developmental accounts we find in psychology and history alike.

Winnicott maintained this radical view of human nature on three counts. First, we thrive as a matter of health, according to an innate tendency to become who we have it in us to be. Second, health is a process that is realized as maturity in the twofold movement towards independence and objective perception. Third, maturation facilitates health as a series of ego processes distinct from drive phenomena. He extended the criterion of maturity along these lines to include, for instance, the realization of a psyche-soma that functions harmoniously with itself, social health (democracy) as an expression of individual health, and healthy living as a phenomenon of primary creativity. The latter comprises related areas of healthy experience, including life, in the world, the inner life, and the life of cultural experience. On this reckoning, health has a relationship with *socius*, the paradigm of the dream, and the contingency of culture as a form of play.

Crucially, Winnicott conceived of health as tolerant of ill health: the discussion in *Human Nature* covers modes of illness and health as conjoined formations of the psychosomatic field of experience. This does not amount to a conflation of the normal and the pathological. Rather, it represents the formulation of a genuine psychoanalytic conception of illness, as distinct from biological and psychological notions of pathology. We have yet to appreciate the full extent to which Winnicott resisted the reduction of psychoanalysis to a regional science. Its implications for our understanding of the normative vitality of human experience are profound. Most importantly, within the Winnicottian framework of psyche-soma, the abnormal points to the normal and, indeed, is as normal as the normal. Health comprises "awkward situations" in which defensive maneuvers operate as a matter of course and, therefore, give rise to symptomatic phenomena. Winnicott treated illness as an "awkward category" this side of disaster, where the norm continues to issue from the nature of psychic life; where the a priori is inherent in living; and where health covers individuals who make good against the odds. In short, he did not mistake structure for life and, at the same time, continued to view the true self as a type of fallible man.

The exploration of the abnormal *from the standpoint of the normal* is not only a matter of theoretical interest and historical import but also has direct implications for analytic practice. This is evident, for instance, in the different approaches to negative therapeutic reaction that prevail in the British Psychoanalytical Society after the so-called Controversial Discussions. The latter might be more accurately described as the Kleinian Controversy, an effort that consolidated what Ricoeur (1970) calls the "hermeneutics of suspicion." From Klein through Hanna Segal, Betty Joseph, and others, psychic change is conceived in terms of the positive evaluation of disbelief, particularly in the treatment of highly narcissistic structures. By contrast, Winnicott ("Transitional Objects and Transitional Phenomena" [CW 4:2:21]) allows for a twofold determination of the negative, comprising a potentially creative as well as an eliminative aspect of "the negative side of relationships." He credits the play of absence as well as unthinkable emptiness, illusion as well as nihilism. This augments the field and functions of negative therapeutic reaction and, as such, represents a genuine break in the history of clinical curiosity and attention.

Together with Milner, Rycroft, and others, and further to the classical Freudian interpretation (the particular and incomparable rigor of which is reductive rather than constitutive), Winnicott established listening on the side of illusion and its psychic necessity, as distinct from demystification. Essentially, the Winnicottian subject is what Green (1983, p. 119) calls "a playing subject" (*un sujet joueur*), reducible neither to the scientific aspirations of medicine nor to the empiricism of psychological doctrine. The capacity for illusion is thus credited as part of the subjectivity of the patient's lived experience, if not an integral part of Lawrence's sensuous flame of life. Prompted by mechanisms in the service of so-called unreachability or non-understanding, Winnicott ([CW 4:2:21]) emphasized the extent to which "the sense of loss itself can become a way of integrating one's self-experience." The moment of hope is paradigmatic here, as distinct from something wishful on the neurotic model.

The whole of Winnicott's argument turns on the idea that the reach for meaning is primarily a reach for life. There is no question of avoiding pain, however. The basic assumption is that the norm invariably issues from life itself in the form of suffering as a "working solution," a way of going on being. The ethics of creative living includes a thoroughgoing revaluation of the value of the symptom, although Winnicott did not attempt to replace the subject of psychology with a constituting ego borrowed from the philosophies of consciousness. He opted instead for a concept of human nature based on the idea that life affects itself; hence the notion of felt life. On the grounds that our potential to thrive is manifest as pure immanence, or what he called "readiness" for life, Winnicott came to the conclusion that maturity admits of the greatest suffering and, indeed, that the healthier the individual, the greater his capacity for suffering. The truth of the true self does not simply do away with illusion any more than it alleviates suffering. The genetic basis of this conclusion (the genesis of the unconscious) is the central preoccupation of *Human Nature*, a preoccupation that unfolds through a retrospective reconstruction moving backwards to the somatic origin of human experience. While the study of human nature proceeds explicitly along developmental lines, as Green (1996, p. 73) points out, it is nonetheless underpinned by the "preliminary postulate" of the body.

Vitality and Reality

The central dialectic of Winnicott's thought, involving the creative imperative ("the inherent growth element") and the element that comes from outside, is described along three related axes: first, the establishment of contact with external reality; second, the realization and integration of the "unit self" from a state of "primary un-integration"; and, third, the dwelling of psyche in soma. Winnicott grounded both Oedipal and earlier psychical scenes in this primordial configuration of the real, narcissistic, and psychosomatic experience. A reconstruction based on this configuration reveals life as the absolute *datum*.

In the second synopsis and the extant text, Winnicott divides his account of emotional development into three parts, starting with the young child and the period of "first maturity." His account of interpersonal relationships, relationships between whole persons with "instincts in charge," recapitulates truths ("facts") formulated in Oedipal terms. Winnicott retained the Freudian Oedipus complex as a psychical arrangement pertaining after infancy and before the latency period, in which each of the three of the triangle is a whole person. He saw no economic value in applying the Oedipal schema and its dramatization of the drives to earlier psychical scenes—that is, where one or more in the three-body relationship is a so-called part-object. The efficacy of the paternal function is not in question, but the Oedipal schema is not seen as sufficiently dominant to warrant the term "pre-Oedipal" for the earliest relationship, which, as we shall see in a moment, functions in accordance with its own logic.

As set out in Part II of *Human Nature*, the central structural series of interpersonal relations comprises body functioning, imaginative elaboration, and fantasy orientated by drives. Thus, Winnicott reconstructs the process of continuing psychic development in terms of Freudian instinct theory, intrapsychic neurotic conflict, the repressed unconscious, and the neurotic transference. It would be a mistake, however, to count this as the Winnicottian matrix of the mind. The link between health and normal emotional development is taken up at an earlier stage in Part III of *Human Nature*, prior to triangular human relations. During this earlier phase of psychosomatic life, the principal developmental task for the infant involves recognizing that the "environment mother" and the "object mother" are one and the same. The former comprises the maternal frame on which the infant depends (Freud's anaclitic relationship), the mother that the infant discovers/invents in and through his quiet moments. By contrast, the object mother is the focus of the infant's instinctual love, which includes the mother whose feeding breasts the infant would devour and destroy. Winnicott's account of the concern the infant begins to feel for a mother towards whom he has directed the instinctual aggressiveness of his life-force, his "ruthless love," represents a reworking of Klein's depressive position. This covers an important axis of Winnicott's work, including the roots of aggression, the unconscious sense of guilt, the capacity to believe in the world, and the formation of the superego.

Winnicott's debt to Klein notwithstanding, he made an original theoretical contribution to this particular formation of emotional development as part of the foundational process of psychic life. He defined the achievement of integration in terms of the "unit" and viewed the "capacity for concern" as a sign that the infant has achieved spatiotemporal "unit status." Where the psyche has come to live in the soma, the infant is able to differentiate between "me" and "other than me"; he is capable of recognizing mother not only as a whole person (*there is one*) but also as separate from him (*there is another*). The idea of integration along these lines raises fundamental questions for our understanding of health. Concern arises at the point where the infant looks back and, retrospectively, gains a larger sense not only of the ruthless nature of his own impulses but also of the inherent difficulties of life. Winnicott posited a genuine sense of *recognition* at the heart of life, even if it occurs only in retrospect as an expression of mature concern. This allows for the fact that sensual and bodily experiences of recognition and love at the beginning, the early feelings of being known and understood, are subject to restructuring at a later date; that is, when new experience and greater maturity may amplify and augment their significance. Winnicott has thus illuminated the plight of the patients we treat whose early experience has convinced them that nobody really wants to know or understand them.

This brings us to the final part of *Human Nature*, which stands at the center of Winnicott's achievement. His account of primitive emotional development in Part IV of *Human Nature* is coextensive with the range of his deepest sympathies in the late works: "Communicating and Not Communicating Leading to a Study of Certain Opposites" [CW 6:4:8], "The Use of an Object and Relating Through Identifications" [CW 8:2:28], and "Creativity and Its Origins" [CW 9:3:7]. The unprecedented nature of human life, the uniqueness of its emergence, is what Winnicott was most concerned to grasp with his notion of vitality, and he elaborated a creation narrative in order to frame this imperative. For Winnicott, life not only posits itself as creative living but is nothing other than creative self-positing. This is what he meant by *primary* creativity, the idea that creativity brings the world into being.

The radical implication of the creative imperative is that the world is created anew by each human being. Winnicott presents his narrative after Genesis 1:2, in terms of the formlessness (*tōhūwabōhū*) and void state of the world before creation. On the other hand, he argues that life posits its own conditions where the infant is "ready" to live creatively. In coming to this conclusion, Winnicott conceived of human nature as a paradox: he maintained that "human nature does not change" ("Morals and Education" [CW 6:3:18]). A concern with the living self and its foundations cannot but result in an essentialist argument. Winnicott demonstrated that the essence of human nature determines the coherence of its concept. However, based on the assumption that human nature is almost all we have, he demonstrated that what matters is what we make of what is given.

The emphasis in this account of creation falls on life's coming into itself. This is not only a theory of being (albeit the most far-reaching ontology we have in psychoanalysis) but also, more importantly, a theory of indefinite possibility modeled on the potential space between the subjective object ("me-extensions") and the object objectively perceived ("other than me")—between primary narcissism and object relationship. Winnicott considered this space, which he identified and defined as "transitional," as natural to infancy, while at the same time allowing for the infant's dependence on the mother's adaptation to need. The concept of transitional space is not explicitly elaborated in *Human Nature*, which remains the single most significant omission in the second synopsis. Nevertheless, the concept is implicit in the central argument concerning creative vitality. The emphasis on creative living is underpinned by the idea of transitional space as the framework of experience per se.

It is important that we do not lose sight of the dialectical nature of this account. The emphasis on primary creativity is maintained in conjunction with the importance accorded to the "external factor." What we make of who we are goes hand in hand with what we make of the world that is presented to us. Winnicott challenged us to think about what we mean by "world" as the place where we are most of the time when we are experiencing life. Conceived as a "spontaneous gesture," life comes into its own beyond the finitude of the world's horizon. In other words, there is more to life than the "details" presented to the infant by the mother. Winnicott described a world that is not merely objective but has to be invented and perceived before it becomes habitable in any meaningful way. The paradox of human nature, therefore, is inscribed in the paradox of birth as the experience of "a great awakening." The latter is conditional on the mother making the world available to an infant who is not yet awake, but in such a way that allows for the spontaneity and excess of creativity as a primordial mode of arousal.

The spontaneous gesture cannot make itself felt without a world; psychosomatic experience is necessarily embedded from the beginning. But it is creativity alone that opts for life. For the infant, the world comes out of nowhere; crucially, Winnicott ("Fear of Breakdown" [CW 6:4:21]) concludes that "only out of non-existence can existence start" and that "emptiness is a prerequisite for eagerness to gather in." Life is originally a shock, an experience of primary emptiness that is not simply over and done with but has to be made hospitable lest it remain unthinkable. Primary narcissistic illusion brings life into a relation with itself, invests the experience of being thrown into the world with the possibility of meaning, and shapes the formless silence. As such, the world is meaningful neither as an evacuation of what has been incorporated nor as a projection of that which has been previously introjected. The reality of the world alone does not account for the kind of concrete universality—the *humanitas* of human beings—that Winnicott envisaged on the model of health and vitality. He conceived of life as both vital upsurge and exterior situation, unprecedented and continuous. The distinction between spontaneity and continuity is decisive: whereas "continuity of being" may be identified with being in the world, the creative imperative originates independently of the world.

Winnicott's interpretation of being as life is based on the earliest phenomena of human experience. Through clinical inquiry into what he called "pre-primitive stages," he raised a series of fundamental questions. How does human nature appear? What state are we in as being emerges out of non-being? Is reality accessible to experience? By concentrating on these questions, he reformulated what Freud had proposed under the title of death drive. To recall the decisive move, Winnicott identified the basic paradox of our existence at an individual level, implying that it is only through our experience of it that human nature appears. This is not to say that human nature is reduced to a subjective object or, alternatively, that the self ends up as one more object among others. Winnicott was neither a solipsist nor a dogmatic realist. Again, based on the logic of transitional functioning, subjectivity is inscribed into the very kernel of objective reality. Where human nature itself requires personal experience as its mode of appearance, Winnicott fleshed out the paradox in terms of a fundamental and inherent "aloneness" that is only manifest as absolute dependence. He named this paradox "the environment-individual set-up."

The world opened up and given form by this articulation, which Winnicott posited as the most elementary structure of life, was evident from the first phase of his mature work in the 1940s. For there to be health, it is necessary that the environment-individual set-up exists; however, further to the "aloneness of pre-dependence," he identified a prior state of "unaliveness." The latter denotes not only a state before dependence is encountered but also a lack of being, a void state of things before creation, out of which aliveness awakes. Moreover, it is only with the acceptance of the fact of dependence that the drive acquires a perceptible and meaningful character. Winnicott's interpretation of being as life is predicated on a state not only before aliveness but also prior to instinct. While he accepted Freud's instinct theory as an indispensable part of psychoanalysis, at the same time, he saw the soma as primary and illusion as prior to instinct.

This represents a thoroughgoing revision of Freudian psychoanalysis. For Freud, the drives account for how there comes to be something, whereas for Winnicott the creative imperative denotes the pure immanence of life. In a related move, Winnicott situated the Oedipus complex within his own developmental framework, identifying the boundary function of externality, or "thirdness" (*tiercéisation*), with the ongoing maturational process of disillusionment (Reeves, 2012). In what amounts to a reworking of Jones's (1927) idea of "aphanisis," Winnicott effectively reformulated symbolic castration by combining separation and aloneness. He draws our attention to the fact that there is division (me/not-me) before triangulation; that primeval silence is riven before the word; and that the phallic signifier, the law of the name of the father, recapitulates the child's earlier experience of disillusionment. Anxiety arising out of pre-dependent aloneness is thus experienced as separation anxiety/intrusion anxiety only in retrospect. While the father institutes separation as loss of the incestuous object of desire and, therefore, releases the son from sexual union with the mother, at the same time, he inscribes pre-dependent aloneness *as separation* in the symbolic structure.

It is only as separation that aloneness cuts into the self, for it is only in the event of separation that a self emerges capable of experiencing aloneness with all its primitive fears. The infant is now liable to feel alone in the world, prior to which there is no one there for aloneness to befall. Thus the pre-subjective state of aloneness is, retrospectively, experienced as "I am alone." The reality of life becomes implicated in the cares of the world, while fears of abandonment and intrusion retain their primitive underbelly, for example, as the fear of falling into empty space or of returning to an undifferentiated state. Castration anxiety in turn enables life to go on as suffering, precisely beyond the primitive agonies of what we might call blank pain. It affords the Oedipal child "psychological release," through the movement from pre-symbolic aloneness to absence and separation, from the pervasive threat of an abandoning or invading environment. Concerned primarily with what it feels like to be alive, Winnicott drew his own conclusions about the Oedipus myth. That Oedipus comes through eventually, oriented towards a world the painful reality of which he cannot but experience, confirms suffering as a "working solution" for going on being. The confirmation of the latter is predicated on the idea that, together with the associated anxieties of annihilation, the structural necessity of aloneness preempts and is continuous with symbolic castration as the point of entry to the universality of the human situation.

Conclusion

The two works that make up Volume 12 represent complementary sides of Winnicott's clinical thinking: the theorist of ruthless vitality on the one hand and, on the other, the therapist primarily attuned to potentiality, intent on adapting technique to meet the needs of the patient. Winnicott reshaped Freud's thought on both counts while at the same time maintaining the basic methodology of psychoanalysis, the inherent logic of its situation and frames of meaning. As regards his topic, he has significant and new things to say about the self and subjectivity, and he has focused our attention above all on the potentiality of the psyche and its transitional modes of functioning. The space of potential is identified as the condition for psychic elaboration. More than an object, Winnicott describes "a space lending itself to the creation of objects" (Green, 1978, p. 285). This presupposes a theory of symbolization based on the play of absence and yet distinct from the perspective of reparation.

Nevertheless, his abiding and defining theme is life. A preoccupation with the aliveness that living requires runs throughout the work from the first phase of its maturity in the late 1940s. In Winnicott, vitality is the lodestone and the basis of his concept of the vocation of psychoanalysis. Most importantly, he derived a criterion of maturity from the pure immanence of life, a conception of maturational processes that afforded him a sounding in the reach for meaning. As such, he traced the creation of meaning from the beginning of life along true and false lines: a twofold determination of the negative demarcates the division into true- and false-self structures. Life itself appears, accordingly, in conjunction with "the negative side of relationships." And while a thoroughgoing reconciliation of clinical realism and negation may not be feasible within a single psychoanalytic school or tradition, the prospect of calling these epistemological and ontological terms of reference together is brought a good deal closer by Winnicott's contribution.

In terms of clinical practice, *The Piggle* reveals Winnicott engaged in the task of transforming delusion into play, allowing the child to enjoy the experience of playing before differentiating between dreams and an inner reality that she experienced as "actual" inside. There is an explicit statement to this effect in the "Thirteenth Consultation" [CW 11:2:14], where Winnicott describes how he played a game with exuberant enjoyment in order to give the patient "the satisfaction she needed." Making the setting available for use in this way as a potential space underpins Winnicott's approach to false-self structures, the fear of breakdown, the antisocial tendency, and so on as so many "special cases." These cases placed new demands on the analytic situation. Thus, Winnicott augments Freud's account of the negative force at work in "repetitions of reactions dating from infancy" (1937b, p. 259), which Freud summed up under the heading "interminable" (1937a). Winnicott rendered the latter as the "unthinkable." Bringing matters to bear unambiguously on experience itself, he concluded that "the original experience of primitive agony cannot get into the past tense" but requires the intermediate area of illusion (transitional space) to "gather it into its own present time experience" ("Fear of Breakdown" [CW 6:4:21]). Emptiness is gathered in as a phenomenon of the threefold schema: setting–transference–countertransference.

Finally, Winnicott concluded that even in the most disastrous circumstances, hope is not futile if the fear of disaster can be experienced through "reliving"; that is, as the equivalent of remembering in classical psychoanalytic treatment. As such, the unthinkable–thinkable dialectic invests experience with both negative and positive evaluations. The wording is crucial. Historically, the negative form precedes the positive one: the negative prefix *un-* predates the suffix *-able* ("*unthinkable*" c. 1430; "*thinkable*" 1805). The prior determination of negativity, therefore, is rooted in the choice of words, demonstrating that the psychoanalytic and the literary are not two separate elements. A measured assessment of Winnicott, notably in cultivating good sense through the use of plain language, would include an acknowledgment of his contribution to our English prose tradition. T. S. Eliot—the cadence of *Four Quartets*—is the explicit recourse for time and experience apropos "this past thing for the first time in the present" [CW 6:4:21]. But we may need to go to Geoffrey Hill rather than to Eliot for the vocabulary of negative and positive impulses inscribed in the central Winnicottian trajectory from *die Unendliche* to the unthinkable, from the "resistances of the id" to early trauma. I have suggested "blank pain"; in any case, wording the otherwise formless silence of primitive agonies is a task that as ever lies before us: unspeakable desolation, impenetrable absence, unaccountable darkness, near unrecognizable. Invariably, the task is oriented by the fact that we are urged into life by living.

References

Freud, S. (1937a). Analysis terminable and interminable. In J. Strachey (Ed.), *The standard edition of the complete psychological works of Sigmund Freud* (vol. 23, pp. 209–253). London: Hogarth.

Freud, S. (1937b). Constructions in analysis. In James Strachey (Ed.), *The standard edition of the complete psychological works of Sigmund Freud* (vol. 23, pp. 255–269). London: Hogarth.

Green, A. (1975/1986). The analyst, symbolization and absence in the analytic setting. In C. Yorke (Ed.), *On private madness* (pp. 30–59). London: Hogarth.

Green, A. (1978/1986). Potential space in psychoanalysis. In C. Yorke (Ed.), *On private madness* (pp. 277–296). London: Hogarth.

Green, A. (1983/1984). Le langage dans la psychanalyse (deuxièmes recontres psychanalytiques d'Aix-en-Provence). In *Langage* (pp. 20–250). Paris: Les Belles Lettres.

Green, A. (1996/2009). The posthumous Winnicott: On *Human Nature*. In J. Abram (Ed.), *André Green at the Squiggle Foundation* (pp. 69–83). London: Karnac.

Hopkins, G. M. (2013). *The collected works of Gerard Manley Hopkins*, vol. II, *Correspondence 1882–1889*, R. K. R. Thornton & C. Phillips (Eds.). Oxford: Oxford University Press.

Jones, E. (1927). The early development of female sexuality. *International Journal of Psychoanalysis, 8*, 459–472.

Little, M. I. (1986). *Toward basic unity: Transference neurosis and transference psychosis*. London: Free Association Books.

Parsons, M. (2000). The logic of play. In E. B. Spillius (Ed.), *The dove that returns, the dove that vanishes: Paradox and creativity in psychoanalysis* (pp. 128–145). London: Routledge.

Reeves, C. (2012/2013). On the margins: The role of the father in Winnicott's writings. In J. Abram (Ed.), *Donald Winnicott today* (pp. 358–385). London/New York: Routledge.

Ricoeur, P. (1970). *Freud and philosophy: An essay on interpretation*. D. Savage, trans. New Haven, CT/London: Yale University Press.

Winnicott, D. W. (1945). Primitive emotional development. [CW 2:7:8]

Winnicott, D. W. (1953). Transitional objects and transitional phenomena. [CW 4:2:21]

Winnicott, D. W. (1963). Morals and education [1962]. [CW 6:3:18]

Winnicott, D. W. (1965). The aims of psycho-analytical treatment [1962]. [CW 6:3:2]

Winnicott, D. W. (1965). Communicating and not communicating leading to a study of certain opposites [1963]. [CW 6:4:8]

Winnicott, D. W. (1968). Playing: A theoretical statement [1967]. [CW 8:2:15]

Winnicott, D. W. (1969). The use of an object and relating through identifications [1968]. [CW 8:2:28]

Winnicott, D. W. (1971). The concept of a healthy individual [1967]. [CW 8:1:4]

Winnicott, D. W. (1971). Creativity and its origins. [CW 9:3:7]Winnicott, D. W. (1974). Fear of breakdown [c. 1963–1964]. [CW 6:4:21]

Winnicott, D. W. (1977). *The Piggle: An account of the psychoanalytic treatment of a little girl*. London: Hogarth. [CW 11:2]

Winnicott, D. W. (1988). *Human nature*. London: Free Association Books. [CW 11:1]

Winnicott, D. W. (1989). D. W. W. on D. W. W. [1967] [CW 8:1:2]

{ INDEX }

Page numbers followed by *f* indicate figures